PREHISTORIC ARCHAEOLOGY OF INDRAVATI BASIN IN KORAPUT, ODISHA

PREHISTORIC ARCHAEOLOGY OF INDRAVATI BASIN IN KORAPUT, ODISHA

SHIBA CHARAN NANDA

Edited by
MANJIL HAZARIKA

With a Foreword by
S. B. OTA

PATHAK PUBLISHER AND DISTRIBUTORS
New Delhi (INDIA)

Prehistoric Archaeology of Indravati Basin in Koraput, Odisha

Editor : Manjil Hazarika

ISBN : 978-93-91952-39-6

Price : 2100/-

First Edition: 2023

Front cover image: A general view of the Indravati river, Odisha (image courtesy: Jitu Mishra, Archaeologist, Author and Traveller)

Back cover image: A general view of clearance of forest for shifting-cultivation in the hilly landscape in Koraput district, Odisha (image courtesy: Jitu Mishra, Archaeologist, Author and Traveller)

Published by :
PATHAK PUBLISHER AND DISTRIBUTORS
E-6/33c & 34, Ground Floor, Sangam Vihar
New Delhi-110080
E-mail: pathakppd@gmail.com

Type Setting by
G. R. Sharma

Printed in India

Contents

Foreword

I feel privileged and it also gives me immense pleasure to write the foreword of this book "*Prehistoric Archaeology of Indravati Basin in Koraput, Odisha*" written by Dr. Shiba Charan Nanda who was not only my friend but also my Guru from whom I got firsthand knowledge on lithic artefact typology. This original work is in fact the outcome of his doctoral dissertation, the contributions can still be considered fresh in many respects.

Even though this work was carried out in the seventies, I feel that it still holds relevance even in the present-day academia as it was ahead of its time in respect of concept and methodologies. This work by Dr. Nanda can be considered as a paradigm shift in its approach to prehistoric research of Odisha.

Dr. Nanda's research was confined to the Indravati basin in the erstwhile Koraput district and conducted in a manner that the writer himself described as a 'single geographical unit in micro-level' irrespective of its administrative boundaries. This region-centric archaeological approach was the first of its kind in Odisha.

It is really admirable how the author carried out his investigation in a virtually inaccessible and densely forested area of the erstwhile Koraput district. Further, it is one such study where the investigation was carried out towards the hinterland with the central focus being restricted to discovering primary sites instead of following the river bank stratigraphic model that was widely practised by the contemporary archaeologists to understand the prehistoric cultural succession. The small geographical area of nearly 2,400 square km that was investigated has yielded 17 Upper Palaeolithic and 85 Mesolithic sites. It is unique in itself when compared with the contemporary prehistoric investigations in the subcontinent. The locational pattern of these sites has been studied in the context of micro-environmental settings. The importance of the research is also notable in terms of the earliest occurrence and identification of Upper Paleolithic sites in Odisha when such sites were just getting reported and understood in other parts of the country.

Besides, this work also involves a comparative analysis of surface and excavated artefacts collection at a site named Girla, where Dr. Nanda had carried out a trial excavation. Moreover, it is probably one of the very few such research where a comparative study of Upper Palaeolithic and Mesolithic assemblages have been carried out in a pan-Indian context.

With an academic background in Anthropology, Dr. Nanda studied the adaptation strategies of various tribal economies in order to understand the ecological suitability for the prehistoric hunter-gatherer to traverse and settle in the area. It is worth mentioning that it is the first such study that has been carried out in Odisha.

It, thus, delights me that such a scholastic work is now on its way to seeing the face of the light in form of a book. I am immensely grateful to Dr. Manjil Hazarika who has stepped forward to get this doctoral dissertation edited, converted and published as a book retaining the original archival illustrations and maps used by the author. This painstaking initiative of Dr. Hazarika would enable our readers to have better access to this treasure that set a new milestone in prehistoric research in Odisha. Certainly, it is a welcome addition to the study of Indian Prehistory in general and Odishan Prehistory in particular.

S.B. Ota
Former Joint Director General
Archaeological Survey of India

Reminiscence of Shiba Charan Nanda

"Knowledge is power. Information is liberating. Education is the premise of progress." —Kofi Annan

Education informs, enlightens and broadens the horizon of our knowledge. It also helps one to explore and discover. The untimely demise of my husband Dr. Shiba Charan Nanda, Reader in Anthropology in 2002 left a huge void in my life. He used to be very passionate about his branch of knowledge – Anthropology. He was very excited and used to talk animatedly about his archaeological surveys and the interesting discoveries from explorations and excavations. His single minded pursuit of his interest in prehistory made him a committed anthropologist. He visited the remote caves, tall mountains and cascading fountains to probe and satisfy his insatiable appetite for learning. He fostered an atmosphere of creative freedom for his students so that he could share knowledge, ideas and concepts with them. His words of encouragement, positive mindset and gestures of kindness will go a long way in shaping his students to grow and mature.

He used to collect archaeological specimens and stone artifacts and study them closely to understand life history, culture, society and religion of Indian tribes. I always find him alive in his thesis, stone specimens, research papers and his excavations in different places of India. So, I had a long cherished desire to publish his thesis "*The Stone Age Culture of Indravati Basin in Koraput district, Orissa*" in the form of a book so that the students will remember him and his devotion to the profession. I shall be extremely pleased if the students, research scholars and researchers find the book beneficial for their study and research. I feel that an appreciation of his works by the young, upcoming and future generations of scholars and students will be the greatest tribute to him.

Bishnupriya Tripathy
Wife of late Shiba Charan Nanda
September, 2023

Acknowledgements

The present research work, which involved a considerable amount of field work and multi-dimensional approach, would not have been completed without the help of many individuals. It is my great privilege to acknowledge my sincere thanks to those persons whose immense help at different moments and in various ways have made it possible to terminate partially the pages of this unending research work.

My first and foremost pleasure and privilege is to acknowledge my deep sense of gratitude and indebtness to my research supervisor Professor V.N. Misra for kindly agreeing to guide me for the present research work. In spite of his tight schedule, he was kind enough to visit my study area, where I could get an opportunity to discuss with him about some of the practical problems, in the field, related to my work. Besides, he always gave me time to discuss a number of problems pertaining to my research. This has enabled me to refine and elaborate my ideas. He took a keen interest in scrutinising my manuscript and made useful suggestions to improve the over-all presentation of the work. However, I take the responsibility of humbly accepting all the drawbacks that might have remained. Beside this, I was lucky enough, for I had the opportunity to work as a Research Assistant for a couple of years under his guidance in the Bhimbetka excavation project. There I got the first hand knowledge on the prehistoric site excavation methods and recording of antiquities, which was a great help in my research work. I am extremely grateful for all the opportunities that I got to work with him and the constant encouragement, valuable advice and help.

I express my deep sense of gratitude to Dr. M.L.K. Murti, who was very kind in granting me some time to discuss various problems connected with Upper Palaeolithic culture which foms a major part in my research. Besides the academic discussion, he has always been helpful, kind and understanding.

I am indeed, very thankful to Dr. M.D. Kajale who took an interest in identifying various plant specimens brought from the field area. He also gave me some suggestions in putting the ethno-botanical data in a systematic way in the present work.

I am also very thankful to Makkhan Lal, S.B. Ota and R.K. Ganjoo, all research scholars of the department, for their help in different ways in completing this work.

My special thanks are due to Dr. S.N. Rajaguru and Dr. (Miss) Malti Nagar, for their constant encouragement throughout the work.

I also thank my friends Rabi, Jacob, Dukhishyam, Vijay and Sathe, for their inspiration and cordiality. I owe my thanks in a special way to my friend Marie Corroa for the help, encouragement and typing of the first draft of the manuscript.

My sincere thanks are due to Niranjan Misra and Karuti Das, residents of the Nawrangpur, whose help and enthusiastic cooperation were with me at every stage of my field work.

In completion of this work the financial assistance provided to me during (1974-76) in the form of Deccan College Scholarship cannot be forgotten. The facilities at the Institute have been utilised at every stage of my research. I sincerely appreciate the cooperation and help of Deccan College authority. I am thankful especially to the Deccan College Library staff. I thank Mr. S.R. Prabhu for the final typing of my research manuscript within a very short period.

I am in loss of words to express my deep gratitude to my parents. My research would not have completed without their advice, concern and financial support. Their blessing was a constant source of strength in completing my research.

Finally I owe my thanks to all those persons who extended help in some way or other during my research work, but are not mentioned and lie sincerely behind the curtains of this achieved goal.

Shiba Charan Nanda

Note from the Editor

It was on a fine morning in Ethiopia in 2015; my colleague Dr. Santosh Mahapatra of the Department of Anthropology at Mekelle University made a request to me if I would be interested in taking the initiative to publish the PhD dissertation of late Dr. Shiba Charan Nanda, submitted to the University of Poona in 1984. In fact, it has been the desire of Smt. Bishnupriya Tripathy, wife of late Shiba Charan Nanda to see the PhD dissertation in a book form. It took several days for me to decide if I should be able to take on this important and challenging task, as I hardly had any exposure to the archaeology and prehistory of Odisha. Nevertheless, I accepted the request of Dr. Mahapatra, who happens to be a relative of Smt. Tripathy; however, due to several unavoidable circumstances, the publication of the book got delayed and took much longer time than initially planned. And finally, with all of our combined efforts, the dissertation has taken this shape and hence, we all are extremely happy to present the book to the readers, researchers and students of archaeology, prehistory and anthropology in India in general and Odisha in particular.

With initial training in anthropology at Utkal University in Bhubaneswar, Shri Nanda went on to learn and study at the Deccan College, PG and Research Institute in Pune for his doctoral dissertation, under the guidance of noted Indian archaeologist late Prof. V.N. Misra. During his association with Deccan College, Dr. Nanda carried out extensive archaeological field surveys in Puri, Keonjhar, and Khurda districts in Odisha. Moreover, he along with Dr. S.B. Ota conducted explorations in Bhubaneswar tehsil in Odisha in 1981-82 and discovered three historical mounds at Dengahuda, Asurikuda, and Parbati near Danapada, Taraboi, and Panikata villages respectively. For a long period of time, he studied the prehistoric Stone Age artefacts recovered from the world-famous site of Bhimbetka in Madhya Pradesh. He was also associated with numerous other archaeological and quaternary geological surveys in Rajasthan, Madhya Pradesh, Andhra Pradesh and Gujarat which is reflected in several of his publications and presentations made at several academic forums along with others. His untimely demise in 2002 left a void in the archaeological fraternity and is an inseparable loss for the subject.

During his PhD, Shiba Charan Nanda made extensive archaeological surveys in the Indravati basin of the undivided Koraput district of Odisha, covering an area of nearly 2,400 sq km. It was one of the first systematic attempts to understand the Stone Age cultures of the

Indravati river valley which brought to the limelight seventeen Upper Palaeolithic and eighty-five Mesolithic sites with a diverse range of archaeological records. The study of the stone artefacts with in-depth analysis of the typology and technology and comparison with other well-known sites of India provides a methodological framework for prehistoric investigations in the regional context. The author has also taken into account the settlement and subsistence patterns of the ethnic communities living in the remote landscape for ages for developing analogies for interpreting the prehistoric cultures from an ethno-archaeological point of view. The works set an early example of combining archaeological evidences with ethnographic data for understanding past human land use and settlement history. Detailed study of the Gadaba community on their settlement pattern, material culture, and subsistence economy focusing on hunting, gathering, fishing and the traditional knowledge associated with the cultural practices form another significant component of the research. The study is supported by many good maps, photographs and drawings of the artefacts and ethnographic objects. He conducted a small-scale excavation at Girla to ascertain the stratigraphy and chronology of the archaeological materials. The excavation provided valuable information on the archaeological contexts of the Upper Palaeolithic and Mesolithic sites in the valley discovered by him. Considering the significance of the work, we felt that the PhD dissertation deserves wider attention and publicity.

It is also heartening to note that Dr. Simadri B. Ota has taken the initiative to publish the work of Dr. Nanda as a chapter in *Gurudakshina: Facets of Indian Archaeology (Part II) - Essays presented to Prof. V.N. Misra*, edited Dr. Alok Kumar Kanungo in 2007, which was a tribute to late Prof. V.N. Misra by his PhD students. The paper co-authored by Nanda and Ota is a welcome addition to the scholarship on Indian prehistory. Dr. Ota shares that his "association with S.C. Nanda goes back to 1981 when ... began to understand the fundamentals of lithic artefact typology. This was the time when typological study was very popular in Indian Prehistory. Being trained under Prof. V.N. Misra, S.C. Nanda was one, from whom many scholars learnt the stone artefact typology". Dr. Ota acknowledges that he owes his knowledge of lithic artefact typology to Dr. Nanda. This is a fitting tribute to Dr. Nanda by a colleague and friend who conducted several field works and research together.

For the benefit of the researchers and students, below are listed some of the publications of Dr. Shiba Charan Nanda:

1) **Nanda, S.C.** 1982-83. A Note on Stone Age Succession of Indravati Valley, Koraput District, Orissa. *Manav* 1(1): 83-85

2) **Nanda, S.C.** 1985. The Mesolithic Culture of the Indravati Valley, District Koraput, Orissa. In *Recent Advances in Indo-Pacific Prehistory*, eds. V.N. Misra and P. Bellwood, pp. 159-163. New Delhi: Oxford & IBH Publishing Co.

3) **Nanda, S.C.** 2000. The Upper Palaeolithic and Mesolithic Cultures of the Indravati Valley, South Orissa: An Ethnoarchaeological study. In *Archaeology of Orissa*, eds. K.K. Basa and P.K. Mohanty, pp. 153-172. New Delhi: Pratibha Publications.
4) **Nanda, S.C.** and S.B. Ota. 2007. Stone Age Cultures of Indravati Basin, District Koraput, Orissa. In *Gurudakshina: Facets of Indian Archaeology (Part II) - Essays presented to Prof. V.N. Misra*, ed. A.K. Kanungo, pp. 1-27. BAR International Series 1665. Oxford: John and Erica Hedges Ltd.

The following are some of the papers presented by Dr. Shiba Charan Nanda at various academic events:

1) Agrawal, D.P., R.P. Dhir, R.V. Krishnamurty, V.N. Misra, **S.C. Nanda**, S.N. Rajguru, G. Singh and S. Sinha. 1978. *Multiple Evidence for Climatic Change in Rajasthan*. Paper presented at the International Symposium on Arid Zone Research and Development, held at Jodhpur, Rajasthan, India, during February 14–18, 1978.
2) Ghosh, H.N., A.K. Dasgupta, G.C. Deo and **S.C. Nanda**. 1977. *Early Man in the Little Rann of Kutch*. Paper presented at the National Seminar on Quaternary Environments with Special Reference to Western India, organised at the University of Baroda, Baroda.
3) Misra, V.N. and **S.C. Nanda**. 1977. *Mesolithic Industry of Rock-Shelter III F-23 at Bhimbetka (Dist. Raisen, Madhya Pradesh)*. Paper presented at the III Annual Conference Ethnographic and Folk Culture Society and Indian Association of Physical Anthropologist, held at Lucknow, on January 23-25, 1977.
4) Misra, V.N., M. Nagar and **S.C. Nanda**. 1978. *Typology of Indian Microlithic Industries*. Paper presented at the IV Annual Conference of Ethnographic and Folk Culture Society, held at Ahmedabad, January 8-10, 1978.
5) **Nanda, S.C.** 1977. *Microlithic Industry of Koraput District, Orissa*. Paper presented at the III Annual Conference Ethnographic and Folk Culture Society and Indian Association of Physical Anthropologist, held at Lucknow, on January 23-25, 1977.
6) **Nanda, S.C.** 1978. *Microlithic Industry of Daitary, Keonjhar District of Orissa*. Paper presented at the IV Annual Conference of Ethnographic and Folk Culture Society, held at Ahmedabad, January 8-10, 1978.
7) **Nanda, S.C.** 1981. *Upper Palaeolithic Culture of Orissa*. Paper presented at the 7th Indian Society for Prehistoric and Quaternary Studies and XIIIth Indian Archaeological Society.
8) **Nanda, S.C.** 1982. *Stone Age Succession of Indravati Valley, Koraput District, Orissa*. Paper presented at the First Annual Conference of Orissa Anthropological Society, Bhubaneswar.

I am extremely thankful to Dr. S.B. Ota, former Joint Director General of the Archaeological Survey of India, New Delhi and a good friend of Dr. Nanda for writing the foreword of the book. I also thank Prof. Sheila Mishra, former Head of the Department of Archaeology, Deccan College in Pune and Dr. Neetu Agarwal of the Department of Anthropology, Avadh Girls' Degree College, Lucknow for providing valuable suggestions. Prof. Vasant Shinde, former Vice Chancellor of Deccan College made some valuable suggestions, for which I am grateful to him. Thanks are also due to Smt. Bishnupriya Tripathy and Dr. Santosh Mahapatra for giving me the opportunity to associate myself with the publication of the book. Our students Sri Jayanta Roy, Smt. Jutimala Misra and Sri Dhiraj Neog of Cotton University helped me type the text and prepare the figures. Hadibandhu Satapathy, Reader (Retd.) in English, Dhenkanal Autonomous College, Odisha and Smt. Shreya Sarmah of Cotton University provided editorial assistance, for which I am thankful to them. I acknowledge Sri Jitu Mishra, an archaeologist, author and traveller for providing the photographs used in the cover pages of the book. My friends Dr. Dibishada Garnayak of Archaeological Survey of India, Puri and Dr. Tosabanta Padhan, School of Historical Studies, Nalanda University, Rajgir are also acknowledged for helpful suggestions. I am thankful to Sri Gangaram Sharma and Sri S.K. Pathak of the Pathak Publisher and Distributors, New Delhi for preparing the manuscript press ready and publishing the book respectively.

I, on behalf of everyone associated with this long-due publication; hope that the book will be beneficial for the students, teachers, researchers and general readers for understanding the prehistory of one of the important regions of India, which has opened new avenues for further studies on the Upper Palaeolithic and Mesolithic cultures of the Indian sub-continent.

Dr. Manjil Hazarika
Department of Archaeology
Cotton University, Guwahati

List of Figures

List of Plates

List of Tables

Chapter - 1

Introduction

Research in Indian prehistory has travelled a long way since the first discovery of prehistoric relics by Robert Bruce Foote in 1863. Research in this direction (especially in Stone Age archaeology) remained somewhat stagnant till the 1940s, however, received a fillip with the arrival of H.D. Sankalia in the scene. Since then researches in the field of Indian prehistory have passed through many developments in methodological and interpretational phases. There has been growing emphasis on quantitative and qualitative analysis of Stone Age artifacts and from 1960s extensive use of statistics is being made in the field of prehistoric archaeology (Misra 1962, Jacobson 1979). The discipline experienced a drastic change in the perspective of prehistoric studies in India since the 1970s, as a corollary to the new advancements, made in other parts of the world, in methodology and theoretical interpretation.

The Indian subcontinent shows varied geographical settings in respect of landforms, vegetation and drainage system. The fundamental assumption which has been realised is that man is a part of environment (natural and social) and that his behavioural patterns (explicated by an appraisal of archaeologically visible residue of human behaviour) reflect his adaptive strategies in time and space. Moreover, it has now become a common practice to subject an archaeological site for intensive investigations to enumerate the sum total of human behaviour: land use patterns, exploitative strategies, dietary habits and the possible type of social organisation. Fortunately, in Indian context, parallels for such exploitation can be drawn from the traditional ethnics (the so called tribal) whose occupational zones, quite often are contiguous with the Stone Age habitats.

Stone Age studies in Indian subcontinent since the 1960s have established on firm grounds the temporal spatial distribution of Lower, Middle and Upper Palaeolithic and Mesolithic periods respectively. Indian prehistorians are focusing attention to evaluate the interaction of man with the environments and the variation within a cultural system (called micro variation) by investigating a single geographical unit at the micro level. This has been adopted since 1970s by the a few archaeologists (Misra 1973, Jacobson 1975, Murty 1982, Paddayya 1982, Cooper 1983).

Against this background, the Indravati basin in undivided Koraput district of Odisha (previously Orissa) has been investigated to understand the cultural remains and behavioural patterns of the prehistoric people within a well defined ecosystem. The study area constitutes ecotones with characteristic land forms, flora and fauna and drainage systems.

The aim of the study on the one hand, is to reconstruct the succession of cultural variations (typo-technologically with a cultural system), distribution pattern etc. and on the other hand predicting models on the subsistence behaviour of the prehistoric fisher-hunter-gatherers of the region, adopting the approach of ethnographic analogy.

Among the previous research in the field of prehistory of Odisha, the contribution of G.C. Mohapatra (1962) and K.C. Tripathi (1972) are noteworthy. They explored almost all the districts of Odisha and reconstructed the prehistoric cultural succession. The present writer conducted a micro level investigation of a geographical area, which approximately covers about 2,400 sq km. This investigation brought to light 17 Upper Palaeolithic and 85 Mesolithic sites. Such an intensive survey of a limited geographical area and interpretation of the data on the basis of ethnographic approach is rather the first attempt in prehistoric study of Odisha. Results of present study are presented focusing the environment and the Stone Age culture, and the ethnographic study of the local tribes with special reference to the subsistence economy of the tribe 'Gadaba'.

Chapter - 2

Present Day Environment of the Study Area

The state of Odisha, located on the eastern coast of India, lies between 17°31' North latitude to 22°31' North latitude and from 81°31' East longitude to 87°29' East longitude. It is bounded by West Bengal and Jharkhand to the north, Chhattisgarh to the west, Andhra Pradesh and Telangana to the south and Bay of Bengal to the east. Geographically the state can be divided into four distinct regions such as Northern Plateau, Central River Basin, Coastal Plains, and Eastern Ghats.

Northern Plateau

The Northern Plateau covers the undivided districts of Mayurbhanj, Keonjhar and Sundergarh and Pallahara subdivision of Dhenkanal district. It is an undulating upland, frequently intersected by hill ranges and rivers. It is a continuation of the Chhotanagpur Plateau. The average elevation of the plateau in the central region is 914 m.

Central River Basin

It lies between the Northern Plateau and Eastern hills and comprises the watershed areas of the principal rivers of the state, namely the Mahanadi, the Brahmani and the Baitrani. These three river valley run almost parallel to each other. Isolated hills rising abruptly from the plains are a frequent sight in this tract.

Coastal Plains

The Coastal Plains of Odisha stretch from the Subarnarekha in the North to the Rushikulya in the South. The Coastal region has been formed by the six major rivers which bring silt from their catchments. The six rivers are the Subarnarekha, the Budhabalanga, the Baitrani, the Brahmani, the Mohanadi and the Rushikulya. The coastal plains cover most of the undivided districts of Balasore, Cuttack, Puri and Ganjam. Balasore, Ganjam and Puri are sandy whereas Cuttack is swampy and marshy.

Eastern Ghats

These are a series of hill ranges of heterogeneous composition, which stretch from the northern border of Odisha through the coastal region of Andhra Pradesh to join Nilgiri in the western part of Tamil Nadu. They cover the undivided Koraput, Kalahandi, Kandhamal and Ganjam districts. The average elevation is 762 m and the highest peak is the Deomali (1,670 m) of Koraput. The Eastern hill comprise wide upland plateau with forests.

ADMINISTRATIVE UNITS

Odisha assumed the status of a Province in 1936, when it comprised six districts (Cuttack, Balasore, Puri, Sambalpur, Ganjam and Koraput) (Fig. 2.1). During 1948 and 1949, 24 Princely States were merged with the province to form the State of Orissa (presently Odisha). The state on the eastern coast of India is presently divided into 30 districts (as on 2021).

PEOPLE

According to 1961 census, the population of Odisha was 1,75,48,846 persons living in 46,500 villages and 62 towns spread over 1,56,000 sq km. The coastal tract is more thickly populated than the inland areas. The least populated areas are the Eastern Ghats.

On the basis of 1961 census Odisha had a tribal population of 42,23,757, which is a little over 24 percent of the total population of the state. Odisha ranks second in the number of tribal population (the first being Madhya Pradesh) and in the number of tribe represented, (the first

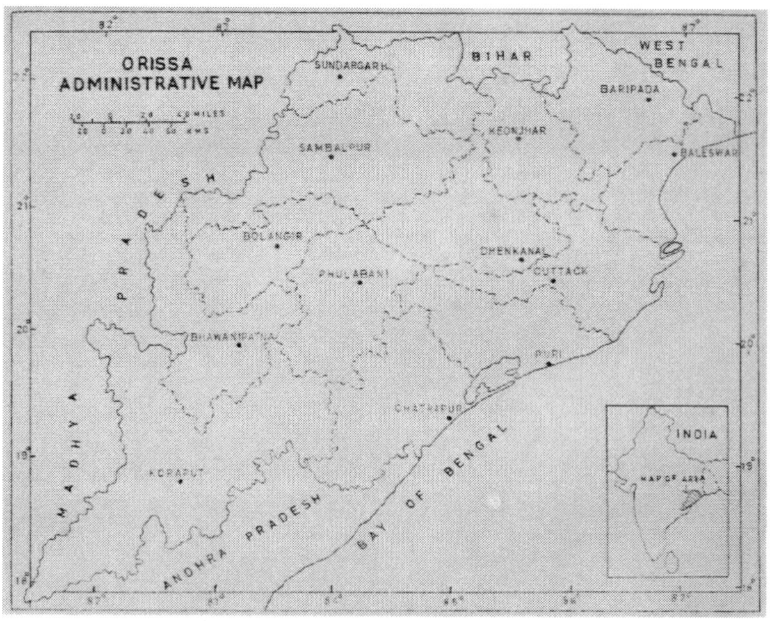

Fig. 2.1: Administrative map of Odisha (as on 1983)

being Assam). There are 62 tribes of which the most numerous are Khond (8,18,847), Gond (4,45,705), Santal (4,11,181), Saora (3,11,614), Munda (2,21,399), Kolha (2,03,515), Shabar (91,95,613), Paraja (1,59,856), Bhottada (1,59,091), Bhuiya (1,56,878), Oraon (1,29,061), Kisan (1,25,668), Bhumij (1,16,181), Baithudi (1,04,542), Kharia (96,691), Binjhal (76,692), Koya (55,284), Bhumia (50,294), Kol (46,397), Sounti (44,409), Gadaba (43,939), Ho (43, 323), Mirdhas (26,660) and Juang (21,890). Among the religious groups, Hindus constitute the majority. They are followed by Muslims, Christians, Sikhs, Jains and Buddhists.

PHYSIOGRAPHY OF KORAPUT

The undivided Koraput[1] district (17°50' and 20°50' North latitude and 81°27' and 84°10' East longitude) was the southernmost district in the state. It is the northernmost extension of the Eastern Ghats. The undivided Koraput district was bounded by Kalahandi district of Odisha and Raipur district of Madhya Pradesh on the north, Bastar district (earlier Madhya Pardesh) on the west, the district of East Godavari and Vishakhapatanam of Andhra Pradesh on the south and by districts of Srikakulam (Andhra Pradesh) and Ganjam (Odisha) on the east. Its southeastern boundary was almost parallel to the sea coast and its shortest distance from the sea was 67 km, whereas the most remote corner of the district was more than 300 km away from sea. It was the largest district of Odisha in 1983 and also one of the largest in India. The area of the district was 27,020 sq km.

Koraput district was established on 1st April, 1936. The present district of Koraput lies at 17°4' to 20°7' North latitude and 81°24' to 84°2' East longitude. It is presently bounded by Rayagada in the east, Bastar district of Chhatisgarh in the west and Malkangiri district in the south.

The district is marked by geographic diversity and can be divided into four distinctively dissimilar tracts, each separated from other by natural barriers. The easternmost tract consists of the valleys of the rivers Nagabali and Vamsadhara, which cover Bissamcuttack, Rayagada and Kashipur Tahsils. The second tract, which is a 1000 m high plateau, extended from the north to the southernmost units and is about 176 km long with an average width of 64 km. The plateau drains westwards into Godavari basin through Indravati, Kolab/Sabari and Machkund/Sileru. The third natural tract is a plateau with an elevation of 650 m. It occupies Jeypore, Nowrangpur subdivisions and extends to the west and north-west into the neighbouring state of Madhya Pradesh. The fourth natural tract is Malkangiri subdivision which contains the valleys of Sileru and Savari. It is a flat plain varying in elevation from 250 m to 60 m.

The district is named after the town of Koraput, which is also the district headquarter. Regarding the origin of the name, the commonly accepted theory is that one Khara Naika

1. The description and discussion is based on the information collected in 1983. In the last four decades there have been considerable changes in the administrative divisions as well as boundaries of the district and the state. Hence, the term undivided Koraput district is used to denote the district of Koraput as on 1983.

got a locality as a gift from Nandapur king of the Nanda dynasty for his faithful services. He established a village as "Khora Putu" after his name which later became Koraput.

The district was formed by the merger of the zamindaris of the area, mainly Kashipur and Jeypore. In the ancient time when Nalas were ruling over this area, Pushkari near modern Umarkote was the capital city. In the medieval period Nandapur became the capital under Silvamsi kings and sometimes under the kings of Solar dynasty. Viravikram Deo of the Solar dynasty shifted his capital to Jeypore in the middle of the 17th century. Koraput was chosen by British in 1870 for better health prospect as a camp near Jeypore. Before 1936, Koraput was part of the Madras Presidency, as a subdivision of Vizagapatanam district (present Vishakhapatnam in Andhra Pradesh). But by the merger of zamindaris, mainly Kashipur and Jeypore, it was formed into a district in 1936.

As on 1983, the district of Koraput (Fig. 2.2) had 6 subdivisions namely – Koraput, Nowrangpur, Joypore, Malkangiri, Nayagoda and Gunupur. There were 14 Tahsils, namely – Koraput, Nandapur, Machhakunda, Jeypore, Kotpad, Borringuna, Nowrangpur, Umerkote, Malkangiri, Notu, Rayagoda, Kashipur, Gunupur and Bissamcuttack. The district had 40 police stations, 42 blocks, 14 towns and 6,124 villages.

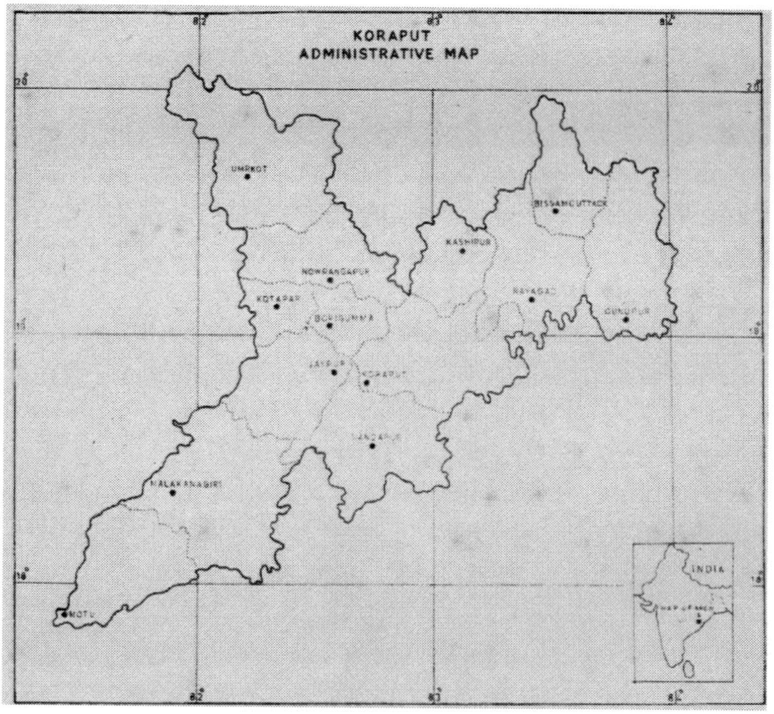

Fig. 2.2: Administrative Map of Koraput district (as on 1983)

The census of India 1961 accounted for 1,561,051 total populations in the Koraput district out of which 1, 97,618 are scheduled castes and 9, 54,338 are scheduled tribes. The tribal population of Koraput district was 61.13% as against 24.06% of the entire state. But if the scheduled castes and scheduled tribes population are added then it goes up to 73.79%. The tribal concentration is more than 50% in all the six subdivisions: Rayagoda (63.2%), Gunupur (58.0%), Malkangiri (57.0%), Koraput (56.6%), Nowrangpur (55.0%) and Jeypore (51.2%). There are 62 tribes in Odisha, of which 51 are founded in Koraput district. The rural population is 88.86% and the density of population is 92% per sq km. A comparative demographic table of Koraput district and Odisha is given bellow in Table 2.1.

Table 2.1: Demography of Koraput district and Odisha (Census of India 1961)

	Koraput	*Odisha*
Geographical area	27,020 sq km	1,55,707 sq km
Population	24,84,005	2,63,70,271
Rural Population	22,03,043	2,32,59,984
Urban Population	2,80,962	32,10,267
Percentage of Rural to Total Population	88.68%	88.20%
Scheduled Tribes Population	13,71,550	59,15,067
Percentage of Scheduled Tribe to Total Population	55.21%	22.43%
Scheduled Caste Population	3,49,307	38,65,543
Percentage of Scheduled Caste to Total Population	14.06%	14.66%
Density of Population per sq km	92	169
Female per 1000 Male	98200.00%	99400.00%
Distribution of Main Workers		
a. Cultivation	53.74%	47.00%
b. Agricultural Labour	28.54%	27.65%
c. House hold Industries	1.90%	3.47%
d. Others	15.82%	21.88%
Literates Percentage of Total Population		
a. Persons	15.83%	34.12%
b. Male	23.17%	46.90%
c. Female	8.44%	21.11%

The main tribal communities are Paraja, Gadaba, Koya, Bonda, Bhottada, Saora, Khond and Gonda. The subsistence pattern of Koya, Gadabas, Paraja and Bonda depends on shifting cultivation, hunting, fishing and gathering. These tribals represent pockets of population who are least affected by cultural contact with advance groups and traditional persist in their subsistence economy.

GEOLOGY

Geologically the undivided Koraput district forms a part of the Indian peninsular shield, one of the oldest rock mass on the earth, which has remained generally stable up to the Tertiary era. The chief rock types comprises Archaean, Cuddapah, Tertiary and recent formation like Laterite and Alluvium (Fig. 2.3).

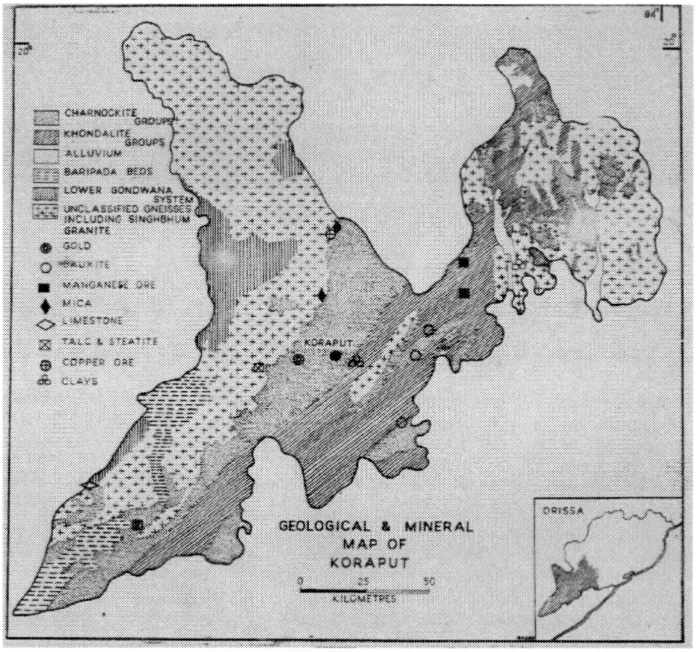

Fig. 2.3: Geological and Mineral Map of undivided Koraput

Archaean

Archaean, the ancient rocks of the Indian peninsular comprises of gneies, a rock, which in mineral composition may vary from granite to gabbro, but which possesses a constant, more or less foliated or banded structures. The gneiss frequently shows great look of uniformity either of composition or of structure and varies from place to place. The Archaean can be divided (Table 2.2) into sedimentary and igneous. Each group is further subdivided into two sub groups as Khondalite, Calc – gneisses, Gneissose granites, and Charnockite series respectively.

Table 2.2: Divisions of the Archaean rocks

Archaean	Sedimentary	Calc – gneisses
		Khondalite
	Igneous	Gneissose granites
		Charnockite series

Khondalite

Khondalite, the name is originated from the Khond inhabitants of Odisha. The Khondalite, a metamorphosed rock (Paraschists), an extremely developed rock-series is essentially garnet–sillimanite schists containing graphite, some quartz and feldspar. It forms a part of Koraput plateau and occurs with the Charnockite. It dominates in the slopes of Eastern Ghats.

Calc – gneisses

Calc-gneisses are associated with the Khondalites, usually at their junction with the gneisses granites. These are believed to be sedimentary origin. Nearly all the minerals of these gneisses are of lime, the rock have been called Caleaveous or Calc-gneisses. These are observed in some parts of Koraput district.

Gneissose Granites

This is the most common rock type of the Jeypore and Malkangiri subdivision. The fine grained biotite gneiss which is quite different from the country crystalline granite gneiss occurs in the Malkangiri subdivision at Eastern Ghats. It is composed of angular grains of quartzs and feldspar. The biotite – gneiss is associated with numerous region or northeast of Tentulikhunti.

Charnockite series

This name is given to a series of granitoid rock of south India, occurring among the older Archaean gneisses and achiest of the peninsula. These rocks are medium to coarse grained, dark–coloured, basic holocrystalline, granitoid gneisses. Charnockite occurs on the western slopes of Eastern Ghats and sometimes in peaks of the Koraput hills. Khondalite constitute the flat topped hills and plateau while the Charnockite forms sharp ridges and hills.

Cuddapah

Cuddapah formation is composed of a number of more or less parallel series or groups of ancient sedimentary strata. Quartzite is the most common rock of this formation. It is seen along the undivided Koraput–Kalahandi border to the north of Nowrangpur. The rocks are normally horizontally bedded. The main part in the series in Koraput district is formed of purple shades and slates with intercalations of lime stone in places overlying a variable thickness of coarse white quartzite. Exposures of these rocks are seen around the Gupeswar Siriveda area near Jeypore and Duma-jodinkondojodi area near Koraput and Nadivadu and Kottanuta near Malkangiri.

TERTIARY AND RECENT FORMATION

Laterite is well developed in some patches of eastern hills region. It can be divided into high level laterite and low level laterite. The high level laterite occurs at an elevation of 915 m to

1220 m. It is also found in Jeypore and Koraput region. The low level laterite is usually found on the plains at the base of the hills, which is comparatively at low level then the high level laterite.

RIVER SYSTEM

The undivided Koraput district is drained by five important rivers. They are Vamsadhara, Nagavali, Indravati, Kolab and Machkund.

Vamsadhara

It originates in Bissamcuttak Tahsil of undivided Koraput district, flows through the extreme north of the district as a small stream up to Gudari village, from there it becomes a major river and flows through Gunupur Tahsil of undivided Koraput and after about 3 km of Gunupur it enters Ganjam district. The total length of the river is 216 km out of which 110 km lies in undivided Koraput. After flowing for a short distance in Ganjam district it enters Andhra Pradesh near Srikakulam district and finally drains in to the Bay of Bengal. The river has a total catchment of 11,465 sq km out of which 9,375 sq km falls within the undivided Koraput district.

Nagavali

Nagavali originates in Kalahandi district, enters undivided Koraput near the village Sindupodar, north of Kalyansingpur, passes through Kalaynsingpur and Rayagoda, and then flows into Srikakulam district of Andhra Pradesh, it flows parallel to the Vamsadhara. The total length of the river is 190 km of which 80 km lies in undivided Koraput. It has a catchment of 9,347 sq km of which 4,457 sq km is within undivided Koraput district. It drains into the Bay of Bengal after flowing for a short distance through Srikakulam district in Andhra Pradesh.

Indravati

Indravati (Plate 2.1 and 2.2) is the second largest river. It originates near Nardiguda village of Kalahandi district. According to legend, it emerged from the base of a mango tree (Ombravrikha) in the form of three small streams. After a short distance these streams join together and form a bigger stream. Further downstream it receives a number of hill streams and forms into a major river and enters undivided Koraput district near the Gaurakurumali village of Tentulikhunti Tahsil. It flows through Kashipur, Nowrangapur and Kotpad Tahsils of undivided Koraput district, than enters Bastar to join the Godavari river. The extreme upstream channel of the river is rocky with a boulderly bed, but as it enters the plains at Nowrangapur the nature of the river bed changes to coarse sandy with thick alluvial banks.

Plate 2.1: River Indravati

Plate 2.2: The Indravati river near Nowrangpur

The total length of the river is 410 km of which 95 km lies in undivided Koraput district. The main tributaries of Indravati are Podagada Nullah, Muran Nullah, Telengiri Nullah and Bhaskel Nullah. The Podagada, Muran and Telengiri Nullahs originate from Dasamantopur of Koraput Taluk and join the Indravati near Khattiguda, Indanpur and Ratali villages respectively.

The Bhaskel originates in the Dandavaranga Hills of Omorkot Tahsil of undivided Koraput and flows to meet the Indravati near Kotpad just before entering Madhya Pradesh (presently Chhattisgarh).

All these rivers originate in Eastern Ghats, flow through the hilly and forested country and enter the plains. Even with a little rainfall in the hilly catchment area the rivers swell and produce flash flood.

Kolab

It originates from the Sinkaram hills of undivided Koraput near Jeypore. The total length of the river is about 340 km of which only 70 km lies in undivided Koraput district. It enters Bastar and finally meets the Godavari.

Machkund

It rises in the Madgol Hills of Visakhapatnam district of Andhra Pradesh on the 914 m plateau near Vondragedda. It flows for a short distance forming the boundary between Andhra Pradesh and Odisha. Then after covering 39 km, it takes a westward direction, about 50 km south of Jeypore and enters the valley through the hills. There are several waterfalls, of which the one at Machkund (165 m) is the most famous. After Kondakamberu it assumes the name Sileru (rocky stream) and joins the Saberi at Moter. The total length of the Machkund-Sileru is 230 km of which 47 km lies in undivided Korput and for next 150 km flows along the border between Koraput district of Odisha and Andhra Pradesh.

SOILS

Soils (Fig. 2.4) of undivided Koraput are very sandy and lateritic in nature. They contain very high percentage of Nitrogen and Phospheric acid. The S102 /R203 ratio of the clay fraction is about 1.8 but that of S102 /A1203 is 3.1 and 2.85 for surface and subsoil, respectively. The water holding capacity is low, but the moisture equivalent appears to be too high in relation to the sandy nature of the soil (ICAR 1958: 81-85). The major soil of Koraput district are Red soil, Laterites and lateritic soils, Black soils and Alluvial soils.

Red Soils

These soils cover large areas in the district. These are derived from weathering of rocks like granites, gneisses, charnockite, diorites and others which are relatively richer in clay forming minerals. The red colour of the soil is due to diffusion of iron, rather than a high proportion of it. The soils are deficient in lime, organic matter, nitrogen and medium on phosphorous and potash. The pH is slightly acidic to neutral. The soil is medium to coarse in texture.

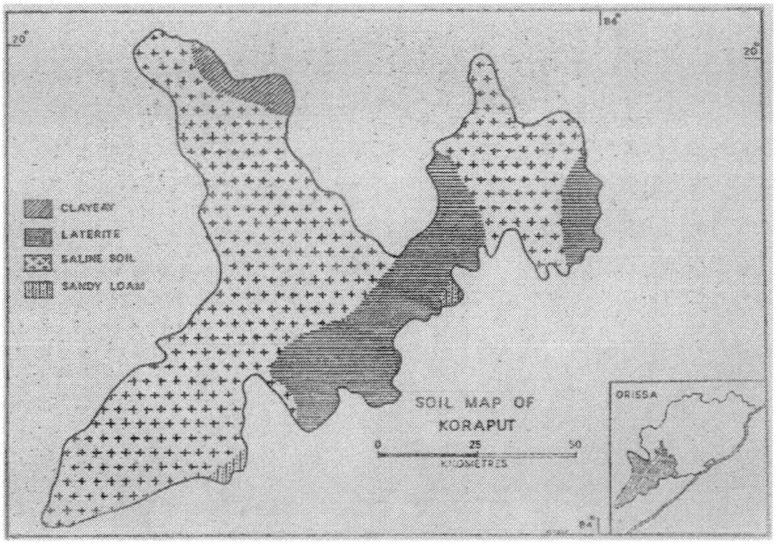

Fig. 2.4: Soil Map of undivided Koraput

These soils are found in whole of undivided Koraput subdivision and partly Jeypore and Nowrangpur tahsil.

Laterite and Lateritic Soils

These are generally reddish or yellowish red in colour. The freshly out laterite bricks on exposure dehydrate and become as hard as granite. The lateritic soils are associated with and derived from laterites. These soils largely occur as cappings on hills over plateaus. The pH is generally low. They are found in Gunupur, part of Koraput and Jeypore tahsils.

Black Soils

These are another soils having characteristically dark colour, varying from dark brown to deep black. These are very fine in texture. They are sticky when wet and very hard when dry. Occasionally these soils are found in Umarkote, Nowrangpur and Gunupur tahsils. The black cotton soils are black in colour, slightly alkaline in nature. It is observed in Umarkote tahsils.

Alluvial Soils

These soils are found along the streams. They are further grouped as:

Fine silt alluvial soils: These soils contain fine sand and silt, as found on both the banks of river Indravati, near Nowrangpur and Boriguma.

Coarse-textured alluvial soils: These soils contain coarse sand silt and clay as observed on both the banks of the Vamsadhara.

Coarse textured sandy soils: These are composed of a large percentage of coarse textured sand and small amounts of organic matter. These soils are found on both the banks of Nogavali and part of Rayagada and Bissamcuttack region.

CLIMATE

Odisha falls under the tropical monsoon climate region. The climate on the west of the Eastern Ghats is more like that of Deccan than the coastal region. Koraput enjoys three distinct seasons in a year: cold season (December to February), hot season (March to May) and monsoon season (June to November). In comparison to other parts of the south-eastern Odisha, Koraput experiences extreme climate during the respective seasons.

Rainfall

The average annual rainfall (Fig. 2.5) of the undivided Koraput district is 1,522 mm about 86% of the total rainfall is received during the monsoon months. The monsoon breaks in the middle of June and continues till the end of November; July and August are the rainiest months of the year. During April and May, most parts of the district receive an average of 101 mm to 127 mm. The average annual rainfall during 1951-60 was 1,868 mm in Kashipur tahsil. The heaviest rainfall in 24 hours was 546.1 mm at Porrangi area on the 4th October 1931.

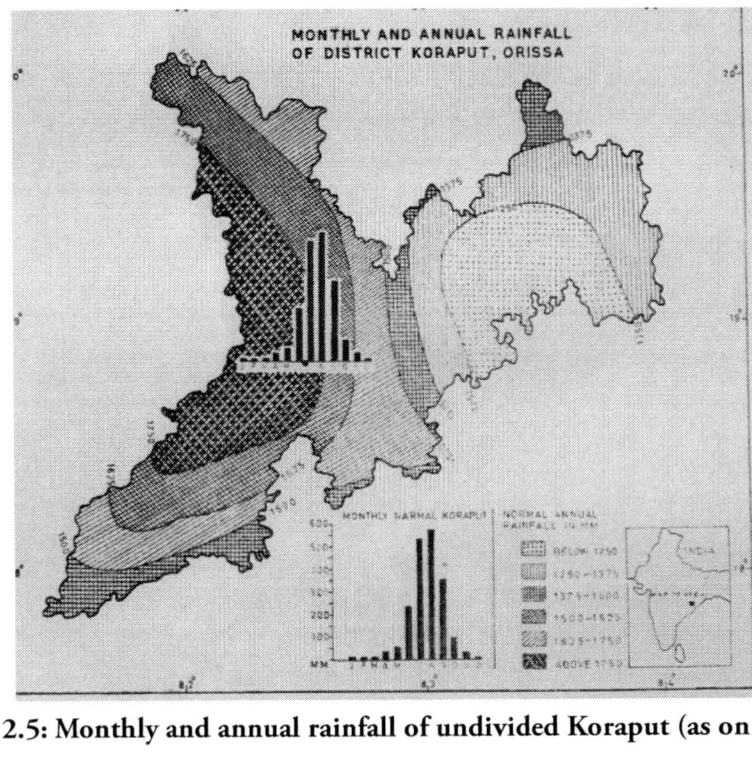

Fig. 2.5: Monthly and annual rainfall of undivided Koraput (as on 1983)

The eastern side of the Ghats gets less rain as it is a rain shadow area. Rayagada region at an elevation of 150 m to 180 m receives an average of 1,300 mm, whereas Koraput region with an elevation of 900 m receives 1,700 mm. The average rainfall at Nowrangpur area is 1658.7 mm.

The rainfall recorded at different rain gauge stations in the district are given in Table 2.3. And the month wise normal and actual rainfall in the district is given in the Table 2.4.

Table 2.3: Normal rainfall in mm at different stations (as on 1983)
(Source: Gazetteer of India, Orissa, Koraput)

Station	*Annual rainfall*
Jeypore	1940.2
Nowrangpur	1658.7
Malkangiri	1671.9
Koraput	1618.5
Padwa	1528.3
Pottangi	1600.6
Gunupur	1213.1
Rayagada	1164.2
Bissamcuttack	1300.2
Koraput District	1521.8

Temperature

March to May is the hot season of the year. December is the coldest month with the mean daily minimum temperature at 11.2°C. But the temperature increases slowly till May. The temperature of the coldest month is between 15°C and 20°C. During summer, at 600 m plateau, the temperature goes up to 112°C while in the Malkangiri region, at 120 m to 240 m; it is 115°C. In Koraput region the temperature (Fig. 2.6) goes up to 103°C. The dry season lasts for four months on the higher elevation towards the southeast of Koraput. The normal temperature (month wise) of the district is given below in Table 2.5.

Humidity

During monsoon and post-monsoon months the humidity is high. In the rest of the year, afternoons are drier. Daily variation of temperature in the cold season causes lot of dew in the morning time. During summer, the wind direction is mainly from south and west, but during monsoon time the winds blow a south-westerly or westerly direction.

Vegetation

The hilly country with a good rainfall, is generally thickly wooded with tall trees, shrubs and grasses. In undivided Koraput, the forest covers about 70 percent of the total area. The total

Table 2.4: Normal and actual rainfall in the district (as on 1983) (Source: Board of Revenue, Orissa Cuttak courted in District Statistical Handbook; Koraput 1976-77)

Year/Month	*Normal rainfall in mm*	*Actual rainfall in mm*	*Deviation from normal rainfall in mm*
1974	1521.8	1009.8	–512.0
1975	1521.8	1580.7	+58.9
1976	1521.8	1145.6	–376.2
1977	1521.8	1750.6	+228.8
Monthly distribution for 1977			
January	6.7	0.1	–6.6
February	11.3	2.1	–9.2
March	16.2	12.3	–3.9
April	53.4	107.3	–3.9
May	75.0	62.2	–12.4
June	205.8	154.3	–51.5
July	351.1	429.7	–78.6
August	380.3	522.2	+114.9
September	262.1	250.5	–11.6
October	116.5	53.7	–62.8
November	35.8	151.7	+115.9
December	7.6	4.1	–3.5

forested area is about 18,914 sq km of which 4118.1 sq km is reserved land, 284.79 sq km is protected land and roughly 12,950 sq km is unreserved land. The existing forest is concentrated in the hilly region and the plains show less vegetation (Fig. 2.7).

The whole forested area has been divided into 15 ranges 8 in Jeypore and 7 in Rayagada division. The Jeypore division covers the whole of Nowrangpur and Malkangiri subdivisions and the Rayagada division covers the Koraput, Rayagada, and Gunupur subdivision (Orissa District Gazetteers: Koraput 1966).

The southern extremity of undivided Koraput possesses:

(i) northern tropical moist deciduous forest which occur in continuation with semi-evergreen type. The western portion of Koraput is covered with

(ii) northern tropical dry deciduous forest. The dry vegetation type includes:

   (a) Tectona-Terminalia series and

   (b) Shorsa-Buchanania cleistanthus series.

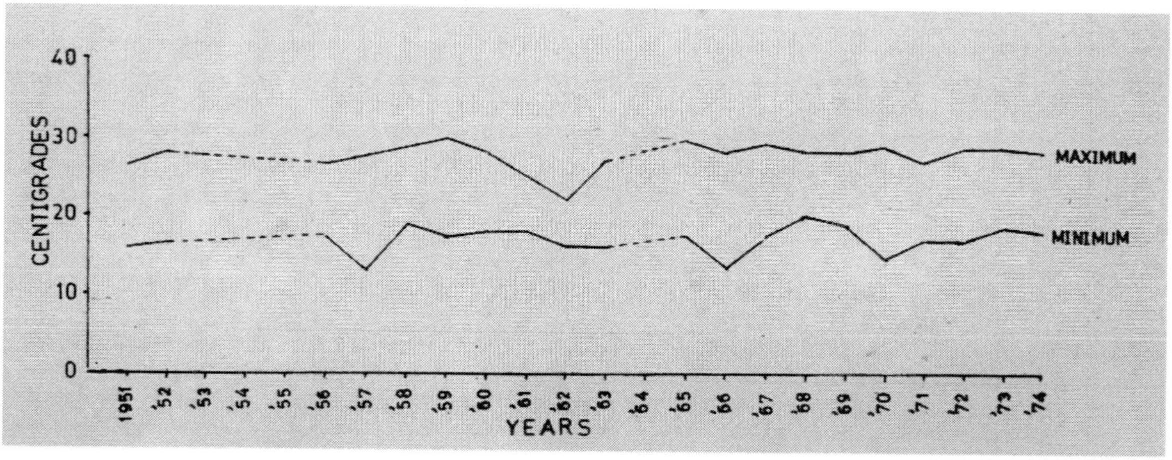

Fig. 2.6: Mean annual temperature of undivided Koraput district during 1951-1974

Table 2.5: Temperature (month wise) of the district (Source: Gazetteer of India, Orissa, Koraput)

Months	*Mean daily Maximum temperature*	*Mean daily Minimum temperature*	*Highest Maximum ever recorded*	*Lowest Minimum ever recorded*
January	25.3	11.9	29.4 1958 Jan 29	6.1 1956 Jan 18
February	28.2	14.1	31.7 1953 Feb 27	6.7 1956 Feb 8
March	31.6	17.7	36.1 1933 Mar 27	10.6 1952 Mar 4
April	33.3	20.6	37.2 1956 Apr 27	15.0 1956 Apr 23
May	34.0	22.6	38.9 1956 May 10	17.2 1955 May 7
June	30.6	22.4	40.0 1953 Jun 12	17.8 1955 Jun 30
July	25.6	20.3	31.1 1932 Jul 12	16.1 1957 Jul 7
August	25.4	20.1	30.6 1958 Aug 10	15.6 1957 Aug 27
September	26.2	19.9	29.4 1955 Sep 27	16.7 1957 Sep 12
October	26.0	18.2	30.6 1957 Oct 16	10.6 1954 Oct 30
November	24.9	13.3	28.9 1957 Nov 16	8.3 1955 Nov 14
December	24.2	11.2	27.8 1957 Dec 17	5.0 1955 Dec 28
Annual	27.9	17.7	–	–

The Tectona-Terminalia series covers a small part of the southwest of Koraput district. This forest type generally grows on tropical black clayey soils and on tropical red soil. The main types of trees in this series are *Tectona grandis, Terminalia tomentosa, Pterocarpus swietenia, Adina cordifolia, Diospyros melanoxylon* and *Lannea coromandelica*. This series consists of a few shrubs, species like *Aristida adscensionis, Aristida hystrix, Cassia auriculata* and *Canthium parviflorum*.

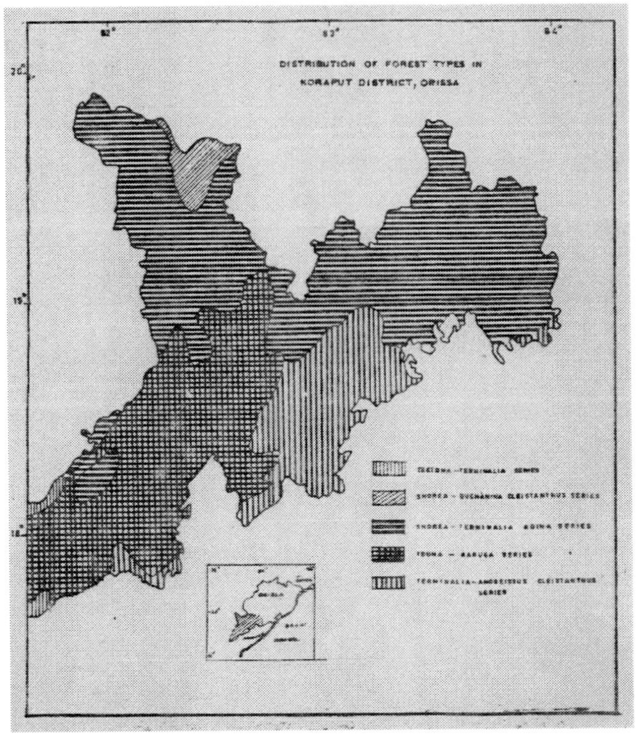

Fig. 2.7: Distribution of forest types in undivided Koraput District, Odisha

The Shorsa-Buchanania cleistanthus series occurs in Koraput up to an altitude of 600 m. It consists of *Shorea robusta, Terminalia bellirica, Semecarpus anacardium,* and *Anogeissus latifolia.* The moist vegetation type includes Shorea-Terminalia-Adins series and Tcons-Garuga series. The Shorea-Terminalia-Adins series occurs in Koraput district and its neighbouring area. This forest type generally grows on red soils either loamy or sandy. The main types are *Shorea robusta, Terminalia tomentosa, Dalbergia latifolia, Adina cordifolia, Xylia xylocarpa,* and *Bambusa arundinacea.* The Tcons-Garuga series is to be found on the Koraput plateau. The series is also associated with red sandy soils. It consists of semi-evergreen species like *Garuga pinnata* and *Salmalia malabarica* and deciduous species are *Pterocarpus marsupium, Terminalia tomentosa* and *Emblica officinalis.*

According to the nature of occurrence the vegetation falls under the following types.

Central Plateau of 900 m and Upwards

Earlier this area must have been covered with sub tropical wet hill type with evergreen vegetation, but due to shifting cultivation a part of this has been reduced to barren land. Above 1200 m grass land is found and tree growth is very much limited. A part of this is covered with deciduous species such as *Pterocarpus marsupium, Bursera serrata, Garuga pinnata, Terminalia bellirica, Dalbergia lanceolaria, Eugenia jambolana, and Bombax malabaricum.* The evergreen species are *Magnolia champaca, Pongamia pinnata,* and *Dendrocalamus strictus.*

Jeypore Plateau of 600 m

The greater part of the plateau is covered with sal forest. The main types of trees in this plateau are *Shorea robusta, Dillenia indica, Gmelina arborea, Bassia latifolia, Phyllanthus emblica,* and Bridelia species Grasses include *Imperata arundinacea* and *Jasminum angustifolium.*

Malkangiri Plateau

Sal is found in the Ghats on the Malkangiri plateau. Teak (*Tectona grandis*) is most common on this plateau. Bamboo is equally widespread in this region. The varities are *Dendrocalamus strictus,* and *Bambusa arundinacea.* Bissamcuttack, Umarkot, Nowrangpur, Jeypore, Kotpad, Gudari and part of Ramagiri range are covered with Sal forest.

The common trees around the present village and forest are Mango (*Mangifera indica*), Penas (*Artocarpus integrifolia*), Ber (*Ziziphus jujuba*), Jamun (*Eugenia Jambolana*), Tentuli (*Tamarindus indica*), Banya (*Ficus benghalensis*) and Neam (*Azadirachta indica*).

The aquatic vegetation found in the ponds and ditches are Padma (*Nelumbium speciosum*), Kain (*Nymphaea lotus*), and Singada (*Lisianthus oristalum*). Following are the species in the forests of Koraput (Table 2.6).

Table 2.6: Floral species found in the forests of undivided Koraput

Sl. No.	*Vernacular name*	*Botanical name*
1	Saguan	*Tectona grandis*
2	Chandan	*Santalum album*
3	Sal	*Shorea robusta*
4	Piasal	*Pterocarpus marsupium*
5	Bandhan	*Ougeinia oojeinensis*
6	Sisoc	*Dalbergia sissoo*
7	Kurum	*Adina cordifolia*
8	Khair	*Acacia catechu*
9	Gambhar	*Gmelina arborea*
10	Kangada	*Xylia xylocarpa*
11	Champa	*Magnolia champaca*
12	Rose wood	*Dalbergia latifolia*
13	Toom	*Toona ciliata*
14	Rakta Chandan	*Pterocarpus santalinus*

15	Assan	*Terminalia elliptica*
16	Kasi	*Bridelia melanoxylon*
17	Mahul	*Bassia latifolia*
18	Mango	*Mangifera indica*
19	Kendu	*Diospyros melanoxylon*
20	Panasa	*Artocarpus integrifolia*
21	Sema	*Bombax ceiba*
22	Jamu	*Syzygium cumini*
23	Bhalia	*Semecarpus anacardium*
24	Ambada	-
25	Amla	*Phyllanthus emblica*
26	Bel	*Aegle marmelos*
27	Gu	*Dillenia indica*
28	Tentuli	*Tamarindus indica*
29	Tal	*Borassus flabellifer*
30	Neam	*Azadirachta indica*
31	Karacmanga	*Averrhoa carambola*
32	Kodamba	*Neolamarckia cadamba*
33	Asok	*Saraca indica*
34	Tentra	*Albizia lebbeck*
35	Dhaura	*Anogeissus latifolia*
36	Rehini	*Soymida febrifuga*
37	Sindha	*Lagerstroemia parviflora*
38	Nitkunia	*Mitragyna parvifolia*
39	Dhaman	*Grewia tiliifolia*
40	Panigambar	*Trewia nudiflora*
41	Ghodolanjia	*Albizia chinensis*
42	Chhachina	*Alstonia scholaris*
43	Mohanim	*Ailanthus excelsa*
44	Gindhini	*Sterculia urens*
45	Kansa	*Hymenodictyon excelsum*
46	Simili	*Bombax malabaricum*
47	Palms	*Butea frondosa*

48	Maladhua	*Erythrina indica*
49	Bara	*Ficus benghalensis*
50	Aswastha	*Ficus religiosa*
51	Dimbiri	*Ficus glomerata*
52	Karanja	*Pongamia indica*
53	Chakunda	*Dalbergia lanceolaria*
54	Khanar	*Phoenix sylvestris*
55	Kantei Koli	*Caesalpinia sappan*
56	Chara Koli	-
57	Bara Koli	*Zexyphus jujube*
Creeper		
1	Kudei	*Wrightia antidysenterica*
2	Pita tarada	*Luffa pluckilina*
3	Kumbhatua	*Smilax macrophylla*
Grass		
1	Mutha	*Cyperus rotundus*
2	Bena	–
3	Beruaghas	*Cyperus tegetum*
4	Duba	–
5	Sabai	*Imperata arundinacea*
6	Bagali	*Polonidium angustifolium*

FAUNA

With its varying and contiguous blocks of different types of forests, undivided Koraput district is rich in game and aerial fauna. As a consequent of deforestation, hunting and poaching wildlife has dwindled in the major part of the district.

Aged tribal informants of Singleari and Haldi villages recall that in the past wild buffaloes, black bucks, and spotted deers existed in large herds in the forests of Pannabeds, Papadanand and Chitra region. Among the existing big game, the spotted deer or chital (*Axis axis*), barking deer (*Muntiacus muntjak*), sambar (*Cervus unicolor*), wild bear (*Sus scrofa cristatus*) are common in the forest of Umarkot, Jhorigam and Kotpad ranges.

Indian buffalo (*Bubalus babalis*) is found in small number in Malkangiri subdivision. The wolf (*Canis lupus*), bison (*Bos gaurus*) are generally found near Ramgiri, Malkangiri and Umarkot area. The tiger (*Panthera tigris*), leopards (*Panthera pardus*), nilgai (*Baselaphus tragocamelus*) and elephants (*Elephus maximus*) are occasionally found in Umarkot, Malkangiri, Dasamntapur area.

The four-horned antelope (*Tetracarus cuadricornis*), blackbuck (*Antilope cervicapra*), swamp deer (*Rucervus duvaucelii*) and the mouse deer (Tragullus) are rarely found. Sambar (*Cervus unicolor*), chital (Axis axis), Bear (*Melursus ursinus*), Indian fox (*Vulpes bengalensis*), wolf (*Camis lupus* pallipes aureus), common jungle cat (*Felis chaus*), wild dog (*Cuon alpinus alpinus*) and Hyaena (*Hyaena hyaena*) are well represented in most of the forests of Koraput district.

Table 2.7: Important fishes found in the rivers and ponds of Koraput

Sl. No.	*Vernacular name*	*Scientific name*
1	Balia	*Wallaga attu*
2	Magur	*Clarias batrachus*
3	Seula	–
4	Singhi	*Heteropneustes fossilis*
5	Pholi	*Notopterus notopterus*
6	Rohu	*Labeo rohita*
7	Bhakur	*Catla buchanani*
8	Chitala	*Chitala chitala*
9	Adi	*Mystus cavasius*
10	Baligarada	*Glossogobius giuris*
12	Mahurali	*Ambly pharyngeodomola*
13	Kanti	*Mystus cavasius*
14	Jails	*Pargarius pangarius*
15	Kao	*Anabas testudineus*
16	Gadis	*Ophiocephalus lata*
17	Kerandi	*Barbus chola*
18	Bodami	*Nandus nandus*
19	Sala	*Ophicephalus marulius*
20	Chenga	*Ophecephalus gachua*
21	Dandikiri	–
22	Sarana	*Puntius sarana*
23	Jills	*Rasbora daniconius*
24	Jalla	*Oxygaster bacaila*
25	Kuji karandi	–
26	Pita karandi	*Puntius sophore*
27	Ranga chandi	*Ambassis ranga*

Among the smaller species, rabbit (*Leous nigricollis ruficaudstus*), striped squirrel (*Fumambulus palmarum*), the large Indian squirrel (*Ratufa indica*), porcupine (*Hystrix indica*), grey mongoose (*Herpestes edwardsi*) are very common in forests of Koraput district. Among the primates the common langur (*Presbytis entellus*) and the common pati (*Macaca mulatta*) are reported from all parts of the district.

Reptiles include, house lizards, monitor lizards (*Varanus monitor*) and various species of makes like dhaman (Homalepesidae) laudankia (*Cyclops vernalis*); water snakes (*Rhabdophis nigrocinctus* and *Nerodis piaster*), cobra (*Naia naia*), Rait (*Bungarus candidus*), Russel's viper (*Daboia russelii*), python (*Python molurus*) and king cobra.

The common birds are koel (*Eudynamys scolopaceus*), crow (*Corvus brachyrhynchos*), jungle crow (*Corvus macrorhynchos*), Indian myna (*Acridotheres tristis*), hornbill (*Tockus birostris*), king-fisher (*Pelargopsis capensis*) blue rock pigeon (*Columba livia*), baya (*Plocous shiliopinus*), harada (*Crocopus phoenicopterus*), rajalapatt (*Dicridotherus aler*), haladi basanta, dahuka. The important fishes found in the rivers and ponds are provided in Table 2.7. The snub-nosed crocodile (*Crocodylus palustris*), the common tortoise (*Testudo elegans*), crabs and snails are found in Indravati, Kolab, Bhaskel and Vamsadhara rivers. Frogs and toads (*Rhacophorus maculatus*) are very common in ponds, pools and streams.

Chapter 3

Prehistoric Investigation in the Study Area

The earliest discovery of Palaeolithic artifacts in Odisha was made nearly one and half century ago by V. Ball from Angul (Kaliakata), Talchor (Horichandanpur), Dhenkanal, and Sambalapur (Bursapali) (Ball 1875, 1976-1980). P. Acharya (1923-24) and R.D. Banerjee (1930) reported Palaeoliths from Baldipur in present day Mayurbhanj district. In 1939 N.K. Bose and his colleagues discovered additional stone implements of Lower Palaeolithic from the same region. Achariya and Norman (1939) reported a number of Palaeolithic sites from Baripada region in Mayurbhanj district (Bose and Sen 1948).

However systematic research in the prehistory of Odisha began only around 1940. In this phase N.K. Bose and D. Sen excavated a few sites at Kuliana in Mayurbhanj and discovered Lower Palaeolithic in a lateritic deposit. This was followed by the investigation of Bose and Sen (1948, 1951, 1958) in Mayurbhanj. The important sites brought to light by those are Amsika, Baripada, Drahsanegaon, Dhuasuni, Buranora, Kakaberia, Kamta and Kuliana. All are open air Lower Palaeolithic sites located on the bank of the river Burhabalang. The Mayurbhanj industry as defined by them is a core dominating industry with choppers, followed by the bifaces, a few cleavers and having a small admixture of flakes showing cruder workmanship.

The assemblage at Kuliana in characterised by core implements with pebble tools and flakes of unprepared or unifacetted striking platform. Between 1956-1959, G.C. Mohapatra carried out a systematic exploration in the valleys of the river Mahanadi, Brahamani and Burhabalang in the northern districts of Dhenkanal, Sundargarh, Sambalpur, Keonjhar, and Mayurbhanj of Odisha, covering an area of 38,560 km (Mohapatra 1962). His works brought to light a succession of prehistoric cultures in Odisha. He discovered twenty two Lower Palaeolithic sites, twenty five Middle Palaeolithic and eight Mesolithic sites. The Lower Palaeolithic artifacts of coarse-grained quartzite, jasper and quartz are reported from graved I and the detrital secondary laterite in Kuliana and Talcher areas. The industry comprises a high proportion of handaxes, cleavers and side scrapers along with flakes and cores. The bifaces are comparable with the Abbevillio-Acheulian tools of Europe and Africa.

The Middle Palaeolithic artifacts of chert, jasper and finegrained quartzite have been reported (Mohapatra 1962) from twenty five sites from gravel II of cliff section and lateritic murram deposits, from the valleys of Khadkei, Baitarani, Brahmani and Mahanadi. The main tools are scrapers, borers, points, burins, cores and flakes of unprepared platform. This industry has some similarity with the Nevasian industry (Mohapatra 1962: 152-153). Mohapatra (1982) has also reported eight microlithic sites without stratigraphical evidence, from three districts (Mayurbhanj, Keonjhar and Sundergarh). The collection includes 42 specimens and comprise of cores, flakes and a few scrapers without any true microliths.

During late 1950s and early 1960s quite a few isolated discoveries of Stone Age have been reported such as microliths from Kaniha in Talcher sub-division by Ghosh (1958-59: 36), Baramandar, Bonikala, Dangusposi in Keonjhar district by Mitra (1961-62: 36-37), from Tel and its tributaries and from the districts of Bolangir, Ganjam, Kalahandi by Raghunath (1963-64: 27), a few microliths from Vanivihar in Bhubaneshwar by Das (*IAR* 1963-64: 90) and from Balangir by Mukharjee (1968-69: 68).

The work of Tripathy (1972) during the early 1970's gave a footing to the microlithic culture along with Lower and Middle Palaeolithic cultural evidence from Tel river basin. He discovered three sites of pebble tool industry, sixteen sites of flake industries (Middle Palaeolithic) and twenty seven sites of flake blade industry (Mesolithic culture), from south western Odisha, covering the districts of Phulabari, Bolangir, Kalahandi and Sambalpur.

The pebble tool industry comprises choppers, scrapers, borers, points, handaxes and worked flakes on quartzite. The flake industry consist of nodules, cores, scrapers on flakes and cores, points worked flakes and miniature handaxe made on chert, jasper and quartzite. The flake blade industry (Mesolithic culture) includes, blades, flakes, fluted cores, scrapers back blades, retouched blades and lunates. Chert is the most popular raw material. This industry is purely a nongeometric one (Tripathy 1972).

THE STUDY AREA

The present study is mainly based on fieldworks carried out during 1975-80 in the Upper Indravati basin in undivided Koraput district. The fieldworks covered an area of about 2400 sq km along the river Indravati and the tributaries. The Indravati originates from the forest Thesamulrampur Block of Kalahandi district near Madriguda village. Further downstream it receives a number of hill streams and enters Koraput district near the Gaurakurumuli village of Tentulikhunti Tahsil. It flows through Kashipur, Nowrangapur and Kotpad tahsils of Koraput district, and then enters Bastar district of Chattishgarh and joins the Godavari. The river has a course of about, 95 km in Odisha.

AIMS AND OBJECTIVES OF THE RESEARCH

The present study is concerned with establishing cultural chronology and for getting an insight into the living patterns of prehistoric societies and aimed at reconstructing the typo-technological evolution during the Upper Palaeolithic and Mesolithic periods, with the help of intensive exploration in the valley, scientific excavation of a site, typo-technological interpretation and material analysis of cultural material. The study is also aimed in delineating the pattern of prehistoric human settlements against the ecological background of the region.

It is attempted here to postulate the life-ways of the Stone Age hunter-gatherers in the Indravati valley by drawing parallels from the ethnographic evidence from the life patterns of tribes of Koraput with special reference to the tribe Gadaba, giving emphasis on their dependence on the eco-system and their subsistence pattern.

EXPLORATIONS

During six seasons of explorations spread over 12 months during 1975 and 1980, 17 Upper Palaeolithic (Table 3.1) and 85 microlithic sites[1] (Table 3.2) in the forested country side in the eastern part of undivided Koraput district along the river Indravati and its tributaries were discovered (Fig. 3.1). Invariably, they are located in the vicinity of present tribal settlements. All these sites are open air surface sites (except Kirki, a cave site) located on the top, slope and foot of hills, on the plain land and elevated waste land covered with wild bushes and trees. The heights of the hillocks vary from 20 m to 250 m above the general ground level. The sites occur uniformly in between 1 and 7 km from the main river course as well as its tributaries. The average distance between adjacent sites is about 2.5 km and the area varies from 8 to 1250 sq m. A few sites are disturbed due to the cultivation. No archaeological material was found in the river deposits. The sites are grouped as foothill sites, hill slope sites, hill top sites, plain land sites, elevated waste land sites and sites on cultivated land.

UPPER PALAEOLITHIC SITES

1. Paidapali A (PDP A, 19°16', 82°13'30")

It is located 12 km to the south-west of the town of Kodinga, about 2 km from the river Bhaskel, near a small stream. The artifacts are found scattered over a chert bed, covering an approximate area of 1200 sq m. The site has yielded 138 artifacts, of which 14 (10.14%) are shaped artifacts and 124 (89.86%) are simple artifacts. Whitish colour chert is most commonly used raw material which is available right on the site. The artifacts are well preserved and have a fresh appearance but most of them have acquired a thin file of brownish patina.

2. Paidapali B (PDP B, 19°16', 82°13')

The site lies 50 m to the north of Paidapali A and covers an area of about 40 sq m. It has yielded 34 artifacts of which 33 (97.06%) are simple artifacts and one is a double side scraper. Typo-

1. The locations of the sites were recorded based on the administrative divisions and the maps of the district of undivided Koraput during 1975 and 1980.

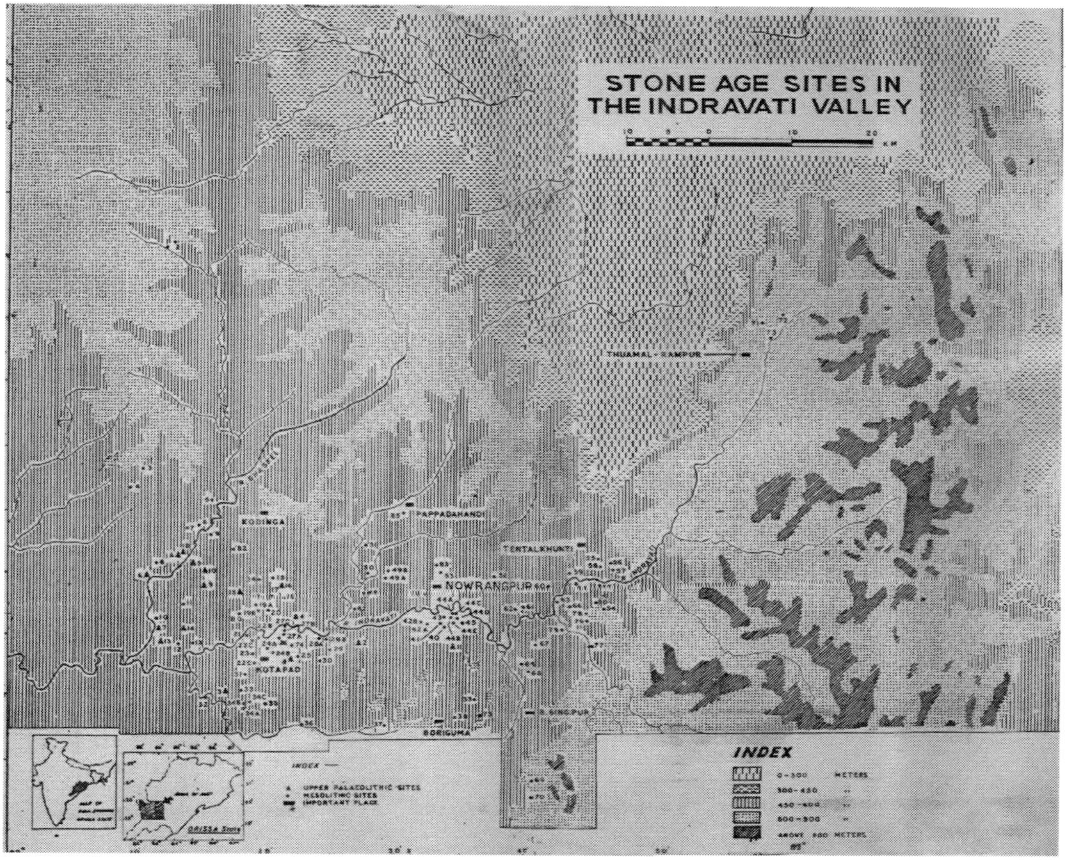

Fig. 3.1: Map of Stone Age Sites in the Indravati Valley

technologically and morphologically they are similar to the Paidapali A assemblage. These are made of chert of yellowish red colour. Most of artifacts are highly patinated.

3. Amota (ATM, 10°10', 82°27')

The village of Amota lies about 15 km north-east of Kotpad town and 3 km south of river Indravati. The artifacts were scattered over an elevated land, stretching about 0.25 km on the right side of the Kotpad-Ghotoria road. The patch covers an area of only 30 sq m. The site has yielded 68 artifacts, of which 60 (88.24%) are simple artifacts and 8 (11.76%) are shaped artifacts. Chert is the raw material used for the manufacture of the artifacts. The artifacts are fresh in condition. The red patination is due to the long time association with red soil.

4. Seamla (SML, 19°4', 82°18')

It is a small village very close to Joura stream. The village is located 8.5 km south-west of Kotpad. A small collection of 40 artifacts was made from a waste land of about 25 sq m. The site is slightly disturbed by recent cultivation. The assemblage comprises large number simple artifacts 32 (80.00%) and 8 (20.00%) of shaped artifacts. The artifacts are made of yellowish red chert. These are fresh.

5. Chirma (CRM, 19°11', 82°22')

The village of Chirma is located north-west of kotpad town at a distance of 6 km approximately. The site is very close to the village. The site is less than a km to the north of Indravati. Sixty six artifacts were collected from a surface of a hillock, over an area of about 50 sq m. The collection comprises 58 (87.88%) simple artifacts and 8 (12.12%) shaped artifacts. Chert is the main raw material. The artifacts are in mint condition.

6. Kosagumura (KOR, 19°16', 82°15')

The village of Kosagumura situated 15 km south-west of Kodinga town and is the block-headquarter of Kodinga. The village is located on the eastern bank of river Bhaskel. The site is situated just behind the block office. The 111 artifacts were found on a rocky waste land covering an area of 150 sq m. Of the total collection 96 (86.49%) are simple artifacts and 15 (13.51%) are shaped artifacts. They are made of quartz chips. The artifacts are highly patinated.

7. Majhidhanua (MDA, 19°15', 82°11')

The village lies 14 km south-west of Kodinga town near the border of Bastar and Koraput. The site is located about 150 m to the left side of the Kodinga-Saraladhanua-Jagdalpur road. The small stream of Bhaskel flows 0.5 km east of the side. Only 36 artifacts were collected from a plain waste land of about 20 sq m. The collection comprises of 35 (97.23%) simple artifacts and 1(2.77%) of shaped artifacts. The artifacts are made of chert exclusively.

8. Ukiapali (UKP, 19°10', 82°11')

The village of Ukiapali is situated about 13 km north-west of Kotpad town, on the right bank of Bhaskel river. A collection of 44 artifacts was made from an elevated land, located north of village Ukiapali at a distance of about 500 m. The assemblage consists of 37(84.10%) simple artifacts and 7 (15.90%) shaped artifacts. Chert is the raw material used for the manufacturing of tools. The artifacts are in mint condition.

9. Chitagaon (CTG 19°8', 82°22')

The village of Chitagaon is situated about 4.5 km south-east of Kotpad, one kilometer north of Kotpad-Vizianogaram road. The artifacts were discovered about 200 m east of the village. These are found scattered over a plain waste land covered with shrub. Only 31 artifacts were collected from this site, out of which 27 (87.09%) pieces are simple artifacts and 4 (11.9%) pieces are of shaped artifacts. These are exclusively made on chert and are fresh on appearance.

10. Kusumpali (KSP, 19°13', 82°13')

The village of Kusumpali lies north of Kotpad at an approximate distance of 20 km. The site is located 0.5 km north of Kusumpali. The Bhaskel river flows north-west of the site at a distance of about 3.5 km. The artifacts were scattered over an elevated land. The site has yielded 21 artifacts from an area of 36 sq m comprises 3 (14.26%) pieces shaped artifacts and 8 (85.71%) pieces simple artifacts, made on reddish yellow chert only. The artifacts are fresh on appearance.

11. Parajasahi (PJS, 19°15', 82°15')

The village lies 2 km south of Kutegura. The site is located 500 m north of the village Parajasahi and about 3 km north-west of Bhaskel river. The site has yielded 151 artifacts, of which 21 (13.9%) are shaped artifacts and 130 (86.09%) are simple artifacts. These are made of yellowish chert with a thin reddish patination.

12. Majiha (MJA, 19°9', 82°34')

The village of Majiha lies 3.5 km north-east of Kotpad and nearly 1.5 km from the river Indravati. The artifacts were scattered over an area of 800 sq m of shrub land. The site has yielded 72 artifacts, of which 8 (11.11%) pieces are shaped artifacts and 64 (88.89%) pieces are simple artifacts. These are exclusively made of yellowish red chert. The redness is the patination due to the long time association with red soil.

13. Sitiliguda (STG, 19°12', 82°22')

The village is situated 15 km north-east of Kotpad town, on the left bank of the Indravati. The site is located on the left bank of Indravati, about 250 m south of the village. The artifacts were found on the top of a hillock and also in the top 2 m of older alluvium. The site is slightly disturbed due to the recent cultivation. Sixty three artifacts were picked up from this area. They comprise 6 (9.52%) pieces of shaped artifacts and 57 (90.47%) pieces of simple artifacts. Chert is the only material used for the manufacture of these artifacts. The artifacts are in mint condition.

14. Borogaon (BGN, 19°9', 82°11')

The village of Borogaon lies one kilometer, east of river Bhaskel and four kilometer north-west of the Indravati. The site is situated to the south of the village over rocky elevated ground. Thirty nine pieces were collected from an area of 28 sq m. Of these, 33 (84.62%) are simple artifacts and 6 (15.38%) shaped artifacts. The artifacts are made of chert only. These are slightly patinated.

15. Gadabaguda (GBG, 19°15', 82°34')

The village of Gadabaguda inhabited by Gadabas is situated 3 km north-east of Nowrangapur. The artifacts are found scattered over on plain area of 40 sq m. The site is disturbed by recent cultivation. The collection includes 166 artifacts, of these 153 (92.17%) are simple artifacts and 13 (7.83%) are shaped artifacts. The artifacts are exclusively made on chert.

16. Rengiguda (RNG, 19°11', 82°20')

The village Rengiguda, a small hamlet of Chirma village, lies 3.5 km north of river Indravati. The site is located at a distance of 30 m north-east of the village. A collection of 62 artifacts was made from an undulating rocky ground. The assemblage comprises 59 (95.16%) simple artifacts and 3 (4.84%) shaped artifacts. The artifacts are made on chert and fresh in appearance.

17. Chatahandi (CTH, 19°11', 82°15')

Chatahandi is situated 6 km north-west of Kotpad. The Indravati flows 2.5 km south of the village and Bhaskel 6 km west of the village. A slightly elevated rocky waste land on the south of the village yielded 140 artifacts, of which 132 (94.29%) are simple artifacts and 8 (5.71%) are shaped artifacts. They are made on chert and patinated with a thin film of red colour.

Table 3.1: Location of Upper Palaeolithic sites of Indravati Basin

Sl. No.	*Name of the sites*	*Abbreviation*	*Latitude*	*Longitude*	*Nearby river*	*Nearby Town*	*Topography*	*Number of artifacts collected*
1	Paidapali-A	PDP-A	19°16'	82°13'30''	Bhaskel	Kodinga	W.P.	138
2	Paidapali-B	PDP-B	19°16	82°13'	,,	,,	W.P.	34
3	Amota	AMT	19°10'	82°27'	Indravati	Kotpad	K.R.W.	68
4	Seamla	SML	19°4'	82°18'	Joura	,,	W.P	40
5	Chirma	CRM	19°11'	82°22'	Indravati	,,	M.T.	66
6	Kosagumura	KGR	19°16'	82°15'	Bhaskel	Kodinga	W.P	111
7	Majhidhanua	MDA	19°15'	82°11'	,,	,,	W.P	36
8	Ukiapali	UKP	19°10'	82°11'	,,	Kotpad	K.R.W.	44
9	Chitagaon	CTG	19°8'	82°22'	Indravati	,,	W.P	31
10	Kusumpali	KSP	19°13'	82°15'	Bhaskel	,,	K.R.W.	21
11	Parajasahi	PJS	19°15'	82°15'	,,	Kodinga	W.P.	151
12	Majiha	MJA	19°9'	82°34'	Indravati	Kotpad	W.P.	72
13	Sitiliguda	STG	19°12'	82°22'	,,	,,	M.T.	63
14	Borogaon	BGN	19°9'	82°11'	Bhaskel	,,	K.R.W.	39
15	Gadabaguda	GDG	19°15'	82°34'	Indravati	Nowran-gepur	W.P.	166
16	Rengiguda	RNC	19°11'	82°20'	,,	Kotpad	K.R.W.	62
17	Chatahandi	CTH	19°11'	82°15'	Bhaskel	,,	K.R.W.	140

MESOLITHIC SITES

FOOT HILL SITES

1. Asanga C (ASN C, 19◦.11', 82◦20')

The village Asanga lies 5.5 km north of Kotpad. The site is located on the right side of the road Asanga-Kokdi at a distance of about 0.5 km from the village Asanga. The artifacts were collected from the foot of a hillock. The site has yielded 221 artifacts, of which 39 (17.64%) are shaped artifacts and 182 (82.35%) are simple artifacts made of chert. These are fresh but with a red stain due to long association with red soil.

2. Hirlidanguri (HLD, 19°13'30", 82°32')

Hirlidanguri is a hill, located behind the weekly market of Nowrangpur town. The river Indravati flows at a distance of about 4 km north of the hill. The approximate height of the hill is 350 m, which is covered with big and small trees, bushes and creepers. The artifacts are thinly scattered at the foot of the hill over an area of about 750 sq m. Only 42 artifacts were collected, of which 39 (92.85%) are simple artifacts and 3 (7.14%) are shaped artifacts.

3. Paljur (PLJ, 19°35', 82°56')

Paljur is a small village of Thuamulrampur tahsil of Kalahandi district. The village lies 7 km east of the Thuamulrampur, on the left side of the Thuamulrampur Bhabanipatna road. The river Indravati flows further east of the site at as approximate distance of 4 km. The river flows through a narrow channel with alluvium of 5 m height on both the banks. Artifacts collected from the foot of a hill consist of 53 specimens. There are 46 (86.79%) simple artifacts and 7(13.20%) shaped artifacts. The tools are made mainly on chert.

4. Dakutha A (DKT A, 19°37', 82°59')

It is a small tribal village in the hilly forested land of Thuamulrampur tahsil. The site is about 2.5 km from Paljur site along the Thuamulrampur-Bhabanipatna road. From an artifact scatter at the foot of a hillock, 24 specimens were collected, of which 22 (91.66%) are simple artifact and 2 (8.33%) shaped artifacts. Quartz is the main raw material, though there are some on chert, chalcedony and jasper.

5. Dakutha B (DKT B, 19°33', 82°58')

The site is located just at the left bank of the river Indravati at a distance of 1.5 km from the previous site. Only 17 artifacts were picked up from an area of 8 sq m. The collection consists of 1 (5.88%) shaped artifacts and 16 (94.11%) simple artifacts. The artifacts are mainly made of chert and are in mint condition.

HILL SLOPE SITES

6. Binjili (BNL, 19°9', 82°14')

The village Binjili is about 9 km north-west of Kotpad town and 0.5 km north of the river Indravati. The artifacts are scattered on a slope of a hillock, located north of the village at a distance of 30 m. One hundred thirty seven artifacts were collected from this site, of these 13 (9.4%) are shaped and 124 (90.5%) are simple artifacts. The predominant raw material is yellow chert and the artifacts show a reddish patination due to long association with red soil. The artifacts are fresh.

7. Asanga (ASN, 19°11', 82°20')

The village is situated 5.5 km north of Kotpad. The site is located north of the village Asanga, about 0.25 km on the left side of Asanga-Kokdi road. The river Indravati flows at a distance of about 3 km south of the site. The artifacts occur as a scatter on the hill slope. Three hundred twenty seven specimens were collected from an area of 40 sq m. The assemblage consists of 38 (11.62%) shaped artifacts and 289 (88.37%) simple artifacts. These are made on chert and are slightly patinated.

8. Kokdi A (KKD A, 19°11', 82°19'30")

The village Kokdi is about 2 km west of Asanga. The site is located on a slope of a hillock, north-east of the village Kokdi, at a distance of 100 m. It has yielded 101 artifacts, of which 92 (91.08%) are simple artifacts and 9 (8.91%) are finished artifacts.

Another locality, labeled as Kokdi B, about 150 m to the north of Kokdi A has an occurrence. From this locality 38 artifacts were collected from an area of about 20 sq m. These consists of 2 (5.26%) shaped artifacts and 36 (94.73%) simple artifacts. These are made on chert.

9. Photaguda (PTG, 19°14', 82°45'30")

The village Photaguda is situated south-east of the village Lambtaguda at a distance of approx. 1.5 km. The site is located on the left bank of the river Indravati. The distance between the Photaguda site and Lambtaguda site is about 2.5 km. The artifacts collected from a slope of hillock are 138. They consist of 13 (9.42%) shaped artifacts and 125 (90.57%) simple artifacts, all on chert.

HILL TOP SITES

10. Umarkot A (UKT A, 19°40'30", 82°11')

Umarkot is situated about 60 km north of Nowrangpur, on Jeypore-Raipur road. A small collection of 54 artifacts was made from the top of hillock, from an area of 25 sq m. The height of hillock is about 30 m located on the left side of the Raipur-Jeypore road at a distance of 1 km from Umarkot bus stand. All are simple artifacts. Chert and quartz are the main raw materials. The tools are well preserved.

11. Umarkot B (UKT B, 19°40', 82°11')

The site Umarkot B is located 1 km north of Umarkot bus stand and 2 km from previous site. The artifacts are found scattered over a rocky surface of about 36 sq m on a top of hillock which is about 35 m high from surrounding level. It has yielded 253 artifacts. The shaped artifacts are 23 (9.09%) and simple artifacts 230 (90.91%). The artifacts are made on chert and quartz. All are fresh.

12. Keragaon (KRG, 19°22', 82°11')

The village Keragaon is situated 7 km north-west of the village of Balenga. The site is located on the side of Notigaon-Keragaon road and less than one kilometer from Keragaon. A small stream flows 0.5 km west of the site. A collection of 33 artifacts was made from an area of 24 sq m. All the specimens are simple artifacts. Chert is the chief raw material.

13. Churchunda (CCD, 19°13', 82°18')

Churchunda is situated 7 km south-west of Kodinga town and is connected by road with Kodinga, Kotpad and Kesagumuda. The site is located to the north of the village about 0.25 km from Kotpad-Kesagumuda road. One hundred thirty three artifacts were collected from an area of 150 sq m. They comprise 15 (11.27%) shaped artifacts and 118 (88.72%) simple artifacts, all made on chert.

14. Girla (GRL, 19°10', 82°23')

The village Girla is situated 8 km north-east of Kotpad town, on the left bank of the Indravati. The topography of the area is characterised by extensive cultivated land with isolated low hills covered with wild shrubs and a few trees. There are three hillocks around this village. These are three working spots of Mesolithic culture. The richest one (GRL A) is located on the top of a hillock, about 12 m high from the ground level and just on the right side of the Kotpad-Girla road and about 1 km south of the village. This site yielded 455 artifacts from an area of 420 sq m of which 67 (14.72%) pieces are shaped artifacts and 388 (85.27%) are simple artifacts. These are made on chert of yellowish red colour. Most of the artifacts are highly patinated, but are fresh.

Girla B and Girla C are located south-west of the site Girla A at a distance of about 0.25 km. The distance between Girla B and Girla C sites is about 150 m. The artifacts are recovered from rocky waste land. Girla B yieled 8 (19.04%) shaped artifacts and 34 (80.96%) simple artifacts; whereas Girla C reported 38 (21.05%) shaped artifacts and 30 (78.95%) simple artifacts. The artifacts are exclusively made on chert and are highly patinated.

15. Phupugaon (PPG, 19°3', 82°23')

The village Phupugaon is situated about 13 km south-east of Kotpad town. The site is located on the right side of the Kotpad-Kundra road, on a hillock, whose approximate height is 8 m from plain land. It has yielded 40 artifacts of which 38 (95.00%) are simple artifacts and 2 (5.00%) shaped artifacts. These are mainly made of chert.

16. Boriguda A (19°3', 82°35')

The site is located near the 2 km on the left side of the Boriguda-Sargiguda road. This is one of the few sites which are away from a tribal settlement. The artifacts are found scattered over a small hill with a few isolated big boulders of granite and a few patches of wild shrubs. The artifacts are found in clusters at the edges of these boulders, suggesting that these might have been fabricated on the boulders and fallen down. It has yielded 56 artifacts, of which 51 (91.07%) are simple artifacts and 5 (8.92%) shaped artifacts. Quartz is the main raw material for the manufacture of artifacts.

17. Rangapiajaguda (RPG, 19°14', 82°39')

The village Rangapiajaguda lies on the east of Nowrangpur town at a distance of 12 km south-east of village Sagarmunda. The artifacts are found on the outcrop of granitic boulders located on the right side of Nowrangpur-Sagarmunda road. A simple collection, of 42 artifacts was made from this site. Of the total collection, 38 (90.47%) are simple artifacts and 4 (9.52%) shaped artifacts. Quartz is the main raw material. A large number of noduler pieces of quartz are noticed around the site.

18. Ekamba A (EKB A, 19°12', 82°39'30")

The village Ekamba is nearly 12 km south-east of Nowrangpur town. The site is located on the top of a hill at a distance of 1 km west of the village with a height of about 75 m and 250 m long (N-S) and 150 m (E-W) approximately. The plains and hill slopes are extensively cultivated by terrace method. The site has yielded 129 artifacts of which 117 (90.70%) are simple artifacts and 12 (9.30%) shaped artifacts. The raw material used for the manufacture of artifacts is chert, qurtz and jasper.

19. Ekamba B (EKB B, 19°12', 82°39')

About 1 km of Ekamba A, there is another hill which has yielded microliths. The approximate height of the hill is 60 m from plain agricultural land and it extends about 200 m N-S and 175 m E-W. The artifacts are found scattered in clusters extending over an area of about 1500 sq m. The total collection is 262 specimens. This comprises of 250 (95.42%) pieces of simple artifacts and 12 (4.58%) pieces of shaped artifacts. Chert is the dominating raw material followed by quartz. These are fresh and a few specimen on chert show staining.

20. Bairagiguda (BRG, 19°13', 82°42')

The village Bairagiguda lies on the right bank of the river Indravati, about 4 km north-east of Ekamba village. At 0.25 km east of the village, there is a hillock of approximately 40 m high from the river bad, which flows just at its feet. Two hundred and twenty four artifacts were collected from this hillock. The collection comprises of 211 (94.20%) simple artifacts and 13 (5.80%) shaped artifacts. Quartz is the predominent raw material. The artifacts are fresh.

21. Phupugaon (PGN, 19°14', 82°45')

Phupugaon lies at a distance of 7 km south of Tentulikhunti town. The river Indravati flows north of the village. The site is about 1.5 km from the village to the east. These are three hillocks adjacent to each other and surrounded by cultivated fields, on the right side of Lambtaguda-Phupugaon road. The artifacts are found scattered over these hillocks. The sampling includes 102 artifacts, of which 94 (92.15%) are simple artifacts and 8 (7.84%) shaped artifacts. The main raw material is qurtz. The artifacts are fresh.

22. Muchagaon (MCG, 19°13', 82°46')

The village Muchagaon is situated about 4 km south-east of Tentulikhunti town and the site is located 0.5 km east of the village. The Indravati flows very close to the hillock. The artifacts are found scattered on the top of hillock over the granitic surface covering an area of 168 sq m. It has yielded 126 artifacts which consists of 117 (91.14%) simple artifacts and 11 (8.59%) shaped artifacts. Quartz is the main raw material used for the manufacture of artifacts.

23. Kumuli (KML, 19°7', 82°41')

Kumuli is a big village of Bhairab Singpur Police Station, from the southwest it is connected by a road to Boriguma and from the south to Bhairab Singpur. From Kumuli, Narigaon village is about 3 km by Kumuli-Bhairab Singpur road. The site is located on left side of Kumuli-Narigaon road at a distance of about 0.5 km. The artifacts are scattered over a hillock. Total 48 artifacts were picked up from this site. The collection comprises of 42 (87.5%) simple artifacts and 6 (12.5%) shaped artifacts. Chert is the main raw material.

24. Dargarkarchi (DGK, 18°59', 82°40'30")

The village Dargarkarchi is situated to the south of Bhairab Singpur at a distance of about 8 km. The site is on the top of a hillock which is about 0.5 km to the north of the village. It has yielded only 30 simple artifacts. Quartz is the most popular raw material. The artifacts are in mint condition.

25. Nagalatal (NGA, 19°10', 82°44')

The village Nagalatal comes under Tentulikhunti tahsil. It can be approached by road, from Bhairab Singpur to Munja then to Chepadi and from Chepadi to Catiguda, which is separated from Nagalatal by the river Muran. Muran is one of the biggest tributaries of Indravati. The village Nagalatal is surrounded by big hills whose average height varies from 800 m to 1400 m covered with dense forest. The hill, locally known as Badaraja has yielded 102 artifacts, a fragment and one complete bead of jasper, two hammer stones and four pieces of ground red ochre. In the collection 6 (5.88%) are shaped artifacts and 96 (94.11%) are simple artifacts. These are made on quartz and chert.

26. Lauguda (LUG, 19°12', 82°45')

The village Lauguda is about 4 km south-east of the river Indravati and 12 km from the town Tentulikhunti. The site is located on the left side of the Jagan-Berapadar road. The artifacts are scattered on a top of hillock of about 45 m heights. A total 100 artifacts were collected from this site. Of these 87 are (87.00%) simple artifacts and 13 (13.00%) shaped artifacts. The artifacts are mainly on quartz and are in fresh condition.

27. Kamata (KMT, 19°75', 82°39')

The village Kamata is south-west of village Kumuli at a distance of 3 km by Kumuli-Boriguma road and the village Ratali is about 3.5 km north of Kamata. The river Tellingiri, a tributary of the Indravati flows at a distance of 0.5 km south of Kamata. The site is located 1 km north of Kamata, on the left side of Kamata-Ratali road. The artifacts are collected from a barren hillock. The collection comprises a total of 22 artifacts of which 2 (0.09%) are shaped and 20 (90.91%) are simple artifacts. Chert and quartz are the raw materials used for the manufacture of the artifacts.

HILL TOP AND HILL SLOPE SITES

28. Komtabadi (KTB, 19°81', 82°18')

The site is located 2 km north-west of Kotpad High School. The river Indravati flows north-west of the site at a distance of about 2 km. The artifacts are scattered on the top as well as on the slope of two hillocks. The distance between these two hillocks is about 60 m only. The artifacts collected from this site are labeled as Komtabadi 'A' and Komtabadi 'B'. These in number are 320 and 35 respectively. Komtabadi A consists of 35 (10.93%) shaped artifacts and 285 (89.07%) simple artifacts where as Komtabadi B has 3 (8.57%) shaped artifacts and 32 (91.42%) simple artifacts. Chert is the only raw material used. The artifacts are in mint condition.

29. Batra Dhargudi (BDG, 19°7', 82°16')

The site is located south-west of Kotpad town at a distance of 8 km on Kotpad-Jagdalpur highway 43, near to the village Batra Dhargudi. The artifacts are found on the top as well as on the slope of a hillock, out by the highway. The approximate height of the hillock is 3.5 m from the road level. The site has yielded 125 artifacts of which 16 (12.8%) are shaped artifacts and 109 (87.2%) are simple artifacts. Chert is the most popular raw material.

30. Boragaon (BRG, 19°11', 82°34')

The village Boragaon lies on the right side of the Boragaon-Nowrangpur road at a distance of about 18 km north-west of Boriguma. This is an adjoining village of Anuli. The river Indravati forms the northern boundary of Boragaon. To the north of the village there is a big hill whose height is about 300 m from the river bed and close to this there are a few hillocks. The artifacts are found in five scatters on these hillocks. The distance between two scatters varies from 30 m to 150 m. The artifacts were collected separately from each scatters. These five scatters are named as Boragaon A, B, C, D and E and they have yielded 71, 180, 49, 53 and 31 artifacts respectively, all on chert, and are highly patinated.

ELEVATED ROCKY WASTELAND SITES

31. Motigaon (MTG, 19°11', 82°12')

The village Motigaon is situated north-west of Kodinga at distance of 18 km approximately. The village itself is located on a rocky elevated land. The site is located at an approximate distance of 1.5 km north-west of the village and about 0.5 km from the nearest stream, a feeder of the river Bhaskel. The artifacts are found scattered over an elevated rocky land. Sixty eight artifacts are collected. Of these 2 (2.94%) are shaped artifacts and 66 (97.06%) simple artifacts. They are chiefly made of chert and are in mint condition.

32. Churahandi (CRH, 19°18', 82°14')

It is a small village, located about 9 km west of Kodinga town and 6 km north of Kosagumura. The eastern part of the village boundary is demarcated by the river Bhaskel and the southern part by a small nullah of the Bhaskel. The artifacts were discovered on an elevated rocky land, located in the north of the village at our distance of about 4000 m. Only 27 artifacts were collected from an area of 96 sq m. All are of simple artifacts group. These are made of chert except a few which are of quartz.

33. Neigaon (NGN, 19°9', 82°15')

The village Neigaon lies east of Binjili. The site is located at a distance of 1 km to the east of Neigaon. The artifacts are scattered over an elevated land, located north of the river Indravati. This scatter has yielded 205 artifacts which comprise of 44 (21.46%) shaped artifacts and 161 (78.54%) simple artifacts. Chert is the chief raw material used for the manufacture of artifacts. There are in mint condition.

34. Asanga (ASN, 19°12', 82°21')

The village Asanga lies 5.5. km north of Kotpad town. The site is located north of the village at a distance of about 1.5 km. The artifacts are scattered over a slightly elevated rocky land spread over an area of 60 sq m. A collection of 84 artifacts was made from this site, of which 9 (10.71%) are shaped artifacts and 75 (89.29%) are simple artifacts. They are exclusively made on chert.

35. Nuagaon (NUG, 19°35', 82°20')

The Nuagaon village lies about 10 km south of Kotpad on Kotpad-Kundra road. The Indravati flows north of the village at an approximate distance of 12.5 km. The Joura, a tributary of Indravati flows about 3.5 km south of the site. The artifacts are found scattered over an elevated rocky waste land covered with bushes and a few isolated trees. Sixty one artifacts were collected from an area of 12 sq m. Chert is the dominant raw material.

36. Bandiguda (BND, 19°10', 82°37')

It is a small village, about 9.5 km north-east of Boriguma town, on the right side of the Indravati at a distance of 1.5 km. The site is located at a distance of about 0.5 km south-west of the Indravati. Thirty six artifacts were picked up from an area of 60 sq m of elevated rocky land. The collection consists of 2 (5.55%) shaped artifacts and 34 (94.45%) simple artifacts. Chert and quartz are the two main raw materials.

37. Kumutitarai (KTT, 19°6', 82°19')

The site Kumutitarai is 6.5 km south-east of Kotpad town, near the village Sarigaon. Forty four artifacts were collected from a scatter on an elevated rocky waste land covering an area of 12 sq m. Out of these 7 (15.90%) are shaped artifacts and 37 (84.09%) simple artifacts. Chert is the main raw material with a few quartz pieces. They are in fresh condition.

38. Ghotorla (GTL, 19°10', 82°25')

The village Ghotorla lies on the right bank of the Indravati, about 7.5 km north-east of Kotpad town. The village is well connected with Kotpad and Nowrangpur by Kotpad-Saragiguda-

Ghotorla road and Ghotorla-Nowrangpur road respectively. Two sites are located to the east of the village at a distance of 150 m between them. The artifacts collected separately from these two localities, called as Ghotorla A and Ghotorla B are 270 and 34 respectively. Of 270 specimens 49 (18.14%) are shaped artifacts and 221 (81.86%) are simple artifacts. The artifacts are made of chert except a few specimens of quartz from respective sites. They are in mint condition.

39. Miriguda (MRG, 19°37', 82°24')

This small village of Miriguda comes under Kotpad tahsil. It is connected by National Highway 43 with Kotpad and Boriguma. The site is located at a distance of 6 km by road from Kotpad towards the east. The artifacts are found scattered on an elevated land covered with bushes. Fifty two artifacts were collected from an area of 56 sq m and these consists of 2 (3.84%) shaped artifacts and 50 (96.16%) simple artifacts. Quartz and chert are the two main raw materials used for the manufacture of artifacts. These are in fresh condition.

40. Site located 5.5 km from Boriguma towards Bhairab Singpur (19°1', 82°36')

There is no village around the site. The artifacts are found scattered on the left side of the road on an elevated land; extending over an area of about 150 sq m. It has yielded 78 artifacts, which consists of 77 (98.72%) simple artifacts and one (1.28%) shaped artifacts. The artifacts are mainly made of quartz with a few of chert.

41. Khandiguda (KDG, 19°10', 82°35')

The village Khandiguda lies about 10 km north of Boriguma town. The river Indravati flows to the north of the village at a distance of 2 km approximately. A collection of 62 artifacts was made from an elevated rocky land of 240 sq m. Of the total collection 3 (4.83%) are shaped artifacts and 59 (95.17%) simple artifacts. All are in mint condition.

42. Deula (DUL, 19°15', 82°29')

The village Deula is situated about 6.5 km north-west of Nowrangpur town. The site is located south of village at a distance of less than 1 km. The artifacts are found scattered over an elevated rocky ground of about 30 sq m. Fifty five artifacts were collected from a locality termed as Deula A and from another (0.5 km north of Deula A) termed as Deula B, 35 were collected from an area of 18 sq m. Of the collection of 55 artifacts, 51 (92.73%) are simple artifacts and 4 (7.27%) shaped artifacts. And of 35 specimens, 3 (8.57%) are shaped artifacts and 32 (91.43%) simple artifacts. Chert is the most popular raw material in both the collection.

43. Bentaguda (BTG, 19°9', 82°23')

A small hamlet lies north-east of Kotpad town at a distance of about 5 km and just before the village Dhanpur. The site is located 70 m southwest of the village Bentaguda. It has yielded 110 artifacts from an area of 102 sq m. The collection comprises of 8 (7.27%) shaped artifacts and 102 (92.75%) simple artifacts. These are made of chert.

44. Bejuguda (BJG, 19°16', 82°46')

The village of Bejuguda is situated 2 km west of the main road Tentulikhunti-Patradora. A small collection of 21 artifacts was made from an elevated rocky ground located at a distance of nearly 3000 m north of the village. The total collection belongs to simple artifact group. They are made of quartz and chert and are in mint condition.

45. Gatiput (GTP, 19°15', 82°45')

The village Gatiput comes under Tentulikhunti police station. The village lies 3 km north of Patradora dam of Indravati. The site is located on the left side of Gatiput-Patradora road at a distance of 2 km from the dam site. This is a hilly and thickly forested area. Only 20 artifacts were picked up from an area of 72 sq m. They are made of quartz except a few specimens which are of chert. The chert pieces are slightly patinated.

46. Site located 6 km from Bhairab Singpur towards Boriguma (19°8', 82°41')

The site is on the left side of the Bhairab Singpur-Boriguma main road at a distance of 6 km from Bhairab Singpur. There is an elevated land extending about 0.5 km which is partly cultivated. In the central part of the land are a few isolated granitic boulders. Fourty six artifacts are collected from near the boulders. The collection comprises of 44 (95.66%) simple artifacts and 2 (4.34%) shaped artifacts. Quartz is the main raw material. The artifacts are is mint condition.

47. Bentaguda (BTG, 19°32', 83°1')

The village Bentaguda lies south of the village Dakutha at an approximate distance of 6 km. The artifacts are sparely scattered on a rocky elevated waste land covering an area of 40 sq m. There are 20 specimens; all are simple artifacts except one shaped tool. They are made on chert and quartz.

48. Sargiguda (SGG, 19°3', 82°36')

The village Sargiguda lies about 6 km east of Boriguma town. An elevated waste land, as one approaches the village, has a scatter of artifacts covering 15 sq m. This has yielded 26 artifacts. Of these 4 (18.18%) are shaped artifacts and 22 (81.82%) simple artifacts. Chert is the main raw material used for the manufacture of artifacts. These are in mint condition.

49. Jagnathpur (JGP, 19°12', 82°44')

This village is about 9.5 km south-east of Tentulikhunti town. About 1.5 km to the north of village is a small stream which joins the Indravati at about 4 km further north of the village. The artifacts are found scattered on an elevated rocky land, 1 km to the north of the village. The 89 artifacts collected comprise 8 (8.98%) shaped artifacts and 87 (91.02%) simple artifacts. These are made dominantly on chert with a few specimens on quartz. They are fresh with a thin film of red patina.

50. Patiaguda (PTG, 19°00', 82°40')

The village Patiaguda lies about 6 km south of Bhairab Singpur. The site is located on the left side of Bhairab Singpur-Kotpad road, close to the road, are elevated rocky land and the artifacts are found on these land. A collection of 29 artifacts was made from an area of 180 sq m approximately. These are made on quartz.

51. Limbata (LMT, 19°11', 82°17')

The village Limbata lies 8 km north-east of Kotpad town. The site is very close to the village and about 1.5 km north-west of the village, Karla. The Indravati flows at a distance of 2.5 km south of the site. Numerically 190 artifacts were collected from an area of 45 sq m. The collection comprises of 178 (93.69%) simple artifacts and 12 (6.31%) shaped artifacts. The artifacts are exclusively made on yellowish red chert and have a thin red patina.

PLAIN WASTE LAND SITES

52. Balenga (BLG, 19°12', 82°15')

The village is located on the left bank of the river Bhaskel. It forms the eastern boundary of the village Balenga, to the northwest of which, at an approximate distance of 6 km is the town of Kodinga. The site lies 0.5 km west of the river. Seventy six artifacts have been recovered from an area of 12 sq m waste land. They comprise of 69 (90.78%) simple artifacts and 7 (9.2%) finished artifacts, made of chert and quartz. The artifacts are in mint condition.

53. Temra (TMR, 19°18', 82°14')

The village Temra is situated about 3.5 km south-west of the village Balenga. The artifacts are found on a plain waste land to the left of Kosagumuda-Temra road. The distance between Temra and Kosagumuda is about 5 km by road. A small stream flows at an approximate distance of 0.5 km in a south-westerly direction where as the river Bhaskel flows in a southeasterly direction at a distance of 1 km from the site. The site has yielded 45 artifacts, of which 2 (4.44%) are shaped tools and 43 (95.56%) are simple artifacts. These are mainly made of chert with a few pieces of quartz. All are in mint condition.

54. Saraladhanua (SLD, 19°15', 82°12')

The village is situated to the south-west of Kosagumuda at a distance of approximately 5 km. The site is very close to the left side of Kosagumuda-Saraladhanua road. The river Bhaskel flows at the distance of 0.5 km north-east of the site. The artifacts are found scattered over a plain bushy land covering an area of about 200 sq m. Only 44 artifacts were picked up from this site. All are simple artifacts. The most popular raw material is chert. The artifacts are fresh in appearance.

55. Bajagar (BJR, 19°12'30", 82°16')

Bajagar is situated about 6 km north-east of Kosagumuda and about 9 km west of Kodinga town. The site is located nearly 200 m north of the village. The river Bhaskel flows at a distance of 1.5 km north-west of the site. The artifacts are found spread over an area of about 60 sq m. Fifty three artifacts were collected from this area. These comprise of only one (1.88%) shaped artifact and 52 (98.11%) simple artifacts. The main raw material is yellowish chert. The artifacts are in mint condition and have a thin red patina.

56. Duragaon (19°11', 82°11')

The village Duragaon is approximately 13 km to the north-west of Kotpad town. The river Bhaskel flows at the periphery of the village and form the border with Bastar district. The artifacts were collected from a plain lateritic surface, on the left side of the Ukipali-Duragaon road. Seventy one artifacts were recovered from this site; comprising of 12 (16.90%) shaped artifacts and 59 (83.09%) simple artifacts. They are made of chert and in mint condition.

57. Bamuni (BMN, 19°12', 82°15')

The village Bamuni lies about 10 km north-west of the Kotpad town. The site is located very close to the village Bamuni on the right of Kotpad-Kodinga road. The Indravati flows 7 km south of the site. One hundred and eighteen artifacts were collected from an area of 180 sq m. They consist of 106 (96.83%) pieces of simple artifacts and 12 (10.16%) pieces of shaped artifacts. Most of the artifacts are made of chert except a few pieces which are of Quartz.

58. Rajoragaon (RJG, 19°14', 82°16')

The village Rajoragaon is about 11 km south-west of Kodinga. The site is to the right side of Kodinga-Rajoragaon road at distance of about 800 m from the village. The artifacts are scattered over a plain land covering an area of about 60 sq m. A collection of 58 artifacts are made from this site. They comprise of 4 (6.89%) shaped artifacts and 54 (93.11%) simple artifacts. Chert is the main raw material. The artifacts are highly patinated.

59. Churahandi (CHD, 19°12', 82°30')

The village Churahandi lies about 5.5 km north-east of Kotpad town and 2 km east of Asanga site. The site is located to the left of Kotpad-Kodinga road. Only 27 artifacts were collected from an area of 35 sq m approximately. All are of simple artifacts group and are made of chert only.

60. Kotpad (KTP, 19°8', 82°19')

Kotpad (Plate 3.1 and 3.2) is situated north-west of Jeypore at a distance of 40 km on the National Highway 43. It is an important tahsil of Koraput district. The site is to the north-east of Kotpad high school, 1 km away from Kotpad police station. The artifacts are found on a plain waste land. Only 34 artifacts were picked up from an area of 30 sq m. Except one specimen, which is a point on blade, the rest are simple artifacts. Chert is the only raw material used for the manufacture of those artifacts. They are in mint condition.

Plate 3.1: Hill slope Mesolithic site of Kotpad A

The locality Kotpad B is only 70 m from Kotpad A. The artifacts are found scattered on the lateritic surface. It has yieded 133 artifacts. They consist of 19 (14.28%) pieces of shaped artifacts and 114 (85.72%) pieces of simple artifacts. The artifacts are exclusively made of chert.

The locality Kotpad C is about 1.5 km north-west of Kotpad police station, 2.5 km from the Indravati and just behind the Inspection Bunglow. Eighty artifacts were collected from an area of 210 sq m approximately. They comprise 9 (11.25%) shaped artifacts and 71 (88.75%) simple artifacts. The main raw material is chert.

Plate 3.2: Mesolithic site of Kotpad B

61. Site located 5 km from Kotpad towards Boriguma on NH 43 (19°8', 82°23')

The site is on the left side of National Highway 43, and 5 km away from Kotpad towards Boriguma town. As this area has thick vegetation, the ground is covered by fallen leaves and grasses and as such, it is difficult to know the extent of artifactual scatter. Only 20 artifacts were picked up, of which 19 (95.00%) are simple artifacts and 1 (5.00%) is shaped artifacts. The artifacts are made of chert only and are in mint condition.

62. Bathasana (BHA, 19°9', 82°24')

The village Bathasana is situated east of Kotpad town at a distance of 8 km by road and about 2 km south of village Ghotorla. The site is located on the left side of Kotpad-Bathasana-Ghotorla road. The artifacts are found scattered over an area of 600 sq m on a plain waste land, at a distance of 0.5 km to the south in Bathasana village. It has yielded 23 artifacts, of which 2 (8.69%) specimens are shaped artifacts and 21 (91.32%) specimens are simple artifacts. Chert is the main raw material.

63. Amlabhata (ABT, 19°7', 82°19')

The village Amlabhata lies south of Kotpad town at a distance of about 4 km by road. The site located north of the village. The artifacts are collected from a lateritic land of 80 sq m. It has yielded 137 artifacts consisting of 122 (89.06%) simple artifacts and 15 (10.94%) shaped artifacts. They are made of yellow chert, and have reddish patina.

64. Narahandi (NHD, 19°6', 82°18')

The site Narahandi is located south-east of the site Amlabhata at a distance of 3 km from Narahandi on Kotpad-Mundaguda road. The artifacts are found over a rocky waste land covering an area of 45 sq m. Only 22 artifacts were picked up from this area. The shaped form are 8 (36.36%) and the remaining 14 (63.63%) are simple artifacts. The artifacts are exclusively made of chert and are highly patinated.

65. Sandhagaon (SDG, 19°4', 82°19')

This village is about 7 km south east of Kotpad on the Kotpad-Mundaguda road. The artifacts are found at three places on undisturbed waste land within a 1 km. The collections from these three clusters (SDG A, SDG B, SDG C) have yielded 69, 30 and 31 artifacts respectively. The clusters SDG A consists of 14 (20.26%) shaped artifacts and 58 (79.72%) simple artifacts, the cluster SDG B consists of 2 (6.66%) shaped artifacts and 58 (79.72%) simple artifacts, and the cluster SDG C consists of 7(22.58%) shaped artifacts and 24 (77.42%) simple artifacts. All are exclusively made of chert with a red stain due to long association with red soil.

66. Parsola (PRS, 19°11', 82°32')

The village Parsola which falls under Boriguma tahsil is 19 km north of Boriguma. There are two artifact occurrences, both being reported by a distance of 40 m near Parsola village. The artifacts are collected separately as PRS A and PRS B assemblage from these two spots. They have yielded 177 and 53 artifacts respectively. The collection PRS A consists of 8 (4.51%) pieces of shaped artifacts and 169 (95.49%) pieces of simple artifacts where as the collection PRS B consists of 12 (22.64%) pieces of shaped artifacts and 41 (77.36%) pieces of simple artifacts. The artifacts are mostly made of chert and are in mint condition.

67. Anuli (ANL, 19°11', 82°33')

The village Anuli lies east of Parsola and 18 km north of Boriguma. The Indravati flows at a distance of 1 km north of the village. The artifacts are found on a plain waste land, just on the left side of the Boriguma-Anuli road. Twenty nine artifacts were collected from an area of 50 sq m. Of the total collection 2 (6.89%) are shaped artifacts and 27 (93.11%) are simple artifacts. These are made of chert and quartz and are in fresh condition.

68. Mahulpadar (MPD, 19°13', 82°28')

The village Mahulpadar lies 2 km south-east of village Siuni. The artifacts are found scattered over a plain undisturbed land, covering an area of 70 sq m approximately, to the north of the village Mahulpadar. The site has yielded 40 artifacts, of which 2 are (5.00%) shaped artifacts and 38 (95.00%) simple artifacts. These are made of chert and quartz. The chert artifacts are patinated.

69. Bikrampur (BRP, 19°15', 82°27')

The village Bikrampur is the adjacent village of Deula. They are separated by Turi nullah. The site is very close to Bikrampur. The artifacts were found on a plain waste land covered with patches of wild bushes. Fifty three artifacts were collected from an area of 150 sq m. The collection comprises 3 (5.66%) shaped artifacts and 50 (94.34%) simple artifacts. The artifacts are made of chert and quartz and are in mint condition.

70. Teliguda (TLG, 19°16', 82°27')

The village Teliguda lies nearly 2 km south of the village Bikrampur. The site is located about 0.25 km north of village Teliguda. The artifacts are found on the left side of the Teliguda-Bikrampur road. The 42 artifacts collected comprise 13 (30.95%) shaped artifacts and 29 (69.05%) simple artifacts. These are mainly made of chert and a few specimens are of quartz.

71. Rangamatiguda (RMG, 19°14', 82°34')

The site (Plate 3.3 and 3.4) is located at a distance of about 500 m south-west of the village Rangamatiguda and about 3 km northeast of Nowrangapur town, just on the right side of Nowrangapur-Ekamba road. The river Indravati flows 5 km north of the site. The site is partly disturbed due to the recent cultivation. The artifacts are found scattered on red soil covering an area of about 725 m. One hundred ninety five artifacts were collected from an area of 40 sq m of which 10 (5.12%) are shaped artifacts and 185 (94.88%) simple artifacts. The artifacts

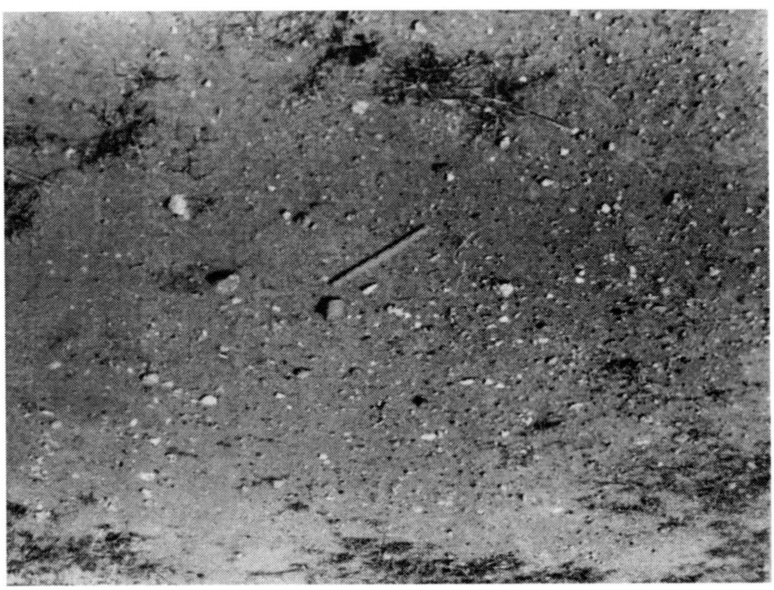

Plate 3.3: Mesolithic site of Rangamatiguda

Plate 3.4: General view of the Mesolithic site of Rangamatiguda

Plate 3.5: Mesolithic site near granite outcrop at Bairagiguda

are chiefly on quartz with only a few of chert, jesper and chalcedony. The artifacts are in mint condition and the ones made of chert are highly patinated.

72. Bairagiguda to Ekamba (BRG-EKM, 19°13', 82°14')

Bairagiguda (Plate 3.5) is a small village, about 0.5 km north of the village Ushuripadar. The site is located on the right side of the Ushuripadar-Bairagiguda-Ekamba road. The artifacts are found on a plain land of red soil. A collection of 109 artifacts was made from an area of 150 sq m. The collection consists of 1 (0.91%) shaped artifact and 108 (99.09%) simple artifacts. These are made of chert with a few pieces of quartz. These of the former are slightly patinated.

73. Kutiguda (KTG, 19°15', 82°17')

The village Kutiguda lies south-west of Kodinga town at a distance of nearly 7 km. The site is located about 150 m to the south of the village. It has yielded 66 artifacts of which 51 (77.28%) are simple artifacts and 15 (22.72%) shaped artifacts. All are made of chert only. These are fresh with a thin film of red patina.

74. Majhiguda (MJG, 19°17', 82°15')

Majhiguda is the neighbouring village of Kosagumura. It is situated 8 km southwest of the Kodinga town. The site is located on the right side of the Kosagumura-Temra road at a distance of 150 m from the village Majhiguda. Fifty two artifacts were collected from a rocky plain land of 35 sq m. The collection consists of 6 (11.33%) shaped artifacts and 46 (88.47%) simple artifacts. The artifacts are exclusively made on chert and are patinated.

SITES ON CULTIVATED LAND

75. Boniaguda (BNA, 19°10', 82°18')

The village Boniaguda is situated about 3 km north-west of Kotpad town. The Indravati flows northwest of the village. The site is located on the left side of the Kotpad-Boniaguda road. The site is slightly disturbed due to recent cultivation. A collection of 41 artifacts was made from an area of 140 sq m approximately. Of the total collection 4 (9.75%) are shaped artifacts and 37 (90.25%) are simple artifacts. These are made of chert except a few which are of quartz. The artifacts are in mint condition.

76. Dhanpur (DPA, 19°9', 82°22')

The village Dhanpur lies 7 km north-east of the Kotpad town. The site is located just opposite the village and right side of Kotpad-Girla road. The Indravati flows about 3 km north of the site. The artifacts are found scattered over an elevated land, which is disturbed due to shifting cultivation. Sixty three artifacts were collected from an area of 250 sq m of the 63 artifacts 2 (3.17%) are shaped artifacts and 61 (96.83%) simple artifacts. All the artifacts except one which is of quartz are made of chert. Most of the artifacts are fresh. Only a few specimens show slight rolling.

77. Siuni (SUN, 19°14', 82°27')

The site is about 0.5 km to the north of village Siuni, which lies south of Bikrampur at an approximate distance of 4 km and 1 km south-east of Turi nullah. Only 41 artifacts were collected from a disturbed area of 35 sq m. Of the total collection 5 (12.19%) specimens are shaped artifacts and 36 (87.81%) specimens are simple artifacts. Chert is the only raw material used in making artifacts.

78. Lambtaguda (LTG, 19°15', 82°46')

This large village falls within Nowrangpur tahsil. The village is connected by two straight roads with Nowrangpur and Tentulikunti towns. The site is located on a hill slope, 3.5 km east of the Indravati and about 1 km south of the village. The height of this hillock is about 40 m. The site is disturbed due to cultivation. One hundred and seventeen artifacts were collected from this site. Out of these 108 (92.31%) are simple artifacts and 9 (7.69%) are shaped tools. The artifacts are made of chert only and are in mint condition.

79. Panaspadar (PPD, 19°15', 82°44')

The village Panaspadar lies 8.5 km south of Tentulikhunti. The site is located near Baghadori nullah, which flows to the south of Panaspadar. The site is 1 km away from the road. Only 59 artifacts were collected from an agricultureal field. The assemblage consists of 1 (1.69%) shaped artifact and 58 (98.31%) simple artifacts. Quartz is the main raw material.

80. Antasar (ATS, 19°14', 82°42')

The village Antasar lies at a distance of 2 km east of village Panaspadar. The Indravati flows about 1 km away from the village in an eastward direction. The site is located just near the village, on the right side of the Dahana-Antasar road. Only 19 artifacts were picked up from an area of 20 sq m. All are simple artifacts made of quartz and are mint condition.

81. Munja to Kumuli (19°9', 82°41')

The village of Munja lies at a distance of 15 km by road from Bhairab Singpur and 5 km from village Kumuli. The site is about 2 km to the south of the village. There is an elevated land at the right side of the Munja-Kumuli road with a rocky exposure at the centre. Recently the land has been brought under cultivation. Most of the artifacts were collected from this exposure and nearby area. Eighty artifacts were collected from an area of about 75 sq m. The collection consists of 3 (3.75%) shaped artifacts and 77 (96.25%) simple artifacts. Chert is the dominant raw material. The artifacts have slightly red stain.

82. Berapadar (BRP, 19°12', 82°46')

Berapadar comes within Tentulikhunti tahsil. The village lies 5.5 m south of Tentulikhunti. The ste is located on the left side of the Jaganthpur-Berapadar road. It has yielded only 39 artifacts, out of which 35 (89.75%) are simple artifacts and 4 (10.25%) are shaped artifacts. The main raw material is chert.

83. Site located 5 km from Nowrangpur towards Boriguma (19°9', 82°33')

The site is located on the left side (200 m away) of the Nowrangpur-Boriguma main road at a distance of 5 km from Nowrangpur. The artifacts are found over a vast area with very poor condition. Only 37 artifacts were picked up from a single spot. The collection consists of 4 (10.81%) shaped artifacts and 33 (89.19%) simple artifacts. Chert is the dominant raw material.

84. Site located 6 km from Nowrangpur towards Boriguma (19°9', 82°34')

This site is on the right side of Nowrangpur-Boriguma road at a distance of 6 km from Nowrangpur. The landscape is characterised by low hillocks 30 m to 50 m height from the plain level. Most of the hillocks are cultivated during the rainy season. The site is located on an elevated land which is disturbed due to cultivation. It has yielded 236 artifacts comprising 18 (7.62%) shaped artifacts and 218 (92.38%) simple artifacts. The artifacts are mainly made of chert with a few specimens of quartz. These are fresh, with a thin film of red patinas on chert specimens.

Table 3.2: Location of Mesolithic sites of Indravati Basin

S. No.	*Name of sites*	*Abbrivation*	*Latitude*	*Longitute*	*Near by river*	*Near by Town*	*Topography*	*No. of artifacts collected*
1	Umarkot-A	UKT-A	19°40'30"	82°11'	Bhaskel	Umarkot	H.T	54
2	Umarkot-B	UKT-A	19°39'	82°14'	Bhaskel	Umarkot	H.T	253
3	Matigaon	MTG	19°24'	82°12'		Kodinga	E.R.W	68
4	Balanga	BLG	19°20'	82°15'	Bhaskel	Kodinga	W.P	76
5	Keragaon	KRG	19°22'	82°11'		Kodinga	H.T	33
6	Churahandi	CHD	19°18'	82°14'30"		Kodinga	E.R.W	28
7	Temra	TMR	19°18'	82°14'		Kodinga	W.P	45
8	Saraladhanua	SLD	19°15'	82°12'	Bhaskel	Kodinga	W.P	44
9	Bajagar	BJR	19°12'30"	82°16'	Bhaskel	Kodinga	W.P	53
10	Duragaon	DRG	19°11'	82°11'	Bhaskel	Kodpad	W.P	71
11	Bamuni	BMN	19°12'	82°00'	Indravati	Kodpad	W.P	118
12	Binjili	BNL	19°9'	82°00'	Indravati	Kodpad	H.S	137
13	Neigaon	NGN	19°9'	82°00'	Indravati	Kodpad	E.R.W	205
14	Rajeragaon	RJG	19°14'	82°00'		Kodinga	W.P	58
15	Churahunda	CCD	19°13'	82°00'		Kodinga	H.T	133
16	Churahandi	CHD	19°12'	82°00'	Indravati	Kodpad	W.P	27
17	Asanga-A	ASN-A	19°11'	82°00'	Indravati	Kodpad	H.S	327

S. No.	*Name of sites*	*Abbrivation*	*Latitude*	*Longitute*	*Near by river*	*Near by Town*	*Topography*	*No. of artifacts collected*
18	Back to Asanga-B	ASN-B	19°12'	82°00'	Indravati	Kodpad	S.R.W	84
19	Kokdi	KKD	19°11'	82°00'	Indravati	Kodpad	H.S	101
20	Asanga to Kokdi-C	ASN-C	19°11'	82°00'	Indravati	Kodpad	H.F	221
21	Bonia	BNA	19°10'	82°00'	Indravati	Kodpad	C.L	41
22	Kotpad	KTP	19°8'	82°00'	Indravati	Kodpad	W.P	34, 133, 80
23	Kumatitarai	KTT	19°6'	82°00'	Indravati	Kodpad	E.R.W	44
24	Komtabadi	KTB	19°9'30"	82°00'	Indravati	Kodpad	H.T.+H.S	320, 35
25	NH 43-5 kms. towards Boriguma	NH 43-5 km.	19°8'	82°00'		Kodpad	W.P	20
26	Dhanpur	DPR	19°9'	82°00'	Indravati	Kodpad	C.L	63
27	Girla	GLA	19°10'	82°00'	Indravati	Kodpad	H.T	455, 42, 38
28	Ghotorla	GRL	19°10'	82°00'	Indravati	Kodpad	E.R.W	270, 34
29	Bathasona	BNA	19°9'	82°00'	Indravati	Kodpad	W.P	23
30	Mirigaon	MRG	19°7'	82°00'	Indravati	Kodpad	E.R.W	52
31	Amlabhata	ABT	19°7'	82°00'	Indravati	Kodpad	W.P	137
32	Batra Dharagudi	BDG	19°7'	82°00'	Indravati	Kodpad	H.T.+H.S	125
33	Narahandi	RND	19°6'	82°00'	Indravati	Kodpad	W.P	22
34	Sandhagaon	SDG	19°4'	82°00'	Indravati	Kodpad	E.R.W	69, 30, 31
35	Nuagaon	NUG	19°3'30"	82°00'	Indravati	Kodpad	H.T	61
36	Phupugaon	PPG	19°3'	82°00'	Indravati	Boriguma	E.R.W	40
37	Bandliguda	BND	19°10'	82°00'	Indravati	Boriguma	H.T	36
38	Sargiguda-A	SGC-A	19°3'	82°00'	Indravati	Boriguma	E.R.W	56
39	5.5 km. Boriguma to B. Singpur		19°1'	82°00'	Indravati	Boriguma	C.L	78
40	6 km. Navrangpur to Boriguma		19°9'	82°34'	Indravati	Boriguma	C.L	236
41	5 km. Navrangpur to Boriguma		19°9'30"	82°33'30"	Indravati	Boriguma	W.P	37
42	Parsola	PRL	19°11'	82°32'	Indravati	Boriguma	W.P	177, 53
43	Anuli	ANL	19°11'	82°33'	Indravati	Boriguma	H.T.+H.S	29
44	Borogaon	BRG	19°11'	82°34'	Indravati	Boriguma	E.R.W	71, 180, 49, 53, 31
45	Khandiaguda	KDG	19°1'	82°35'	Indravati	Boriguma	H.F	62
46	Rirlidanguri	RLD	19°13'30"	82°32'	Indravati	Nowrangapur	W.P	42
47	Mahulpadar	MPD	19°13'	82°28'		Nowrangapur	W.P	40
48	Siuni	SUN	19°14'	82°27'		Nowrangapur	C.L	41

S. No.	*Name of sites*	*Abbrivation*	*Latitude*	*Longitute*	*Near by river*	*Near by Town*	*Topography*	*No. of artifacts collected*
49	Doula	DUL	19°15'	82°29'	Turi	Nowrangapur	E.R.W	55, 35
50	Bikrampur	BRP	19°15'30"	82°27'30"	Turi	Nowrangapur	W.P	53
51	Teliguda	TLG	19°16'30"	82°27'30"	Turi	Nowrangapur	W.P	42
52	Rangpiajguda	RPG	19°14'	82°39'		Nowrangapur	H.T	42
53	Rangamatiguda	RMG	19°14'30"	82°34'		Nowrangapur	W.P	195
54	Bentaguda	BTG	19°9'	82°23'	Indravati	Kotpad	E.R.W	110
55	Bejuguda	BJG	19°16'	82°46'	Indravati	Tentulikhunti	E.R.W	21
56	Gatiput	GPT	19°15'	82°47'	Indravati	Tentulikhunti	E.R.W	20
57	Lambtaguda	LTG	19°15'	82°46'	Indravati	Tentulikhunti	C.L	117
58	Photaguda	PTG	19°14'	82°47'	Indravati	Tentulikhunti	H.S	138
59	Panaspadar	PPD	19°15'	82°44'	Baghadiri	Tentulikhunti	C.L	59
60	Antasar	ATB	19°14'	82°42'	Baghadiri	Tentulikhunti	C.L	19
61	Ekamba-A	EKB-A	19°12'	82°39'30"		Nowrangapur	H.T	129
62	Ekamba-B	EKB-B	19°12'	82°39'		Nowrangapur	H.T	262
63	Bairagiguda	BRG	19°13'	82°42'	Indravati	Tentulikhunti	H.T	224
64	Phupugaon	PPG	19°14'	82°45'	Indravati	Tentulikhunti	H.T	102
65	Muchagaon	MCG	19°13'	82°46'	Indravati	Tentulikhunti	H.T	128
66	Bairagiguda-Ekamba		19°13'	82°41'	Indravati	Tentulikhunti	W.P	109
67	Munja to Kunuli		19°9'	82°41'30"	Indravati	B.Singpur	C.L	80
68	Kumuli	KML	19°7'	82°41'	Indravati	B.Singpur	H.T	48
69	6 km B. Singpur to Boriguma		19°8'	82°41'	Indravati	B.Singpur	E.R.W	46
70	Dangarkarchi	DGK	19°58'	82°40'30"	Indravati	B.Singpur	H.T	30
71	Paljur	PLG	19°35'	82°56'	Indravati	Kalahandi District	H.F	53

S. No.	*Name of sites*	*Abbrivation*	*Latitude*	*Longitute*	*Near by river*	*Near by Town*	*Topography*	*No. of artifacts collected*
72	Dakutha-A	DKT-A	19°37'	82°59'	Indravati	Kalahandi District	H.F	24
73	Dakutha-B	DKT-B	19°33'	82°58'		Kalahandi District	H.F	17
74	Bentaguda	BRP	19°32'	82°1'			E.R.W	36
75	Sargiguda-B	AGA	19°3'	82°36'		Boriguma	E.R.W	26
76	Berapadar	JGP	19°12'	82°46'	Nuran	Tentu-likhunti	C.L	39
77	Mangalatal	PTG	19°10'	82°44'		Tentu-likhunti	H.T	102
78	Jagnathpur	LUG	19°12'	82°45'	Telingiri	Tentu-likhunti	E.R.W	89
79	Piteiguda	LMT	19°0'	82°41'	Indravati	B.Singpur	E.R.W	29
80	Laugura	KTG	19°12'	82°45'	Indravati	Tentu-likhunti	H.T	100
81	Limbata	LMT	19°11'	82°17'	Indravati	Kotpad	E.R.W	190
82	Kuntigura	KTG	19°15'	82°17'	Bhaskel	Kodinga	W.P	66
83	Majhiguda	MJG	19°17'	82°15'	Bhaskel	Kodinga	W.P	52
84	Kamta	KMT	19°7'34"	82°39'	Telingiri	B.Singpur	H.T	22
85	Kharki	KRK	19°19'	82°30'		Papada-handi	Cave	143

CAVE SITE

85. Kharki (KRK, 19°19', 82°30')

The village of Kharki comes within the area of Pappadahandi police station. Pappadahandi is situated south of Nowrangpur at a distance of 12 km by State Highway 2 and Kharki is about 10 km by road from Pappadahandi in north-east direction. Behind the Kharki village, there is a hill range which extends for about a 1 km in length and 0.75 km in breadth. It is largely a barren hill with a few patches of vegetation.

There are about 30 rock shelters in this hill range. The size of the shelters varies from 2 m to 5 m in length and less than 1 m to 6 m in breadth. The height of shelters varies from 0.5 m to 2 m. On the roof of one shelter, there are some historic paintings in red colour. Outside the shelters and on the flat rocks, large numbers of microliths are noticed. The artifacts occur in veneral scatters. A simple of collection of 143 artifacts are made from one of the scatter. They comprise of 7 (4.89%) shaped artifacts and 136 (95.11%) simple artifacts. Chert and quartz are the main raw materials. The artifacts are in mint condition.

Chapter 4

The Upper Palaeolithic Culture

Research in prehistoric archaeology in India has led to the discovery of a large number of Lower and Middle Palaeolithic and Mesolithic sites (Sankalia 1974), but the evidence for the Upper Palaeolithic cultural phase is very scanty. Even till late 1960s little was known about the Upper Palaeolithic phase. The history of Upper Palaeolithic begins with the discovery by Robert Bruce Foote (1884) of a few bone artifacts having resemblance with Magdalenian tools of France and associated with Late Pleistocene fauna from Sillasurgan caves of Kurnool district, Andhra Pradesh. Later, Comniade and Burkitt (1930), and de Terra and Paterson (1939) reported a blade Soan 'B' of the Potwar Plateau, respectively. Chronologically the assemblages belong to the Post-Middle Palaeolithic and Pre-Mesolithic phase.

After a lull of two decades, Sankalia (1956) reported the element of Upper Palaeolithic from Pravara basin in Maharashtra. Later on Upper Palaeolithic blade and burin tools were reported by Srinivasan (1960) from Papaniya Tekdi in Maharashtra, Issac (1960) from Gundalkanna valley of Kurnool, Andhra Pradesh and Sen (1960-61) from South Mandle in Madhya Pradesh. Seshadri (1962) reported further data from Karnataka for establishing Upper Palaeolithic as an independent cultural phase in the Indian Stone Age sequence. The other important discoveries pertaining to the Upper palaeolithic are:

1. Flake-blade industry consisting of large size blades, (usually backed) flake-blades and hollow scrapers of jasper from Ellora in Maharastra (Soundrarajan and Sengupta 1962).
2. The Upper Palaeolithic artifacts from uncemented gravel, in a sequence underlain by Lower Palaeolithic and Middle Palaeolithic and underlain by Mesolithic, from clay deposit of the Son river near Hanumanpura in Uttar Pradesh (Varma and Misra 1968, 1969).
3. The blade and burin industry at Renugunta of Chittor district in Andhra Pradesh in a definite and stratified context (Murty 1966, 1968, 1970).
4. An Upper Palaeolithic assemblage from Vemula of Cuddapah district of Andhra Pradesh, comprising blades, blade flakes and blade tools representing a transitional phase between

the Middle and the Late Stone Ages (Reddy 1968).

5. A blade industry at Salvedgi, Culbal, Kulabhari etc. in Bijapur and Gulburga districts, Karnataka (Paddayya 1968).
6. A flake-blade industry from 15 sites in the Singhbhum district of Bihar, with high proportion of blades and scrapers, providing a clue to the existence of Upper Palaeolithic in Eastern India (Ghosh 1970).

Subsequently quite a large number of sites have been reported by Murty (1974, 1975, 1979), and Murty and Reddy (1976) from limestone caves of Kurnool; by Misra (1974, 1979) from Bhimbetka; by Sali (1974, 1979) from Inamgaon and Patna; by Paddayya (1970) from Shorapur Doab and by Joshi *et al.* (1979) from Bhokar. However, the evidence for the Upper Palaeolithic in eastern India is poorly known, excepting a few blades in the Middle Palaeolithic collections from Odisha made by Mahapatra (1961) and Tripathy (1962).

Before discussing the details of the Upper Palaeolithic of the Koraput region, it would be useful to discuss the salient features of the Indian Upper Palaeolithic assemblages. On the basis of typo-technology, Murty (1979: 303-12) has grouped the Upper Palaeolithic into:

(a) Flake-blade industry,

(b) Blade tool industry and

(c) Blade and burin industry.

Flake-blade Industry

Blade is the predominant tool type of this industry. These are moderately broad, thick and irregular in shape with a prominent bulb. This industry comprises side scrapers, end scrapers, borers, points made on flakes, blade flakes and blades in a smaller proportion.

Blade Tool Industry

This includes blades of varying sizes with parallel and blunted back blades, scrapers, points, awls, burins on flakes and blades or blade-like flakes. The frequency of backed blades and burins is small.

Blade and Burin Industry

Blades and burins are the main tool types of this industry. The backed blades, burins, points, penknives, macro-lunates, macro-triangles, macro-trapezes and scrapers on blades as well as flakes and blade-like flakes constitute the major portion of the industry.

The present study represents seventeen Upper Palaeolithic sites in Koraput district of Odisha. Of these, sixteen sites are located on isolated small hill-topes, slopes, foot-hills, low plateau, and one site is located on the flat bank of the small stream, called Bhaskel at Paidapali.

All these sites are located in the vicinity of present tribal villages. The artifacts are found scattered over leteritie soil or on red soil covering an area varying between 40 sq m to 1200 sq m. The industry under discussion from Koraput region falls into the flake-blade groups, with minor variations.

THE INDUSTRY

On the basis of typo-technology the industry (Plate 4.1) is divided into two groups:

(a) shaped artifacts and (b) simple artifacts.

Shaped Artifacts

They show deliberately on one or more edges with the exception of the knife. This group consists of:

(a) scrapers, (b) denticulates,
(c) notches, (d) knives,
(e) borers, (f) burins,
(g) backed microblades and (h) micro-crescents.

Simple Artifacts

These artifacts are the intermediary and by-products of the shaped tools. They are unmodified or unretouched artifacts and might not have been used as tools with the exception "utilised flakes and utilised blades". These are classified into:

(a) cores, (b) flakes,
(c) blades, (d) chips and
(e) worked nodules.

The total number of artifacts from 17 sites consists of 1,282 pieces, out of which 129 (10.06%) are shaped and 1,153 (89.94%) simple artifacts. The typological analysis in respect of the sites is given in Tables 4.1 and 4.2, with percentage and frequency.

Shaped Artifacts (129: 10.06%)

The artifacts are made on: side struck flakes (23: 17.85%), end struck flakes (31: 24.03%), indeterminate flakes (61: 47.28%), cores (4: 5.10%), blades (5: 3.87%), and microblades (5: 3.87%). This group includes the following types.

(a) ***Scrapers***: The shaped tool group is dominated by scraper element (91: 70.53%). These are further classified as

(i) side scrapers,

Table 4.1: Site and main type-wise distribution of Upper Palaeolithic artifacts from Indravati basin

								Chips		*Blades*		*M. Blades*		*Flake Cores*				*M. Blade Cores*		*Worked Nodules*		*Total*
S. No.	*Type/Site*	*No.*	*%*	*No.*	*%*	*No.*	*%*	*No.*	*%*	*No.*	*%*	*No.*	*%*	*No.*	*%*	*No.*	*%*	*No.*	*%*	*No.*	*%*	
1	Paidapali -A	14	10.14			40	28.98	41	29.71	27	1.056	2	1.45	7	5.07	3	2.17			4	2.9	138
2	Paidapali -B	1	2.94			6	17.65	17	50	6	17.65			2	5.88			2	5.88			34
3	Amota	8	11.74			12	17.65	32	47.05	8	11.74	1	1.47	1	1.47					6	8.82	68
4	Semela	8	20			6	15	11	27.5	6	15			2	5	2	5	1	2.5	4	10	40
5	Chirma	5	12.12			14	21.21	16	24.24	9	13.64	1	1.51	9	13.64			2	3.03	7	10.61	66
6	Kosagu-muda	12	10.81	3	2.7	10	9	46	41.44	29	26.13	3	2.7	3	2.7	4	3.6	1	0.9	3	2.7	111
7	Majhidh-anua	1	2.78			7	19.44	20	55.55	5	13.89			1	2.78					2	5.55	36
8	Ukiapali	7	15.9			7	15.9	15	34.09	4	9.09	1	2.27	5	11.36			1	2.27	4	9.09	44
9	Chitagaon	4	12.9			8	25.8	9	29.03	3	9.67	1	3 22			1	3.22	1	3.22	4	12.9	31
10	Kusumpali	3	14.28			4	19.05	9	42.86	2	9.52									3	14.28	21
11	Parajasahi	21	13.91			29	19.2	57	37.35	10	6.62	1	0.66	8	5.3	1	0.66	6	3.97	18	11.92	151
12	Majhia	7	9.72	1	1.39	15	20.83	26	36.11	8	11.11	2	2.77	4	5.55			4	5.55	6	8.33	72
13	Sitiliguda	6	9.52			21	33.33	22	34.92	8	12.7			1	1.59			4	6.35	1	1.59	63
14	Borogaon	6	15.38			8	20.51	10	25.64	4	10.26			5	12.82	1	2.56	2	5.13	3	7.69	39
15	Gadaba-guda	13	7.83			26	15.66	60	36.14	14	8.43	4	2.41	9	5.42	1	0.6	14	8.43	25	15.06	166
16	Rengiguda	3	4.84			16	25.81	21	33.87	5	8.06	1	1.61	3	4.84	1	1.61	4	6.45	8	12.9	62
17	Chata-handi	7	5	1	0.71	8	5.71	79	56.43	20	12.29	5	3.37	10	7.14	3	2.14	8	5.71			140
		124	9.67	5	0.39	237	18.49	491	38.3	168	13.1	22	1.71	70	5.46	17	1.33	50	3.9	98	7.64	1282

Table 4.2: Site and main type-wise distribution of Upper Palaeolithic shaped artifacts from Indravati basin

S. No.	Type/Sites	SS-1 St.		SS-1 Conc.		SS-1 Conv.		SS Tra nsve		SS-2		SS. Steep		Den-ticu-late		ES		ES-+SS		Notch		Bor-er		Bu-rin		Knife		M. Backed Blade		TotalM. Cresc.
		No	%	No.	%	No.	%	No.	%	No.	%	No.	%	No.	%	No.	%	No.	%	No.	%	No.	%	No.	%	No.	%	No.	%	No%No.
1	Paidapali-A			2	14.28	3	21.42					3	21.42			2	14.28			4	28.57									14
2	Paidapali-B									1																				1
3	Amota	1	12.5	4	50	1	12.5									2	25													8
4	Semela			1	12.5	2	25							2	25	1	12.5	1	12.5							1	12.5			8
5	Chirma			1	12.5	1	12.5			1	12.5					1	12.5			2	25			2	25					8
6	Kosagu-muda	1	8.33	1	8.33	2	16.66	1	8.33							2	16.66			1	8.33			1	8.33			1	8.33	1216.662
7	Majhidha-nua																							1						1
8	Ukiapali	2	28.57	2	28.57											1	14.28			1	14.28	1	14.28							7
9	Chitagaon	1	25													2	50			1	25									4
10	Kusmpali			1	33.33					1	33.33													1	33.33					3
11	Parajasahi	2	9.52	1	4.76	3	14.28							1	4.76	7	33.33	1	4.76	4	19.04	2	9.52							21
12	Majhia			1	14.28							2	28.57							3	42.85									714.281
13	Sitiliguda	1	16.66							2	33.33					3	50													6
14	Borogaon					3	50			1	16.66	1	16.66							1	16.66									6
15	Gadaba-guda	2	15.38	2	15.38	2	15.38									5	38.46			1	7.69					1	7.69			13
16	Rengiguda					2	66.66									1	33.33													3
17	Chatah-andi	1	14.28							2	28.57					1	14.28			1	14.28			1	14.28					714.281
		11	8.52	**16**	**12.4**	**19**	**14.72**	**1**	**0.77**	**8**	**6.2**	**6**	**4.65**	**3**	**2.33**	**28**	**21.7**	**2**	**1.55**	**19**	**14.73**	**3**	**2.33**	**6**	**4.65**	**2**	**1.55**	**1**	**0.77**	**1293.14**

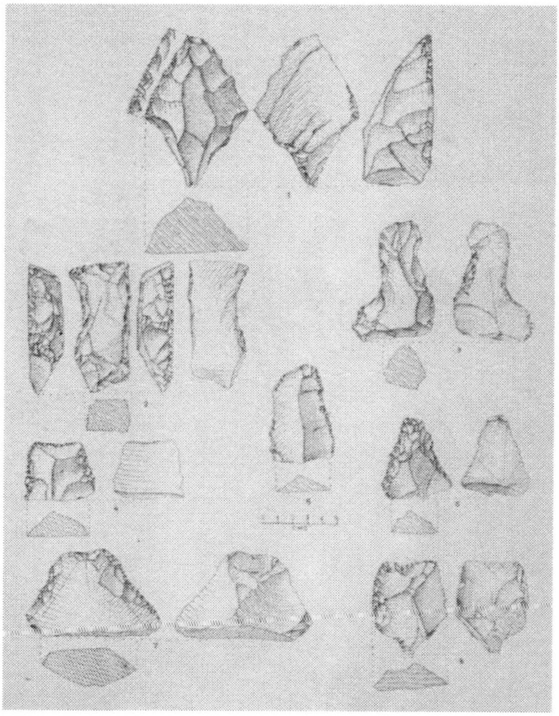

Fig. 4.1: Upper Palaeolithic scrapers

Plate 4.1: Upper Palaeolithic artifacts – surface collections

(ii) end scrapers (Fig. 4.2), and

(iii) end and side scrapers.

(b) ***Side Scrapers:*** Within the scraper group, the side scrapers occur in high frequency (61: 47.28%). These are further divided into

(1) single side scraper and (2) double side scraper.

Single Side Scrapers (53: 41.08%)

Among these specimens the working edge is formed on one of the lateral margins, parallel to the longer axis (with exception for transverse scrapers). They are made on blades, blade-like flakes and on flakes. On the basis of technology, orientation and form of working-edge, this group is divided into:

(a) Straight working edge (11: 8.25%)
(b) Concave working edge (16: 12.40%)
(c) Convex working edge (19: 14.72%)
(d) Transverse working edge (1: 0.77%)
(e) Steep working edge (6: 4.65%)

In the case of the single scraper with transverse retouch working edge the convex margin of the artifact possesses secondary retouch at right angles to be bulbar axis. The category of scrapers with steep retouch working edge, the scraping edge is perpendicular or nearly perpendicular to the ventral surface. The mean working angle is 94°. They are made on cores (66.66%) as well as on thick flakes (33.34%).

Double Side Scraper (8: 6.20%)

Among these specimens the two non-adjacent long margins show retouches. This type comprises 8 specimens which are further divided into:

(a) both the working edges concave (2: 1.55%),

(b) working edges are straight and concave (2: 1.55%) and

(c) working edges straight and convex (4: 3.10%).

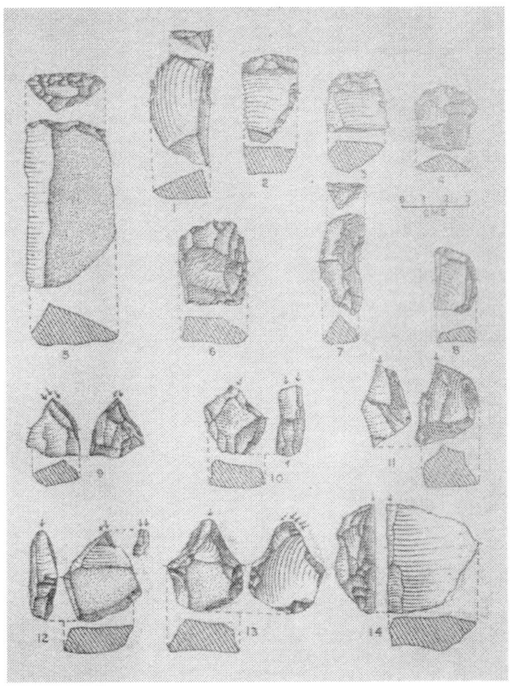

Fig. 4.2: Upper Palaeolithic end scrapers and burins

End Scrapers (28: 21.70%, Fig. 4.2)

This category comes from 13 sites but is absent at site Nos. 2, 7, 10 and 12. The height frequency occurs at site No. 15 (5: 38.46%), a plateau site. These are characterised by working edge at the end. The nature of retouch in the tool types may be classified as follows:

(a) convergent (2: 1.55%),

(b) semi-convergent (1: 0.77%), and

(c) non-convergent (25: 19.37%).

On the basis of shape of the working edge they are grouped as asymmetrical, pointed, and flat-end.

End and Side Scrapers (2: 1.55%)

This type is represented by two specimens, one each from site Nos. 4 and 11. The working edges occur on one of the lateral margins parallel to the longer axis and on the end, usually at right angles to the lateral working edge.

(a) ***Denticulate (3: 2.33%):*** These are made on flakes on blades. They are characterised by more than two consecutive notches on the longer margin or margins giving a denticulated profile. One specimen is made on a blade-like flake and two on flakes.

(b) ***Notches (19: 14.73%):*** The notched specimens in none respects resemble the concave side scraper. But these can be distinguished by a smaller and narrow working edge. Typically the depth is more than the length of working part. They occur on blades and flakes, the latter being higher in percentage. The highest frequency is found at site Nos. 1 (4: 28.57%) and 11 (4: 19.04%). At site Nos. 6, 8, 9, 11, 15 and 17, they are represented by a single specimen each, while at site Nos. 5 and 12 they are represented by 2 and 3 specimens respectively. On a few specimens from site Nos. 1 and 12, the retouches are executed from the ventral side while at other sites they are on the dorsal surfaces.

(c) ***Borers (3: 2.33%):*** There are only three specimens of this type. These are small implements below 25 mm in greater dimension and fashioned on flakes only. The tool is characterised by a projecting pointed end, formed by two small notches closer to both sides of the tip. These two notches may be on the same surface or one each on either surface of the flakes. They occur at sites Nos. 8 (1: 0.77%) and 11 (2: 1.55%) only.

(d) ***Burins (6: 4.65%):*** There are six specimens of this type (Fig. 4.2) and occur with the frequency of one each at sites Nos. 6, 7, 10 and 17 and two at sites Nos. 5. These are made on thick flakes (2: 33.33%) and cores (4: 66.66%). Based on working edges burins are classified as angled (3: 3.32%), central (2: 55%) and retouch (1: 0.77%).

(e) ***Knives (2: 1.55%):*** There are only two specimens in this type, one from site Nos. 4 (1: 12.5%) and the other from site Nos. 15 (1: 69%). At the back of the sharp cutting edge, a thick natural back is a characteristic feature of these artifacts. The cross-section of the artifacts is a right-angled triangle.

(g) ***Backed microblade (1: 0.77%):*** There is only one specimen and it occurs at site No. 6.

(h) ***Micro-Crescents 4: 3.10%):*** There are 4 specimens of this type. These occur with the frequency of one each at the site Nos. 12 and 17 and two specimens at site No. 6. This type comprises symmetric (1: 0.77%) and asymmetric (3: 2.32%) forms. In three specimens blunting is by directional and in one unidirectional.

Simple Artifacts (1153: 89.94%)

The simple artifacts are grouped into:

(a) cores,
(b) flakes,
(c) blades,
(d) chips, and
(e) worked nodules.

(a) Cores (137: 11.88%)

The cores (Fig. 4.3) are further classified into: (i) flake cores, (ii) blade cores, and (iii) micro blade cores.

Flake cores (70: 6.06%): The flake cores are further grouped into two types depending on the nature of shaping. They are: (i) amorphous cores, and (ii) discoidal cores.

(i) **Amorphous cores (65: 5.65%):** With irregular cross section these specimens do not have any particular shape. The frequency of the cores ranges from one each at site Nos. 3, 7 and 13 to a maximum of 9 and 10 specimens at site Nos. 15 and 17 respectively.

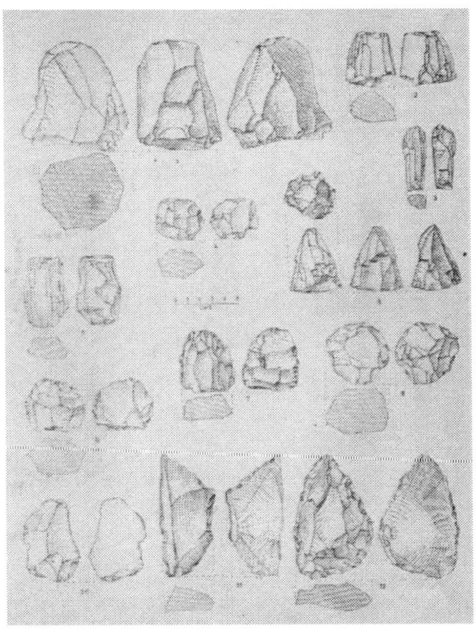

Fig. 4.3: Upper Palaeolithic cores and flakes

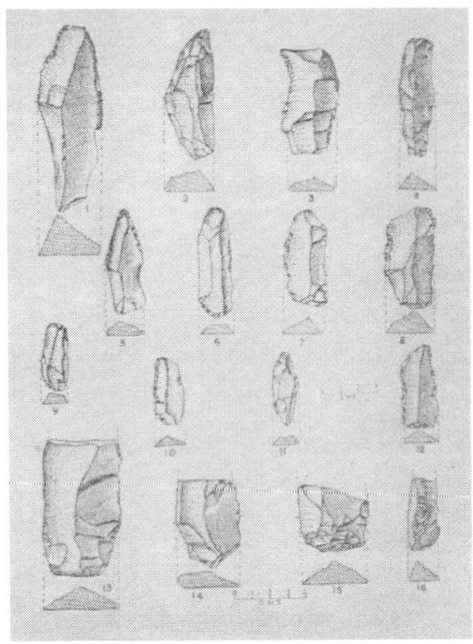

Fig. 4.4: Upper Palaeolithic blades

(ii) **Discoidal cores (5: 0.43%):** These specimens are discoidal in appearance with biconvex or lenticular cross section. Flakes are struck off from the periphery and terminate in the centre. These occur at site Nos. 1, 11, 14 and 16. The discoidal cores occur in a small proportion as compared to the amorphous type (1: 13).

Blade cores (17: 1.47%): These are large-sized cores. The occurrence of these specimens ranges from one each at site Nos. 9, 11, 14, 15 and 16, two specimens at site No. 4, three specimens at site Nos. 1 and 17, and four specimens at site No. 6. Based on shape, they are grouped as pyramidal (2: 11.76%), rectangular (2: 11.76%), cylindrical (3: 17.64%), and irregular (1: 58.82%). On the basis of platform they can be classified as prepared platform (11: 64.70%), plain platform (5:29.41%) and platform with cortex (1: 5.88%). The shaped at the platform is rounded, rectangular and irregular in form. The number of platform varies from one to three. The cores show 3 to 5 scars, and many incomplete scars.

Micro blade cores (50: 4.33%): These cores are represented on all sites, except Nos. 1, 3, 7, and 10. On the basis of shape, they are grouped as conical (24.49%), cylindrical (9.18%), and pyramidal (17.34%). Two cores from site Nos. 11 and 15 are with two platforms and others have a single platform.

(b) Flakes (237: 20.55%)

Flakes form the main component of the simple artifacts group. These specimens are classified into (a) simple flakes, (b) core rejuvenation flakes and (c) utilised flakes.

Simple flakes (177: 15.33%): These are grouped into side stuck flakes (52: 7.45%), end struck flakes (86: 7.45%) and indeterminate flakes (38: 3.29%). These are of rectangular, pointed, triangular, oval and irregular shape. The platforms of the flakes are plain (70: 39.54%), with cortex (112: 65.27%), and prepared (19: 10.75%) types.

Core rejuvenation flakes (5: 0.43%): These are grouped into (i) straight (CRF- st), and (ii) top (CRF- top).

(i) **Straight (3: 0.26%):** These are characterised by relatively thick flakes, with a few blade scars on the dorsal surface parallel to the longer axis and rarely at right angles to it.

(ii) **Top (2: 0.17%):** They are almost rounded with complete platform of the blade core and possess apart of blade scares around it.

Utilised Flakes (50: 4.33%): These specimens are characterized by discontinuous indentation on the margin or margins due to use.

(c) Blades (106: 14.57%)

This group is second to flakes in the simple artifacts group. They are further divided into (1) simple blades, and (2) utilized blades.

Simple blades (168: 14.57%): This type is the most important element of the Upper Palaeolithic industry. Of these eighteen show utilisation. A few of the blades have a ridge, partly or fully, in the centre of the dorsal surface. Generally they have a single ridge and in some cases double ridges. Forty-four specimens are complete and one hundred twenty four are broken. They are classified as regular blades, divergent blades, convergent blades and irregular blades. There are 112 (66.66%) specimens with triangular cross section 34 (20.24%) with trapezoidal cross section 13 (7.74%) with planoconvex cross section, and 9 (5.35%) with irregular cross section (Fig. 4.5). in case of planoconvex cross section, the blades are comparatively thin. In those with irregular cross section the blades do not have any fixed number of ridges. The scars on the dorsal face are parallel to the longer axis, or perpendicular to longer axis, of irregular in orientation. The dorsal surface has two flake scars (77: 45.83%), three flake scars (50: 29.76%), four flake scars (5: 2.97%), and in a few cases with cortex (28: 16.66%, Fig. 4.5). Four specimens (2: 38%) retain cortex on the whole of dorsal surface. It shows that the artificer sometimes exploited the natural ridge of the slab or pebble or nodule, for the removal of blades.

In respect of platform 7 (4.17%) specimens possess cortex, 74 (44.05%) have plain platform and 2 (1.19%) have dihedral platforms. In 77 (45.83%) the platform is broken and in 8 (4.76%) specimens it is not clear (Fig. 4.5). A significant percentage, 22.72% of the blades fall in the length range of 46-50 mm, 43.18% of the blades fall in the breadth range of 12-17 mm and 50% of the blades fall in the thickness range of 4-9 mm (Fig. 4.6).

(d) Chips (491: 42.58%)

Specimens less than 1.5 cm in the greater dimension are considered as chips.

Table 4.3: Length range of Blade from Indravati

Range (in mm)	*Blades No.*	*%*
26-30	1	2.27
31-35	3	6.82
36-40	4	9.09
41-45	5	11.36
46-50	16	22.73
51-55	4	9.09
56-60	7	15.91
61-65	3	6.82
66-70	2	4.54
Above 70	5	11.36
Total	44	99.99

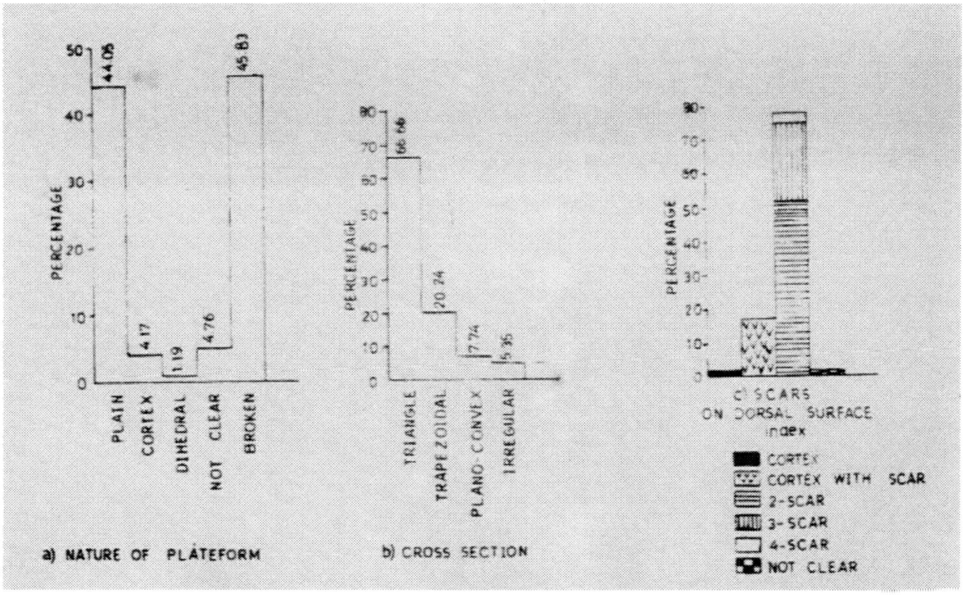

Fig. 4.5: Distribution and nature of scar, platform and cross section of blades

Table 4.4: Breadth range of Blade from Indravati

Range (in mm)	*Blades No.*	*%*
12-17	19	43.18
18-22	11	25.00
23-27	10	22.73
28-32	4	9.09
Total	44	100.00

Table 4.5: Thickness range of Blade from Indravati

Range (in mm)	*Blades No.*	*%*
1-3	1	2.27
4-6	11	25.00
7-9	11	25.00
10-12	9	20.45
13-15	9	20.45
16-18	3	6.82
Total	44	99.99

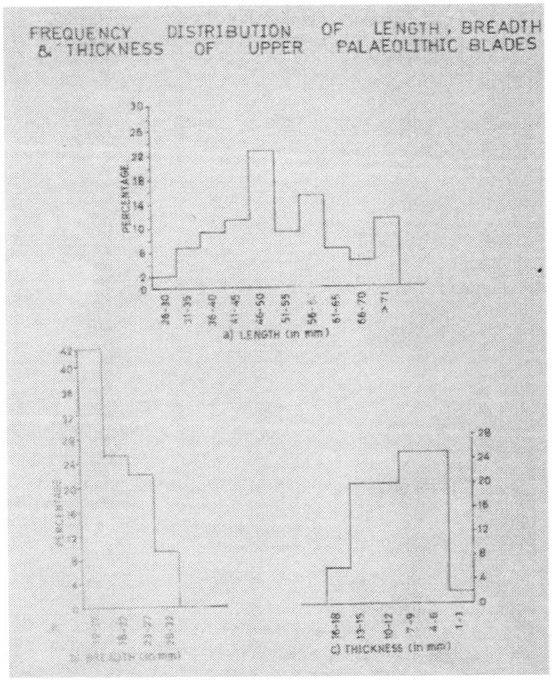

Fig. 4.6: Frequency distribution of length, breadth and thickness of Upper Palaeolithic blades

Table 4.6: Maximum, minimum and mean values of length (L), breadth (B) and thickness (T) of complete blades from Indravati (in mm)

	Length	Breadth	Thickness
Maximum	104	31	17
Minimum	29	13	3
Mean	53	19	9

Worked nodules (98: 8.49%)

The type itself suggests that these are nodules which show a few flake scars. These are the reject pieces at the sites. They have come from all the sites except Nos. 2 and 17.

DISCUSSION

There is no marked difference among the tools from the 17 sites even though they have varying geomorphological setting. They represent a single homogenous industry. The whole collection of artifacts comprises 1262 specimens of which 129 (10.06%) are of finished and 1153 (89.94%) are simple artifacts. The ratio of these two broad groups is 1:9. All are surfacial sites and in association with these artifacts no organic remains have survived.

The industry falls under the category blade-tool industry following the classification of Murty (1979). The industry is dominated by side (47.28%) and end scrapers (21.70%), followed by notches (14.73%), burins (4.65%), borers (2.33%), denticulates (2.33%), knives (1.55%), backed micro blades (0.77%), and micro blade crescents (3.10%). The simple artifacts group is represented by cores (11.88%), flakes (20.55%), chips (42.58%), blades (14.57%), micro blades (1.90%) and worked nodules (8.49%). The high proportion of chips, flakes, blades, flake cores and blade cores at all the 17 sites suggests that these must have been workshop sites. And at the site Parajasahi, the presence of a good proportion of shaped tools and simple artifacts clearly suggests that it must have been a workshop-cum-camp site. Chert is the main raw material used for manufacture of artifacts.

TECHNOLOGY

That the nodules are first dressed with a stone hammer is attested by the primary flakes with cortex (a major portion) on the dorsal surface. After dressing, these nodules were used for the removal of blades. But the proportion of blade cores (1.47%) is very small in comparison to the number of blades (14.57%). This is also noticed in the Bhimbetka assemblage (a cave side in the Raisen district, Madhya Pradesh), in which there is not a single blade core whereas there are as many as 105 (4.90% of total collection) blades. Referring to this characteristic, Misra (1980) had explained that: "this is probably so because blades were produced not from specialised blade cores but from flake cores, and secondly because blade cores may have been worked to produced micro-blades and thereby got converted into micro blade cores." The Upper Palaeolithic industry from the Indravati valley corroborates Misra's hypothesis. The Indravati industry comprises 2.25% blade cores and 4.33% micro blade cores with 14.57% blades and 1.90% micro blades. Such a less representation of the blade cores might be for the reason that they were further exploited for the removal of micro blades.

The blades with plain platform and tiny prominent bulb suggest the application of indirect percussion of punch technique. There is no evidence of elaborate preparation of the platform. In most cases a single flake was removed on the horizontal axis. The blades are generally irregular or somewhat parallel and are comparatively thick, and some of them show use marks of the edges.

Flakes are thick, large and irregular with prominent positive or negative bulb. These were indently removed with a stone hammer. The flakes are eventually finished by pressure chipping, by punch, and by soft hammer into various forms. The steep retouched scrapers possess laminar retouching. Levalloisian flakes are completely absent but there are some which can be called as pseudo Levalloisian. One specimen shows, alternate preparation of guided ridge. As a whole the industry represents a crude craftsmanship.

RAW MATERIAL

On the basis of raw material these sites differ from most of the classic sites of India, like Renigunta (Murty 1966-68), Nagarjunkonda (Sundar Rajen 1958), Betamcherla (Murty 1976), and Bhimbetka (Misra 1974). The main raw material at the above mentioned sites is quartzite (excepting Betamcherla) of different colour and textures; for the present assemblage it is chert. In typological and morphometric features the Indravati industry displays similarities with that of Bhimbetka, with slight variation. This variation may be due the different raw material at these two sites. For instance the mean length, breadth and thickness of blades of Bhimbetka is more when compared to those of the Indravati industry, which is shown in the following table (Table 4.7).

Table 4.7: The maximum, minimum, and mean values in length (L), breadth (B) and thickness (T) of blades

	Bhimbetka			*Indravati*		
	L	B	T	L	B	T
Maximum	8.5	3.4	1.9	10.4	3.1	1.7
Minimum	4.2	2.0	0.7	2.9	1.3	0.3
Mean	6.2	2.6	1.2	5.3	1.9	0.9

CAVE SITES

The rock shelter III F-23 at Bhimbetka excavated by V.N. Misra (1980) has received the prehistoric cultural sequence from late Acheulian to Mesolithic period. This is the only cave in India which has yielded all the four lithic phases and considerable quantities of cultural material in stratigraphical context. At Bhimbetka, blades occur right from the Acheulian level. The frequency of blades rises considerably from Acheulian to Mesolithic level. Microblades occur in a negligible proportion in the Acheulian and Middle Palaeolithic level, where as they are such higher in Mesolithic phase and form a significant representation in Upper Palaeolithic phase.

In the Indravati collection the blade element is 13.1% against 4.28% at Bhimbetka and microblades are 1.71% and 1.57% respectively in the Upper Palaeolithic phase. The proportion of flake tools is 9.67% in Indravati and 16.1% in Bhimbetka collection. In both the industries scraper is the dominant tool, followed by blade category. The variation between these two assemblages can be explained as follows:

1. Being due to the different raw material
2. On account of a lot of difference between two samples

3. Bhimbetka is an excavated cave site whereas Indravati assemblages are open air surface sites.

The metrical analysis of blade from both assemblages shows that they do not differ much. The blades of Bhimbetka are long, thick and broad than the blades of Indravati assemblage. This can be explained as:

1. Raw material used at Bhimbetka is quartzite whereas chert is used at Indravati sites.
2. Only 7 pieces of complete blades are taken for material analysis at Bhimbetka whereas 44 pieces are taken from Indravati assemblages.
3. The proportion of broken blades is equally high in both assemblages. The blades are generally broken on their longer axis.

The above comparative analysis shows that Upper Palaeolithic culture of Indravati valley has a close similarity with Bhimbetka Upper Paleolithic industry.

MUCHCHATLA CHINTAMANU GAVI

It is a cave near Betamcherla in a Kurnool district of Andhra Pradesh and has been excavated by M.L.K. Murty (1974: 196-230). This is the early Upper Palaeolithic site which has yielded bone tools in a high proportion (90.30%). The lithic assemblage comprises cores, flakes, blades, chips, scrapers, chisels, and shouldered points. The flakes show irregular, convergent and crossflaking on dorsal surface with diffused bulb on their ventral face. The blades are parallel sided, pointed and irregular in form. The following table gives a comparative analysis of simple artifacts from Indravati and Betamcherla cave complex.

Table 4.8: Type wise distribution of simple artifacts

	Betamcherla		*Indravati*	
Flakes	57	25.90	237	20.55
Blades	91	41.36	168	14.57
Cores	12	5.45	235	20.38
Chips	60	27.27	491	42.58
Microblades	–	–	22	1.90
Total	220	99.98	1155	99.98

From the above table it is clear that the assemblages do not have such similarity in the frequency of different types of simple artifacts. But the occurrence of blade element is quite significant in both the assemblages. And the frequency of flakes is more or less the same in both the industries, whereas the distribution of cores is much higher in the Indravati valley. The probable explanation for this is that the Indravati assemblages are from open air-surfaces sites collected randomly, whereas Betamcherla collection is from an excavated cave site. This cave site is a habitational site whereas the Upper Palaeolithic sites in Indravati valley are open air workshop-cum-camp sites.

OPEN AIR SITES

As there are several open-air Upper Palaeolithic sites from different parts of India, an attempt is made to compare the industries of the Indravati valley, with those from other parts of the country.

EASTERN INDIA

Since the late 1950's, evidence of Upper Palaeolithic culture has been reported from Bihar. Blades were reported by S. Roy from Prattapur and Marvania in Palmau district (*IAR* 1959-60: 12), from surface. In 1965-66 more sites were reported from Dhekulia also in Palmau district (*IAR* 1965-66: 8). The tool kit comprises of scrapers, points, burins, knives, awls, blades, flakes and cores. The above artifact types are common to both the industries.

Latter a large number of surface sites have been reported by A. Ghosh (1970: 1-58) from Singhbhum district of Bihar. The important sites are Chandil, Sini, Ghataila gua, and Ghaibasa. The artifacts are fashioned on agate, jasper, and other silicious rocks. The collection from these sites amount to 210 artifacts and these consists of choppers (25: 11.9%), side scrapers (112: 55.3%), points (25 11.9), knives (4:1.9%), borers (20: 9.5%) and blades (19: 9.0%). As all these sites, stratified though, are secondary sites, the above mentioned types cannot be regarded as the only types, especially when other simple artifacts like flakes, chips and dabitage are not reported. Hence attention can be given only to the fact that industries from both the regions display typological similarities and that scraper is the most dominant tool type in both the industries. The chopper, which is an important tool type of Singhbhum industry, is absent in Indravati collection.

WESTERN INDIA

S.A. Sali (1957: 157-167) has been able to document excellent evidence from Patne of Jalgaon district in Maharashtra. Excavation conducted by him at this site revealed total cultural horizon of 10 m thickness covering Middle Palaelithic to Mesolithic phases. The Upper Palaeolithic phase is divided into five sub-phases such as A, B, C, D and E. These sub-phases are mainly on the basis if stratigraphical evidence and on slight variation in typology. These five sub-phases are again grouped as early Upper Palaeolithic (A, B and C) and late Upper Palaeolithic (D and E). The difference lies in raw material, size of the tools and typological variations. Jasper is the dominant raw material in the early phase and chalchedony in the late phase. Blade is the most dominant type which is well represented in the Indravati industry also. Occurrence of triangle and trapeze at Patne, show the advanced nature of Upper Palaeolithic, which are absent in the Indravati collection. The scraper is the most dominant tool type in the Indravati Upper Palaeolithic, whereas at Patne the proportion of scraper is very low. One more advanced feature of Upper Palaeolithic culture of Patne is the size of the tools. They are smaller in size than those of the Indravati. As a whole the Patne Upper Palaeolithic seems to be more advanced than that of the Indravati.

Another site of Maharashtra, Bhokar from Nanded district has yielded Upper Palaeolithic artifacts (Joshi and Pappu 1979). The tool kit is dominated by scrappers along with borers, burins, points and knives. This assemblage has such affinity with the Indravati assemblages.

Another assemblage recently discovered at Naikund in Nagpur district (Pandey 1980: 223-230) shows similarities to that of the Indravati assemblage. The artifacts have come from a 1 m thick gravel layer resting over the gneisses with quarts veins covered by a thin band (0.5 m) of Kankar. The gravel is capped by 2 m thick fine sand and dark clay (1 m) layer. Chert is the only raw material used for the manufacture of artifact at Indravati sites whereas at Naikund it represents 60.55%. Side scrappers on flakes and cores of different geometrical form are the common tool type in both. The side scrapper makes up 47.28% in Indravati and 56.6% at Naikund collection respectively. Chopper is absent at Indravati but it is highly significant (5.0) in Naikund collection.

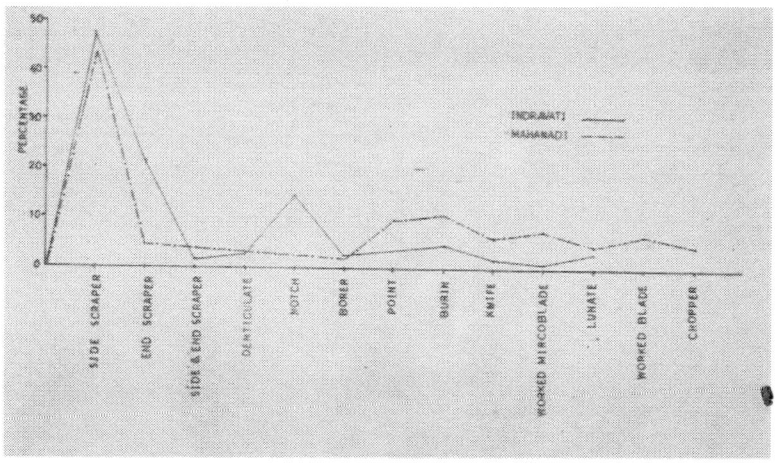

Fig. 4.7: Comparative distribution of Upper Palaeolithic shaped artifacts from Indravati and Mahanadi

R.P. Pandey's (1982) work in the upper Mahanadi valley brought the evidence of Stone Age cultures from Acheulian to Mesolithic phases. These are open air surface sites. The blade and burin industry of Upper Mahanadi valley has come from gravel II. The total collection of artifacts from four sites is 1512, out of which 291 (19.25%) are shaped tools and 1212 (80.75%) are simple artifacts; whereas Indravati industry consists of 10.06% of shaped artifacts and 89.94% of simple artifacts. The tool kit of Upper Mahanadi valley comprises side scrappers

(104: 35.73%), end scrappers (14: 4.81%), cores scrappers (23: 7.90), borers (5: 1.72%), knives (18: 6.18%), burins (30: 10.32%), points (29: 9.96%), lunates (13: 4.47%), retouched blades (30: 10.32%), backed blades (12: 4.12%), choppers (13: 4.47%), microblades (154: 12.62%), cores (175: 14.33%), flakes (355: 28.26%), blades (183: 15.0%), chips (220: 18.0%), worked nodules (102: 8.35%) and rejects (42: 3.44%). The proportion graph (Fig. 4.7) of finished artifacts of Mahanadi and Indravati complex shows that side scrapper is the most dominant tool type in both; frequency of end-scrapper is high at Indravati (21.77%); chopper is absent in Indravati but it is well represented (44%) in Mahanadi and burin is 10.3% at Mahanadi against 4.65% in Indravati.

Metrical analysis of blades shows that the length of the blades from Indravati is longer than those from Mahanadi, the thickness is more or less the same, and there is negligible difference in breadth. These details are given in the following table.

Table 4.9: The maximum, minimum and mean value in length (L), breadth (B) and thickness (T) of blades

	Mahanadi			*Indravati*		
	L	B	T	L	B	T
Maximum	77	23	13	104	31	17
Minimum	24	12	4	29	13	3
Mean	34	15	8	53	19	9

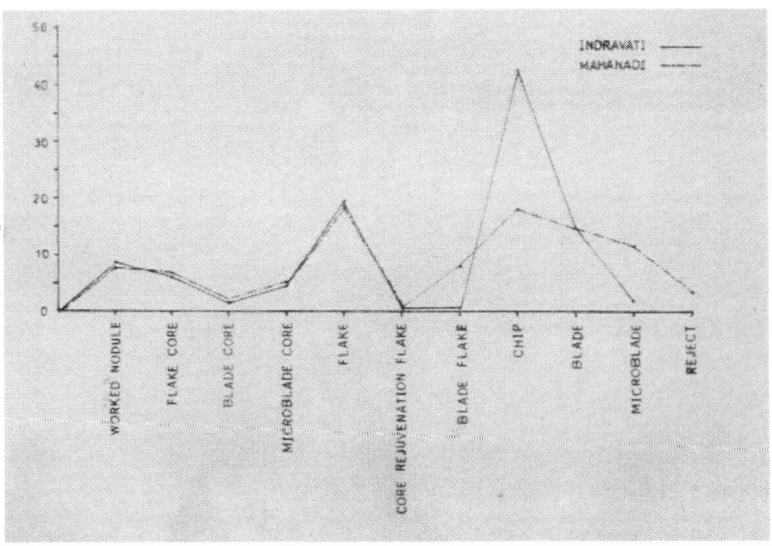

Fig. 4.8: Comparative distribution of Upper Palaeolithic simple artifacts from Indravati and Mahanadi

The comparative histogram (Fig. 4.8) of unfinished or simple artifacts of both the industries shows that blade is well represented whereas the blade core is very poorly represented in both the industries. Perfection in blade technique is clear in both the industries.

Typo-technologically, Indravati has much similarity with the upper Mahanadi Upper Palaeolithic industry.

SOUTH INDIA

In the Shorapur Doab of Karnataka, there are several open-air Upper Palaeolithic sites, and also stratified sites. The blade tool industry has come from a layer of loose pebbly gravel of 21 cm thickness, sandwiched between Middle Palaeolithic and Mesolithic culture (Paddayya 1970: 165-190). The artifacts are exclusively made of chert of different shades. The platforms of blades and flakes are usually plain with a single flake scare. Blades with faceted platform are of less frequency. It is the same case with the industry in the Indravati valley. The total kit of Shorapur Doab comprises edged tools, non-edged tools, and multy-edged tools. The non-edged tools consist of artifacts like points (15.31%), borers (6.11%), and burins (8.39%). In the Indravati industry, borers amount to 2.31% and burins 4.65%, points are absent. Among the simple artifacts, blade (78.9%) is the most dominant type and flakes are only 7.49% in the Shorapur Doab industry, in that of the Indravati, flakes are 20.38% and the representation of the blade element (14.57%) is almost the same. The edged tools of the Shorapur Doab are fashioned on blades, which is rare in the Indravati valley.

The Upper Palaeolithic site at Nagarjunkonda, Andhra Pradesh yielded artifacts fashioned on flakes, blade like flakes and blades. The use of punch and pressure technique is well attested in this industry. Scrappers are quite common and blades and burins also make a significant percentage. The Indravati industry compares with that of the Nagarjunakonda technologically.

A large number of Upper Palaeolithic sites are discovered by Issac (1960) in the Nallamalai and Erramalai areas of Kurnool district. Typologically the industry is well represented with blades, blade tools and scrappers, the proportion of shaped tools being higher than that of simple artifacts. It is just the reverse in the Indravati industry. In the Kurnool industry, flakes and chips are not reported and the occurrence of cores is negligible. Point is the most significant tool type, in the Kurnool industry, which is absent in that of the Indravati. Scrapers are well represented in both the regions. A few other tool type like axe and picks of the Kurnool are absent in Indravati.

Yerragondapalem, is an open air Upper Palaeolithic site, in Markapur taluk of Prakasam district (Thimma Reddy 1970) in the Eastern Ghats. This site has yielded 2129 artifacts. The finished or shaped artifacts comprise scrapper (84: 3.94%), backed blades (62: 2.91%), knives (22: 1.03%) and awls (5:0.23%). Blades (720: 33. 82%) form the major component of the assemblage. The proportion of blades is very high at Yerragondapalem, whereas at Indravati blade occurs to a significant proportion. One interesting feature of the Yerragondapalem industry is the absence of end scrappers and microliths. A detailed typological comparison (Table 4.10) of the Yerragondapalem and Indravati industries is given in Table 4.10.

Table 4.10: Upper Palaeolithic artifacts from Yerragondapalem and Indravati

	Yerragondapalem		*Indravati*	
	No.	*%*	*No.*	*%*
Scrapers	285	18.58	94	7.32
Choppers	34	2.23	–	–
Backed blades	62	4.05	–	–
Knife blades	22	1.43	2	0.15
Burins	24	1.58	2	0.15
Points	56	3.66	–	–
Awls	5	0.33	–	–
Borers	–	–	3	0.23
Notches	–	–	19	1.48
Backed microblades	–	–	1	0.08
Crescents	–	–	4	0.31
Blades	120	7.86	168	13.10
Cores	191	12.49	137	10.68
Core flakes	124	8.12	5	0.39
Flakes	250	16.36	232	18.10
Chips	356	23.28	491	38.30
Utilized flakes	–	–	50	3.90
Microblades	–	–	22	1.72
Worked nodules	–	–	98	7.64
Total	15–29	99.99	1282	99.99

Points and choppers are totally absent in the Indravati collection. In general, the Indravati Upper Palaeolithic industry does not differ much in typology from that of the Yerragondapalam.

VEMULA

Vemula is another Palaeolithic surface site located 10 km south-east of Pulivendla town of Cuddapah district (Thimma Reddy 1970). The site has yielded 180 artifacts, out of which 67 (37.22%) are shaped tools and 113 (72.27%) are simple artifacts. The artifacts are made

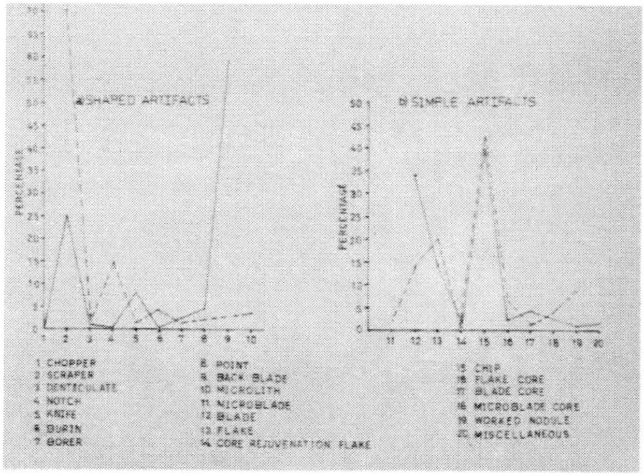

Fig. 4.9: Comparative distribution of Upper Palaeolithic artifacts from Indravati and Cuddapah (surface)

on reddish chert. Typologically the Vemula industry falls in blade flake group of Murty's classification. The tool kit comprises flakes, blades, flake-blades, prismatic cores, chisel edged blades and a couple of true burins. It has some affinity with the Indravati Upper Palaeolithic industry.

RENIGUNTA

Renigunta Upper Palaeolithic industry is mainly made on fine grained quartzite and to a very limited extent on black lydianite, whereas Indravati industry is chiefly on chert. The typical feature of this industry is that the tools are fashioned on blades and a few are on flakes. The most dominant tool type is the backed blade (63.30%), followed by burins (16.26%), scrappers (7.56%), awls (13.7%), choppers (3.7%) and points (2.0%). Among the simple artifacts blade is the second dominant tool type. The blades are massive to slender with parallel or irregular sides and longitudinal ridges, and triangular and trapezoidal cores section. Length of the blades varies from 11 to 105 mm and the average, fall within 36 to 40 mm close group. Typologically the Indravati industry shows greater variation than that of Renigunta. Indravati industry has high proportion of flake tools (90%) with a low proportion of backed blades (3.67%) and burins (4.65%). Typo-technologically the Indravati Upper Palaeolithic industry belongs to crude facies and could belong to an earlier phase than that of Renigunta.

CUDDAPAH

Recent work in the Cuddapah district of Andhra Pradesh, D.R. Raju (1981) has brought to light ten Upper Palaeolithic sites in the Gunjana river valley. The blade and burin industry of the Gunjana valley comprises 14,825 artifacts out of which 1,926 (12.19%) are shaped tools

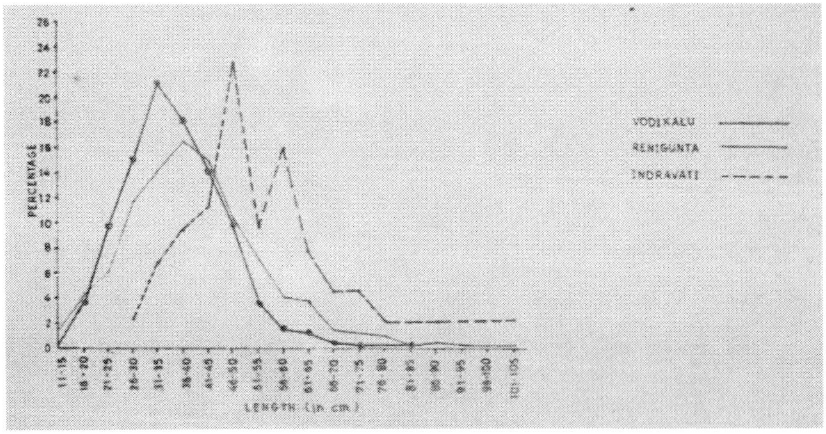

Fig. 4.10: Comparative distribution of length of Upper Palaeolithic blades from Vodikalu, Renigunta and Indravati

and 12,892 (86.96%) are simple artifacts and other category is 7 (0.055). Among the shaped tools, the most dominant tools type is the backed blade variant (58.98%), followed by scrapper (28.28%). Blade is the second dominant tool type (33.86%) in the simple artifacts group. A detailed comparison of simple artifacts group of the two industries (Fig. 4.9 and 4.10) is given in table Table 4.11.

Table 4.11: The comparative analysis of simple artifacts from surface Upper Palaeolithic sites of Cuddapah and Indravati

		Cuddapah		*Indravati*	
Sl. No.	*Artifacts type*	*No.*	*%*	*No.*	*%*
1.	Microblades	–	–	22	1.90
2.	Blades	4365	33.86	168	14.58
3.	Flakes	1885	14.61	182	15.78
4.	Core rejuvenation flakes	127	0.99	5	0.43
5.	Chips	5161	40.03	491	42.58
6.	Flake cores	368	2.85	70	6.07
7.	Blade cores	617	4.79	17	1.47
8.	Microblade cores	–	–	50	4.34
9.	Worked nodules	168	1.30	98	8.50
10.	Utilized flakes	–	–	50	4.34
11.	Miscelleneous	203	1.57	–	–
		12982	100.00	1153	99.99

The Upper Palaeolithic industry of Gunjana based on blade tools technology. In length range of the blades the Vodikalu site of Gunjana and Renigunta display close affinity (a significant percentage of blades from Vodikalu and Renigunta fall in the length ranges of 31-35 mm and 36-40 mm respectively), while the blades of Indravati collection differ from them showing a significant percentage of the blades fall in the length range of 46-50 mm (Fig. 4.10). The Upper Palaeolithic industry of the Gunjana valley is much advanced than that of the Indravati.

Chapter 5

The Mesolithic Cultures

ORIGIN AND DEVELOPMENT OF THE CONCEPT OF MESOLITHIC

Sir John Lubbock, in his book *Pre-historic Times* published in 1865, first suggested the division of Stone Age into Palaeolithic and Mesolithic (Wilkins 1959). Palaeolithic was characterised by chipped stone tools and hunting and gathering economy while the Mesolithic was associated by tools made by grinding and as well as chipping and by food producing economy. In 1866, Hodder M. Westropp, introduced the term 'Mesolithic' in his three phase Stone Age classification, i.e. Palaeolithic, Mesolithic and Kainolithic or recent Stone Age (Wilkins 1959: 130-31). With more clarity and explanation, Brown (1895) gave a classification of Stone Age as: Eolithic, Palaeolithic, Mesolithic and Neolithic and defined Mesolithic as the intermediate age between the Palaeolithic and Neolithic periods.

M.C. Burkitt (1926) gave a detailed account of Mesolithic culture in his book *Our Early Ancestor*. In this he included Azilian, Tardenoisean, Astrurian, Maglemosean, Kitchen-Midden and Campignian cultures in the Mesolithic period. Afterwards J.G.D. Clarke (1932, 1936, 1962) gave a clear picture of the Mesolithic phase as an independent, distinct culture on the basis of geological time period (stratigraphy), technological variation and economical difference (quoted from Misra 1965). And now it is a well established, widely accepted cultural phase in the lithic evolution.

Mesolithic phase in India is more wide spread than the preceding or succeeding cultural phases. The credit goes to A.C.L. Carlleyle, for the first discovery of microliths in the caves and rock-shelters of the Vindhya in Bundelkhand, Mirzapur and Biwa, in the eighties of the 19th century, while he was an assistant of General Cunnigham, the Director General of the Archaeological Survey of India (Brown 1889, Allchin 1958). In the year 1883, Rivell-Carnal also had collected microliths from the same area. Here evidence of Mesolithic culture comes to light after the discoveries of Robert Bruce Foote, from South India and Gujarat. After that, the work of Cammiade (1924) in the Godavari delta, Cammiade and Burkitt (1930) in the

Eastern Godavari, Todd (1932) in west coast, Hunter (1935-36) in Mahadeo hills and Gordon (1938) in Peshawar region confirmed the wide spread of Mesolithic culture in India.

In the early forties of 20th century Sankalia (1946: 55) undertook a systematic investigation at Langhanaj in Gujarat and gave new information about the environment, food habit and burial practice of Mesolithic people. Subbarao (1948) brought to light a stratified Mesolithic deposit of Bellary district, in Karnataka, which was followed by Todd's (1949) reports of microlithic industry in Bombay area, Mundar Rajan (1952) in the Siagrauli basin, Subbarao (1952) in the Mahi valley, Zeunar and Allchin's (1956) discovery of Teri industry and Allchin's (1958) rediscovery of microlith from Morhana Pahar. The knowledge of Mesolithic cultural distribution was widen by the work of Khatri (1958) in Malwa, Issac (1960) in Kurnool, Mahapatra (1960), Misra (1961), Pappu (1966), Murty (1966), Paddayya (1968) and Reddy (1968). Latter the excavation reports of a few sites have helped to understand the different aspects of Mesolithic cultures, such as technological development, chronology, food habits, art and decoration and social life. These excavated sites include Birbhanpur (Lal 1958) in West Bengal, Adamgarh (Joshi 1969), Joshi and Kharu (1966) in Madhya Pradesh, Sangankallu (Sankalia 1969) in Karnataka, Bagor (Misra 1971a, 1971b, 1973) and Tilwara (Misra 1971) in Rajasthan, Mathkamna and Pachad (Joshi and Bopardikar 1972) in Maharashtra, Bhimbetka (Wakankar 1973, Misra 1980) in Madhya Pradesh and Sarai Nahar Rai (Sharma 1972) and Pratapgarh district in Madhya Pradesh.

ODISHA

Until 1970, the evidence for microlithic industries in Odisha was sketchy. The first microlithic evidence was reported from Saraikala, which was formerly a Princely State of Odisha but now it is in Bihar (Ghosh 1948). During 1957-1959, G.C. Mahapatra (1960) discovered eight microlithic sites in three districts of Sundargarh, Mayurbhanj and Keonjhar. They have been reported from the surface and river beds. Sometimes microliths occur along with Middle Palaeolithic culture. The assemblage comprising 42 artifacts made on jasper, chert and opal. The other discoveries for Mesolithic culture are made from Baranda, Bonaikala, Danguerpose of Keonjhar district by Mitra (*IAR* 1958-59); Udaigiri of Puri district by Mitra (*IAR* 1958-59: 73); Kuchai in Mayurbhanj district by Thapar (*IAR* 1961-62: 36), the Tel valley by Raghunath (*IAR* 1963-64: 27), the campus of Utkal University of Bhubaneshwar by Das (*IAR* 1963-64: 90) and near the confluence of the Tel and Puul river of Bolangir district by Mukharjee (*IAR* 1968-69: 68). All are open air sites. As the reports about these sites carry little informations about the industries and their relation to their ecosystem, it is difficult to draw any detail information about the typological variation and development in the site or among the sites. R.G. Tripathy (1972) during 1967-69 discovered 27 microlithic sites from three districts of Kalahandi, Sambalpur and Bolangir. All those are open air sites located along the river Tel and its tributaries.

However, till then, work on the southern part of Odisha was very limited. Subsequent works by the present investigator, during 1975-79, in the district of Koraput in southeastern Odisha, along the river Indravati have reported high concentration Mesolithic settlements. The field investigations have revealed 85 Mesolithic sites. All are open air surface sites excluding the site of Khirki. With the exception of Girla, no occupational deposit was encountered at any of the sites. Since the assemblages are sufficiently homogenous, they are treated as belonging to a single cultural complex and single assemblage.

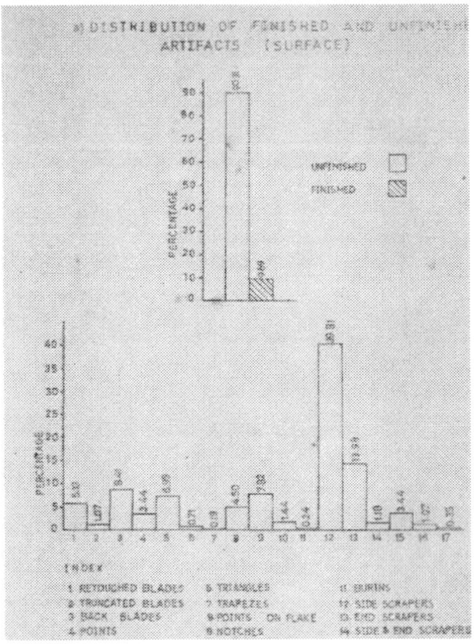

Fig. 5.1: A: Distribution of finished and unfinished artifacts (surface) and B: Distribution of shaped artifacts (surface)

INDUSTRY

The industry (Plate 5.1) is divided into three broad groups, viz. (a) shaped artifacts, (b) simple artifacts and (c) others. The total collection of artifacts from all the 85 sites comprises 8709 specimens. Typologically, the assemblage is classified into two main groups as shaped artifacts or finished artifacts (844: 9.69%) and simple artifacts or unfinished artifacts (7865: 90.32%) (Fig. 5.1A). Shaped artifacts comprise 220 (26.07%) microliths and 624 (73.93%) flake tools. The industry is discussed as follows:

(a) Shaped artifacts (844: 9.69%) (Fig. 5.1B)

The artifacts are distinguished by an intentional retouch and blunting on micro blades, blades and flakes etc. The shaped artifacts are grouped into two main groups: (i) microliths and (ii) flake tools.

(i) Microliths (220: 26.07%, Fig. 5.2 and Fig. 5.3):

This group comprises 2.52% of the total assemblage and 26.07% of shaped artifacts. These are made on micro blades. Based on nature and position of retouch on microliths, this group is again categorised into eight groups:

(i) retouched blade,

(ii) truncated blade,

(iii) blunted back blade,

(iv) blunted back and truncated blade,

(v) point,

(vi) crescent,

(vii) triangle blade and

(viii) trapeze.

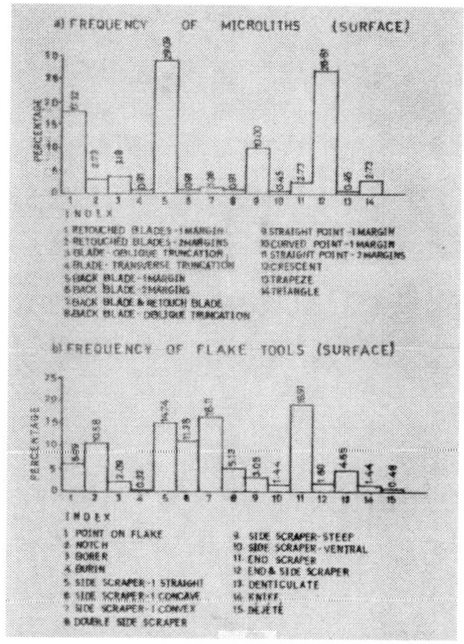

Fig. 5.2: A: Frequency of microliths (surface) and B: Frequency of flake tools (surface)

Group I: Retouched blades (45: 20.45%)

This group is characterised by marginal retouch which extends along either one, or both edges of a blade. The nature of retouch is flat or slightly oblique in microscopic form. This group is divided into two, as:

(i) blade with flat retouch on one margin and

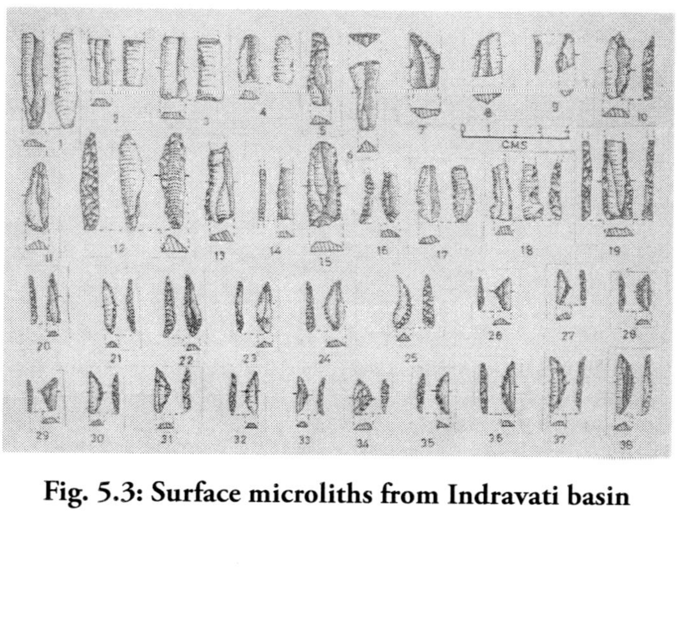

Fig. 5.3: Surface microliths from Indravati basin

(ii) blade with flat retouch on two margins.

On the basis of location of retouch they are further grouped as:

(i) ventral surface retouch,

(ii) dorsal surface retouch and

(iii) dorse-ventral retouch.

The group is represented by retouched blades (45: 20.45%) comprising blades with single margin retouch (59: 17.52%) and blades with two margins retouch (6: 2.73%). The single margin retouch blades are represented from 23 sites and both margins (Fig. 5.2 and Fig. 5.3) retouch blades are represented from 5 sites.

Most of the specimens are broken particularly either at proximal or at distal end. The retouching is very frequently found on the dorsal surface of the blades and a few pieces show retouch on ventral face of the blade with a proportion of 3:5:1.

Plate 5.1: Mesolithic artifacts – surface collections

Group II: Truncated blades (9: 4.09%)

This class includes the specimen with fine or irregular retouch without reducing the size of the blades by the removal of spall. The working edge is perpendicular to the longer axis. Therefore the blades have been retouched on one, or both the ends.

This group is split into two sub-groups, such as blades with transverse truncation (2: 0.91%) and blade with oblique truncation (7: 3.18%). Oblique truncation is more frequent than transverse truncation. These occur at nine sites with a frequency of single specimen. Two are complete and the roots (seven) are broken from the distal end. Therefore it is difficult identify the sides (left or right) of retouch incase oblique truncated blades.

Group III: Blunted back blade (69: 31.36%)

This group is represented by the steep edge, developed through the reduction of blade to a certain width for either hafting or holding. 'Ihis category is again split into three sub-categories *i.e.*

(i) blade blunted on one margin (64: 29.09%),

(ii) blade blunted on two margins (2: 0.91%) and

(iii) blade blunted on one margin and having flat retouch on the other (3: 1.37%).

On the basis of the extent of blunting these can be classified again as:

(i) heavy backing,

(ii) medium backing and

(iii) light backing.

Considering the cross-section, the backed blades are grouped into two categories, *i.e.*

(i) triangular cross-section and

(ii) trapezoidal cross-section.

The blunting may be unidirectional (either from ventral face or from dorsal face) and, sometimes, bidirectional. Single margin blunting type (64: 29.09%) represents major part of group III. The single margin blunting specimens are from 39 sites, whereas double margin blunting and blunting with one major retouch, are from the two sides each. It shows that the backed blade element is the significant character of this microliths industry.

Group IV: Blunted back and truncated blades (2: 0.91%)

This category is represented by the combination of groups II and III. The lateral margin or margins are blunted, with truncations at one or both the ends of the blade. This is the least represented group among the B groups, and is characterised by oblique retouching at the proximal end of a single margin backed blade. These occur at sites, Nos. 53 and 78.

Group V: Points (29: 13.18%)

These are made on microblades. These are characterised by the pointed tip resulting from the fine retouching at the tip (distal end of the blade or one or two margins, completely or restrictively at the tip. These occur in three distinct groups as:

(i) single margin retouch, straight point (22: 10.00%),

(ii) single margin retouch, curved point (6: 2.73%) and

(iii) both margin retouch, straight point (1: 0.45%).

i) **Straight points (22: 10.00%):** These occur at 17 sites with a frequency of one or two specimens except at site No. 2, which has yielded 3 specimens. This group is characterised by the pointed tip, produced by a regular and continuous retouching on one lateral margin till the tip, or partial retouching confined to the tip. Five specimens possess partial retouch. Out of 22 pieces, 15 (68.18%) are broken and 7 (31.81%) are completed. The breaking is from the proximal end or distal end.

ii) **Curved points (6:2.72%):** In this type, the retouch or blunting is formed on the curved margin producing a pointed tip at the distal end. These specimens occur at four sites. Four pieces are complete and two are broken. This occurs with a ratio of 1:3.6 between curved and straight points.

iii) **Both margins retouched, straight point (1: 0.45%):** This single specimen is from site No. 58. The specimen is slightly broken from the base.

Group VI: Crescents (59: 26.81%)

The outline of this artifact shows at least one convex edge, with retouch/blunting. The blunting may be unidirectional or bidirectional. The other margin is left unretouched. Generally, these are made on microblades sometime on microflakes. On the basis of size of the tool they are divided into long and short crescent. Further each group is split into symmetric and asymmetric crescent. This group comprises 59 species of crescents. These are further grouped as: (i) long crescent (18: 8.18%) and (ii) short crescent (41: 18.63%). This is the second dominating typological variant among the microliths. These occur at 27 sites. Only 15.25% of specimens are broken and four pieces have used marks on the inner margin of the crescent.

Group VII: Triangles (6:2.75%)

These are triangular in shape and made on narrow microblades. The blunting is generally confined to the two sides of the implement leaving a sharp straight margin. This group represents specimens from four sites. They are of scalene shape with two margins blunted. Two pieces are broken at one of the pointed ends and four are complete. The longer lateral margin has edge damage (No. 63).

Group VIII: Trapeze (1: 0.45%)

This is of trapezoidal form. The terminal ends of the blades are blunted leaving the parallel lateral margin. But in some cases the short parallel margin is also blunted. In every case the longest margin is left unretouched. Simple trapeze occurs at site No. 63. It is asymmetric in shape with two oblique blunted margins.

Flake tools (624: 73.94%): This group includes artifacts made on flakes and consists of:

(i) side scrapers,
(ii) dejete scrapers,
(iii) denticulates,
(iv) notches,
(v) end scrappers,
(vi) points,
(vii) borers,
(viii) burins and
(ix) knives.

These occur in 4:1 ratio with microblade tools (microliths).

Side scrappers (336: 53.84%): This category is divided into:

(a) single sided scrapper and
(b) double sided scrapper.

This division is strictly on basis of the number of working edges on a flake. This group is represented by 336 specimens. Out of these;

(a) single-sided scrappers are 304 (48.71%) specimens and

(b) double-sided scrappers are of 32 (5.12%) specimens.

a) Single-sided scrappers (304: 48.71%)

The working edge is confined to any one of lateral/longer margins of the flakes, blades or cores. They are further divided into:

(i) scrapper with a straight working edge,

(ii) scrapper with a concave working edge and

(iii) scrapper with a convex working edge,

(iv) single sided scrapper with steep retouch and

(v) single sided scrapper with ventral retouch.

Single-sided scrappers with straight working edge (92: 14.74%)

This group consists of 92 specimens representing by 45 sites with one or two, specimens, site No. 13, 27A and 27B have yielded 9, 6 and 11 pieces respectively. These are made on flakes only. The metrical values of the scrappers are given in Table 5.1.

Table 5.1: Metrical values of the scrappers

	Length	*Breadth*	*Thickness*	*Working edge*
Maximum	59	58	26	45
Minimum	15	13	4	13
Mean	34	29	10	15

Single-sided scrappers with concave working edge (71: 11.37%) (Fig. 5.4: 9, 10)

There are 71 (11.37%) artifacts, from 45 sites. The frequency of occurrence varies from 1 to 8, only one site (No. 27 A) has yielded 8 specimens. The rest of the sites have yielded a frequency of 1 to 4 specimens. The metrical values are given in Table 5.2:

Table 5.2: Metrical values of single-sided scrappers with concave working edge

	Length	*Breadth*	*Thickness*	*Working edge*
Maximum	68	66	22	40
Minimum	19	11	3	10
Mean	54	29	11	22

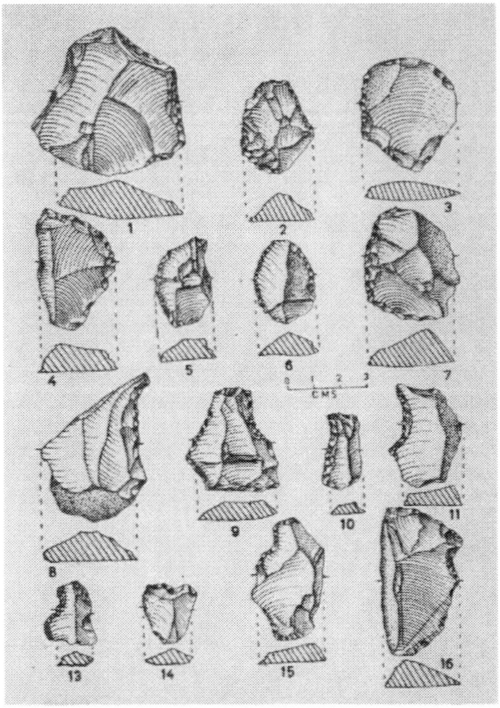

Fig. 5.4: Surface Mesolithic scrapers and notches

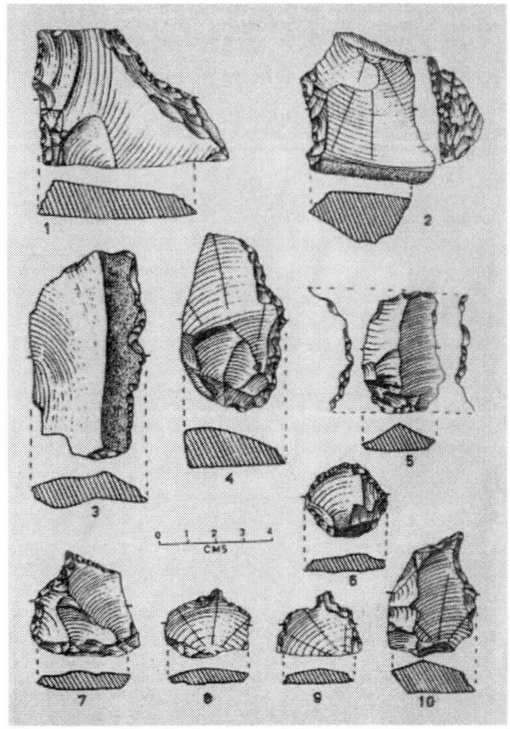

Fig. 5.5: Surface Mesolithic scrapers

Single-sided scrapper with convex working edge (113: 18.10%) (Fig. 5.4: 4, 5, 7, Fig. 5.5: 6)

This is the second larger group among the shaped tools. Fifty sites have yielded 113 specimens the occurrence of this artifact varies from 1 to 3. But sites like No. 13, No. 20, No. 24A, and 28A have yielded 5, 5, 11, 13 and 7 pieces respectively. The metrical values of the artifacts are given in Table 5.3.

Table 5.3: Metrical values of single-sided scrapper with convex working edge

	Length	*Breadth*	*Thickness*	*Working edge*
Maximum	60	58	26	52
Minimum	16	13	5	11
Mean	35	27	10	26

Single sided scrapper with steep retouch (19: 3.05%) (Fig. 5.4: 8)

These specimens occur at 12 sites with a frequency of 1 and 2 except site No. 42B, which has yielded 5 (41.66%) specimens. The metrical values are given in Table 5.4.

Table 5.4: Metrical values of single sided scrapper with steep retouch

	Length	*Breadth*	*Thickness*	*Working edge*
Maximum	64	59	26	48
Minimum	25	21	8	20
Mean	44	36	17	33

Single sided scrapper with ventral retouch (9: 1.44%) (Fig. 5.4: 3, 11)

These are made on flakes only. Only six sites represent this category with a varying frequency of one and two specimens. In the scrapper group this category gives the lowest representation. The metrical values of the artifacts are given in Table 5.5:

Table 5.5: Metrical values of single sided scrapper with ventral retouch

	Length	*Breadth*	*Thickness*	*Working edge*
Maximum	45	43	12	31
Minimum	21	27	6	18
Mean	31	32	10	24

(b) Double sided scrappers (32: 5.12%) (Fig. 5.5: 1, 2, 5, Fig. 5.4: 6)

The two working edges are opposite to each other and parallel to the longer axis. The ratio of this type with single sided scrappers is about 1: 9.5. The metrical values of the specimen are given in Table 5.6.

Table 5.6: Metrical values of double sided scrappers

	Length	*Breadth*	*Thickness*	*Working edge*	
				Left	*Right*
Maximum	108	90	33	73	69
Minimum	23	19	5	17	15
Mean	48	40	15	32	33

Dejete scrapper (3: 0.48%)

Dejete occurs at site No. 27A and 34B as two pieces and one piece respectively. Two pieces are made on end flakes and one is on side flake.

Denticulates (29: 6.64%) (Fig. 5.5: 3, 4)

Denticulates are tools which have a working edge or edges formed by the combination of more than two notches conjugatively. This group comprises 29 specimens from 18 sites. These are made of side and end flakes. The frequency of occurrence is at site No. 20 and 27C (3 specimens each). The metrical values are given in Table 5.7.

Table 5.7: Metrical values of denticulates

	Length	*Breadth*	*Thickness*	*Working edge*
Maximum	57	75	25	68
Minimum	26	17	5	19
Mean	35	32	11	31

Notches (66: 10.57%) (Fig. 5.4: 13, 14, 15, 16)

Notch is a micro form of concave scrapper. It is more or less deep or small, with a small radius of curving and occupies a small part of the side of the tool. These represent 34 sites with a frequency varying from 1 to 7. Sites like No. 13. No. 22B, No. 24A, No.27A and No. 32 have yielded 4, 4, 6, 7 and 4 pieces respectively. These are made on flake only. In general the notch occurs at the lateral margin of the flake but retouching on the transverse margin is also seen. The metrical values are given in Table 5.8.

Table 5.8: Metrical values of notches

	Length	*Breadth*	*Thickness*	*Working edge*
Maximum	78	47	25	20
Minimum	17	13	4	6
Mean	36	25	10	15

End scrapper (118: 18.19%) (Fig. 5.6: 1-7)

These specimens are characterised by retouch on either the distal end or the proximal end, or both in a narrow curved area. This group is represented by the highest number of specimens in shaped artifacts group. This is a dominating character of the assemblages. Among the total shaped artifacts it represents with 13.36%. These are made on end flake and blade flake and a very few are on cores. These represent 46 sites with a frequently varying from 1 to 12. The site like No. 27A and No. 28A have yielded 8, 6, 7, 12, 7 pieces respectively. The metrical values of end scrappers are given in Table 5.9.

Table 5.9: Metrical values of end scrapper

	Length	*Breadth*	*Thickness*	*Working edge*
Maximum	57	52	26	29
Minimum	18	10	4	9
Mean	33	23	10	16

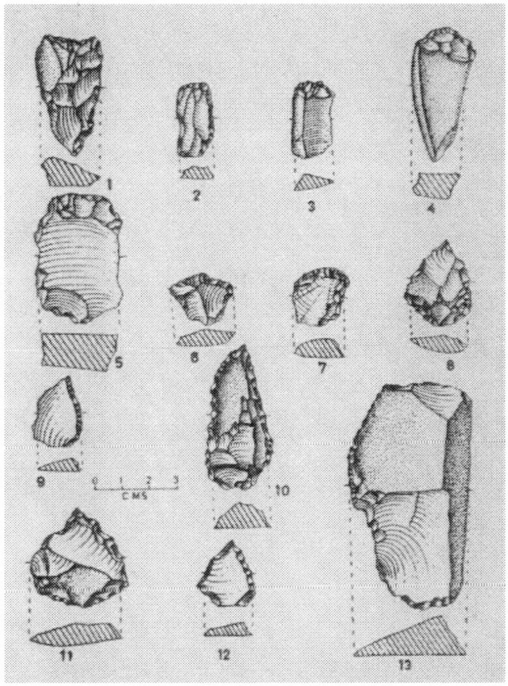

Fig. 5.6: Surface Mesolithic end scrapers, points and knifes

Point on flakes (38: 6.08%) (Fig. 5.6: 9-12)

These are 38 pieces made on small flakes with retouch (Fig. 5.6) at one, on two margins of the tool, partly or wholly producing a pointed tip. These occur at 24 sites, and the site No. 17 and 27A have yielded 6 and 3 specimens respectively by specimens of 1 to 2. The metrical values of the artifacts are given in Table 5.10.

Table 5.10: Metrical values of point on flakes

	Length	*Breadth*	*Thickness*
Maximum	74	58	19
Minimum	23	11	4
Mean	35	28	9

Borers (13:2.08%) (Fig. 5.5: 7-10)

This is defined by borer tip formed by the small notches at two margins conjugatively oriented giving an impression of a borer tip. There are 13 specimens, made on small flakes only. This group represents 10 sites. Except site No. 15 and 17 others have yielded one each and the sites 15 and 17 have yielded 2 and 3 specimens respectively.

Burins (2: 0.32%)

They represent sites No. 20 and 51. One is of angle and other one is bevel. This type is the poorest group in the shaped artifacts group.

Knives (9: 1.445) (Fig. 5.6: 13)

This is the only type of shaped tool without retouching. Knives are characterised by long sharp working edge with a thick back, opposite to the working edge, with an elongated triangular cross section. The site No. 20 has yielded 2 specimens, and all the remaining seven are from 7 sites. Except two pieces all are of natural backed knife. Three specimens show edge damage. The metrical values of these artifacts are given in Table 5.11.

Table 5.11: Metrical values of knives

	Length	*Breadth*	*Thickness*
Maximum	18	43	18
Minimum	43	21	11
Mean	62	29	14

(b) Simple artifacts (7865: 90.31%) (Fig. 5.8)

This group represents ratio of 9:1 with shaped tools. This comprises six main groups as:

(i) cores,

(ii) flakes,

(iii) blades,

(iv) chips,

(v) worked nodules and

(vi) microburins.

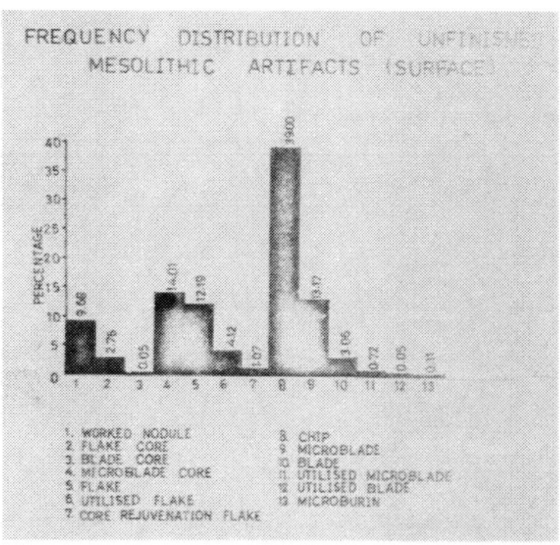

Fig. 5.7: Frequency distribution of unfinished Mesolithic artifacts (surface)

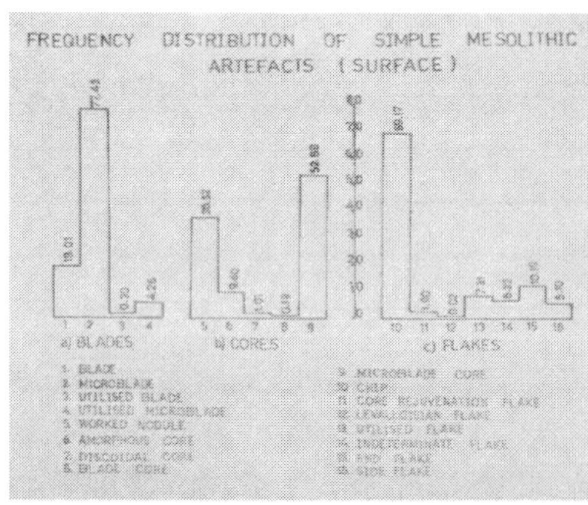

Fig. 5.8: Frequency distribution of simple Mesolithic artifacts (surface)

Table 5.12: Site and type wise distribution of Mesolithic simple artifacts

S. No.	W.N.	A. Core	Disc. core	Blade core	M.Bl. core-1	M.Bl. core-2	M.Bl. core-3	Side. fl.	End. fl	Ind. fl	Ut. fl.	Lev. fl.	CRF. st.	CRF. obl.	CRF. top	CRF. base	Chips	B. comp.	Bl. br.	M. Bl. comp.	M. Bl. br.
1	8				8												29		2	1	5
2	5				20	1		1	2		4						114		14	4	65
3	8	1			5			2	1	8	2						33				5
4	5				9				1	4	1						31			2	14
5	3		1		3			3	3	2	2			1			11			1	3
6	4				2						1						16				2
7		3			8						2					1	18		2		9
8	11	1			5				4		2		1			1	16				3
9	2				5			1	1								36				7
10	4	2			13	1		2	6		3						23	1	1		3
11	10				3			4	9	2	4						69		1		4
12	13	13			15	5		2	12	3	7						37		3	2	11
13	35	14			18	4		4	5	7	7					2	50	7	4	1	3
14	4		1		10			2	2	3							25			2	4
15	16	10			4	1		5	6	9	10						41			1	13
16	6				2						1						16				2
17	11	3		3	57	2		8	18	2	6		1	1	2	1	103	11	16	1	41
18	12				11			3	11	2	1						31		1		3
19a	18	6			10			2	5	2	2		1				41			1	4
19b	4	1			2				1		1						22				5
20	8	5	2		17	3		8	15	6	10	1	5			1	72	6	4	6	10
21	5				2				1		2						24				3
22a	12				3					4	2						7				4

S. No.	W.N.	A. Core	Disc. core	Blade core	M.Bl. core-1	M.Bl. core-2	M.Bl. core-3	Side. fl.	End. fl	Ind. fl	Ut. fl.	Lev. fl.	CRF. st.	CRF. obl.	CRF. top	CRF. base	Chips	B. comp.	Bl. br.	M. Bl. comp.	M. Bl. br.
22b	25	4			3			3	8	3	12						49			2	5
22c	11	3			4	1		6	7	15	2						16			2	4
23	5	1	1		4	3		5	3	3	2						9				1
24a	79	10			14	4	1	12	19	20	24		1			2	68	3	19	2	5
24b	11	1			3			1	3		2						9			2	
25	1				2			1	2	1							9				3
26	5	2	2		10	1		5	9	3	5					1	15				3
27a	58	3	1		97	3		14	23	29	42		3	2		3	88	5	2	7	4
27b					6	3		3	6	2	4						6			1	3
27c	1				10			1	3	2	3					1	4			2	3
28a	1	2			60	9		10	11	14	28		4	1	2	2	25	3	4	29	25
28b					5				2		2		1				7	1	2		5
29	2				4				1				1				11			2	
30	13				2				1	2	1						28				2
31	15	3			21	2		2	8	5	1				1		48	1	2		12
32	24				14					3	4						48	2	2	8	4
33	1	2			5				1	2	1						1				1
34a	3	1			14			2	6	3	4		1				16	2	1		5
34b			1		3			2	10	3					1		8				
34c					4				6		8						5				1
35	2				5			6	4	8	2			1			20			1	10
36		1			5			2	4		1				1		14			3	7
37	8		1		7					2	3		1				7				3
38	8	2			3			2		8	2						20			2	8

S. No.	*W.N.*	*A. Core*	*Disc. core*	*Blade core*	*M.Bl. core-1*	*M.Bl. core-2*	*M.Bl. core-3*	*Side. fl.*	*End. fl*	*Ind. fl*	*Ut. fl.*	*Lev. fl.*	*CRF. st.*	*CRF. obl.*	*CRF. top*	*CRF. base*	*Chips*	*B. comp.*	*Bl. br.*	*M. Bl. comp.*	*M. Bl. br.*
39	5	3	2		5			4	3	3							53			5	14
40	5	3	2		39	2		3	8	5	8		4	1			87	1	4	15	14
41	5				3				3	1	3						15				3
42a	18	4			33	4		5	15		5		1				67		3		14
42b	3	2			5			2	2	2	2						21				2
43	2				2				3	7	3			1			6				3
44a		4			12			1	7	5	3						34	2			
44b	6				17			3	7	5	2		2		1		92	6	5	4	18
44c	3	2			5				3		3						27			1	
44d	2	3			3			2	7		2		3		1		26			1	
44e		2	1		2				1	6	3						11			1	
45	4	4			6	2		1	4	2			4				22			1	9
46	5	1			4				2								21				6
47	5	1			4				2	5							19				3
48	5	1			4				5								18			1	2
49a	2	4		1	3	2				1	2						27	1	5		3
49b	7				4				2	1							15			1	2
50	9				1				1		1						33				5
51	3	1			1			2	1	1	3						15	7	4		1
52	2	1	1		6				1		1						24				2
53	9	1			31	2		1	7		8						80	1	6	7	28
54	8	2			7			4	4		2						35		1	5	22
55	2				6			1	3	1							5				
56	4				1				1		1						9		1		1

S. No.	W.N.	A. Core	Disc. core	Blade core	M.Bl. core-1	M.Bl. core-2	M.Bl. core-3	Side. fl.	End. fl	Ind. fl	Ut. fl.	Lev. fl.	CRF. st.	CRF. obl.	CRF. top	CRF. base	Chips	B. comp.	Bl. br.	M. Bl. comp.	M. Bl. br.
57	3				21	2		1	3	1	1		2				54		1	7	10
58					11			7	8		1				3	2	51	1	2	4	32
59		3	1		6	1		3	4				1				28	3		3	5
60	4				3				3								8				1
61	10	14			18	3		2	6	2	4		1			1	30		1	2	19
62	7	3	1		35	2		14	12		1		2				91		8	6	64
63	11				23	3		2	3	1	6		2				71	7	11	26	43
64	12	1			17	2		3	6	1	4				1		33		3		10
65	16	4			21	2		1	6	3			1				42	1	5	3	12
66	10	2			13	1		2	7		5		1				48	2	1	7	9
67	4	1			8			6	4	5	3						34				12
68	5	3	1	1	2			2	4	5							14				6
69		2			5			2	2	4	3						13	2	3		8
70					1				2	2	1						18		2		4
71	2	2			1				2	2	1						18		2		4
72	3				1				2	2	1						18		2		4
73	2				1				2	2	1						18		2		4
74	6				1				2	2	1						18		2		4
75		1			1				2	2	1						18		2		4
76					1				2	2	1						18		2		4
77	2	2			1				2	2	1						18		2		4
78	5				1				2	2	1						18		2		4
79		1			1				2	2	1						18		2		4
80		1			1				2	2	1						18		2		4

S. No.	W.N.	A. Core	Disc. core	Blade core	M.Bl. core-1	M.Bl. core-2	M.Bl. core-3	Side. fl.	End. fl	Ind. fl	Ut. fl.	Lev. fl.	CRF. st.	CRF. obl.	CRF. top	CRF. base	Chips	B. comp.	Bl. br.	M. Bl. comp.	M. Bl. br.
81	37	12	2		1				2	2	1						18		2		4
82					1				2	2	1						18		2		4
83					1				2	2	1						18		2		4
84	4				1				2	2	1						18		2		4
85	14	9			1				2	2	1						18		2		4
	761	**196**	**21**	**4**	1				2	2	1						18		2		4

(i) Cores (1323: 16.92%) (Fig. 5.8B)

These are grouped into flake cores, blade cores and micro-blade cores.

Flake cores (217: 10.41%)

This group consists of amorphous core or irregular cores (196: 9.40%) and discoidal cores (21: 1.01%). These are made on nodules. A few of the irregular cores retain original cortex part. About 70% cores possess more than two platforms. A minor preparation shows a single platform. The metrical values of the cores are given in Table 5.13.

Table 5.13: Metrical values of flake cores

	Length	*Breadth*	*Thickness*
Maximum	91	73	41
Minimum	46	34	22
Mean	27	17	10

The discoidal cores are more or less discoidal in shape. They are made on chert nodules excepting two quartz pieces. These occur at 16 sites with the frequency of one or two.

Blade cores (4: 0.19%)

These are collected from sites No. 17 and 49. They have yielded 3 and 1 specimens respectively. Three of them are cylindrical in shape and one is of an irregular shape. One specimen has half cortex on the reverse side and another specimen retain a part of prepared flaking on the reverse side and they rest of the part is exhausted with blade scare. The number of blade scares varies from two to five only. One specimen possesses two platforms whereas the other three are with single platform.

Microblade cores (1102: 52.88%)

This is the major group among the cores. It comprises three sub-groups on the basis of the number of platforms which are as follows:

(a) **Single directional Microblade cores (1027: 48.28%):** The group is represented at all sites. These are distinguished by a single platform. The platform is prepared prior to the blade removal. As this possesses a single platform the blade scares are in one direction. On the basis of morphology these are grouped as cylindrical (23.76%), triangular (27.16%), rectangular (9.54%) and irregular (39.53%). The average number of blade scares on core is about 9. The metrical values are given in Table 5.14.

(b) **Double directional (74: 3.55%):** There are 24 specimens in this group. They occur at 30 sites, the lowest frequencies being 9 pieces. These specimens have two platforms therefore

Table 5.14: Metrical values of single directional microblade cores

	Length	*Breadth*	*Thickness*
Maximum	56	50	34
Minimum	30	22	14
Mean	13	9	4

the orientation of blade scares are in two different directions. Sometimes they are opposite to each other or perpendicular to each other. These are grouped into cylindrical, tabular and rectangular on the basis of their shape.

(c) **Tridirectional (1: 0.04%):** This group is represented by a single specimen from the site No. 24. It possesses three platforms. It is irregular in shape.

(ii) Flakes (1367: 17.38%) (Fig. 5.8C)

This group consists of 1367 specimens. These occur from 85 sites with a varying platform. This group is classified into side flake, end flake, indeterminate flake, Levallois type flake, cores rejuvenation flake and utilized flake.

Side flakes (226: 16.53%)

This group comprises of primary and secondary flakes. The shapes of this group of flakes are rectangular, oval, elliptical, trapezoidal and irregular with plain (49.9%), cortex (5.10%), prepared platform (8.16%) and not clear (40.81%). Most of the pieces possesses prominent bulb. The metrical values are given in Table 5.15.

Table 5.15: Metrical values of side flakes

	Length	*Breadth*	*Thickness*
Maximum	56	87	28
Minimum	15	19	4
Mean	30	42	11

End flakes (452: 33.06%)

This group consists of primary and secondary flakes. These are end struck flakes. On the basis of morphology these are further classified as pointed, triangular, irregular flakes. These flakes possess plain platform with good proportion (44.51%), then comes the cortex platform (4.05%) which is followed by prepared platform (2.89%). The cross sections are triangular, trapezoidal, plano-convex and irregular. The metrical values are given in Table 5.16.

Table 5.16: Metrical values of end flakes

	Length	*Breadth*	*Thickness*
Maximum	85	61	25
Minimum	19	13	4
Mean	40	28	11

Indeterminate flakes (280: 3.56%)

This constitutes 280 specimens occurring at most of the sites. They are irregular, pointed, rectangular and parallel in outline.

Utilized flakes (324: 23.70%)

This type is characterised by edge damage, probably due to use. These are noticed on end flake side and also on few chips. Only on the secondary flakes it is recognised. This occurs in a ratio of about 1:3 with simple flakes. The metrical values are given in Table 5.17.

Table 5.17: Metrical values of utilized flakes

	Length	*Breadth*	*Thickness*
Maximum	*58*	*42*	*21*
Minimum	13	8	3
Mean	32	24	9

Levallois type flake (1: 0.07%)

This group is represented by and specimen from the sites No. 20. It is more or less pentagonal in shape with fine flake seen on its dorsal surface with a plain platform. The size of the flake is 45 mm × 32 mm × 8 mm.

Core rejuvenation flake (84: 6.14%)

There are 84 (6.84%) specimens in this group. They are from 33 sites. This group comprises core rejuvenation flake straight (44: 52.38%), are rejuvenation flake-oblique (8: 9.52%), core rejuvenation flake-top (14: 16.66%) and core rejuvenation flake-base (18: 21.43%).

(iii) Blades (1330: 17.01%) (Fig. 5.8A)

This group consists of two types of blades: (a) simple blades and (b) microblades. The ratio between blade and microblade is 1:4.5.

(a) Simple blades (245: 18.31%):

These are long, slender thin flakes with one, or more ridges on the dorsal surface. And the breadth is more than 12 mm, whereas the length is more than double the breadth. These are parallel sided, having sharp edges without retouching.

There are 245 (18.31%) specimens from 39 sites. It is further divided into two sub-groups as blade and utilised blades. Blade comprises 79 (32.78%) complete type and 162 (67.22%) broken ones. There are triangular and trapezoidal in cross-section with regular and irregular form. The utilised specimens constitute only 4 (1.63%) specimens and of these 3 are broken and one is complete.

The metrical values of blades (Fig. 5.9) display that the distribution of breadth frequency of blades from the (Fig. 5.9A) Mesolithic sites fall in high proportion within the class group of 12-14 mm, while the blades from Upper Palaeolithic sites fall in high proportion within the class group of 18-20 mm. The Fig. 5.9B shows that the blades from both Mesolithic and Upper Palaeolithic sites fall high frequency within the class group of 7-9 mm. And the Fig. 5.9C shows frequency of blades from Mesolithic sites fall within 36-40 mm whereas from Upper Palaeolithic sites high frequency of blades fall within the class group of 41-45 mm. This shows the gradual reduction in length and breadth of blades from Upper Palaeolithic culture to Mesolithic culture.

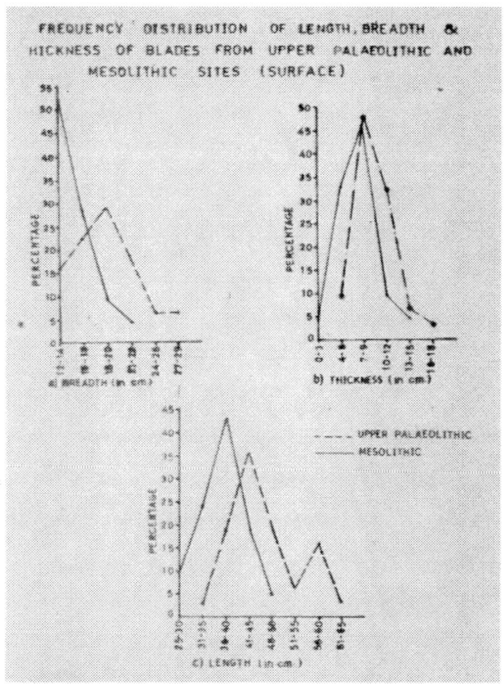

Fig. 5.9: Frequency distribution of length, breadth and thickness of blades from Upper Palaeolithic and Mesolithic sites (surface)

(b) Microblades (1036: 77.42%)

These are micro form of blades. The only distinguishing factor is that the breadth of the artifact is less than 12 mm. There are 1036 (77.42%) specimens in this group. The ratio between the microblade core and microblade is about 1:1. The blades are split into two groups; complete microblade (177: 13.22%) and broken microblades (859: 64.20%). These blades possess one or two mid-ridges sometimes it is difficult to trace the mid-ridge. The blades show triangular (47.23%), plano-convex (16.66%) or trapezoidal (27.77%) or irregular cross-section (8.33%). The metrical values are given in Table 5.18.

Table 5.18: Metrical values of microblades

	Length	*Breadth*	*Thickness*
Maximum	39	11	7
Minimum	19	6	2
Mean	26	8	3

On the basis of the nature of the platform of the blade this group can be classified as follows: (a) microblade with plain platform (22.54%), (b) microblade with prepared platform (7.42%), (c) microblade with cortex platform (0.96%) and (d) platform not clear (69.2%).

(iv) Chips (3067: 38.99%)

These occur in high frequency, than the other categories. These are very small irregular flake piece which come out during the dressing of nodules, detachment of blades and retouching. In the present classification those less than 15 mm in length are considered as chips.

(v) Worked nodules (761: 9.675)

This type is represented with specimens of 761 cores from most of sites except 13; sites and 449 are of chert, 309 are of quartz, 2 are of jasper and 2 are of quartzite.

(vi) Microburin (9: 0.114%)

It is represented by nine pieces from 6 sites. The site No. 58 has yielded 3 specimens. This is a by-product of the process of microlith manufacture. One is partly broken and 8 are complete. All the pieces are from the distal end of the blades, they posses bulbs and the platforms of the microblades.

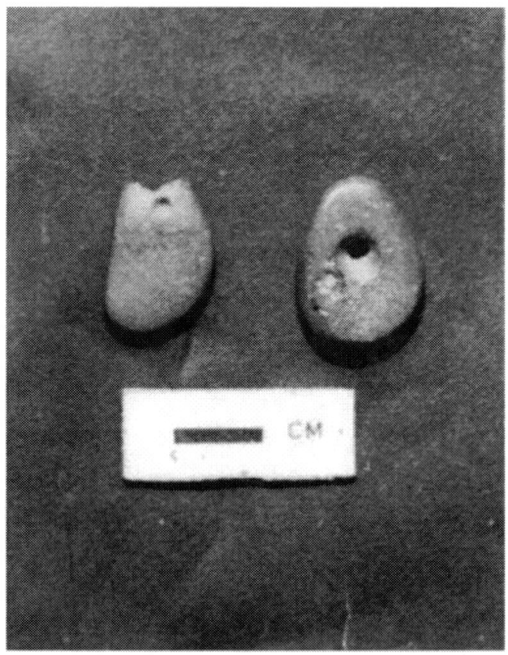

Plate 5.2: Jasper beads from Mesolithic context

(c) Others

The other type includes 4 hammerstones, from site No. 27, 39, 46 and 63, one fragment of ringstone, from site No. 18, two grindstones from site no. 51 and 77 and two jasper beads (Plate 5.2) from site No. 48 and 81. The stone hammers are of quartz pebble of size varying from 3.4 cm to 5.2 cm on length, 2.4 cm to 3.9 cm in breadth and 1.3 cm to 2.2 cm in thickness. Two of them (site No 39 and 46) are of in shape and broken. They have retained a large number of bettering marks at two narrow ends and a few on two sites. The third one is (site No. 27) round in shape and broken at one end and the 4th one (site No. 63) is also round, complete and with a few battering marks. The fragment of ringstone is of basalt having a thickness of 2.1 cm. The two rubber stones are of 4.5 × 2.1 × 4.0 cm and – × 3.8 ×1.7 cm (broken) and one of quartz pebbles. The two surfaces are flat and smooth, due to rubbing and the two margins retain a few bettering marks. The beads are of red jasper pieces of size 2.0 ×1.5 × 0.4 cm and 1.9 × 1.4 × 0.2 cm. One is centrally bored from both sides and the second one is partly broken near the bored end. From sites Nos. 7, 29, 63 and 73, fire rubbed haematite pieces have been collected which are dark red in colour.

Raw Material

Chert (71.03%) is the most common raw material (Fig. 5.11 and 5.12) exploited by the stone knappers of Mesolithic phase, less commonly used raw materials are quartz (27.68%), chalcedony (0.77%), granite (0.29%) and jasper (0.23%). Seven sites (8.23%) are exclusively of chert industry, at 54 sites (63.52%) chert is more common and at 24 sites (28.24%) quartz is more common. The cherts occur in slab form, varying in size at the site or within a range of one to two kilometers from the site. Chert occurs in a number of shades, such as grey, yellowish, white, yellowish red, reddish, reddish brown and green. The cherts implements are highly patinated with a reddish stain, because of long time association with red soil and

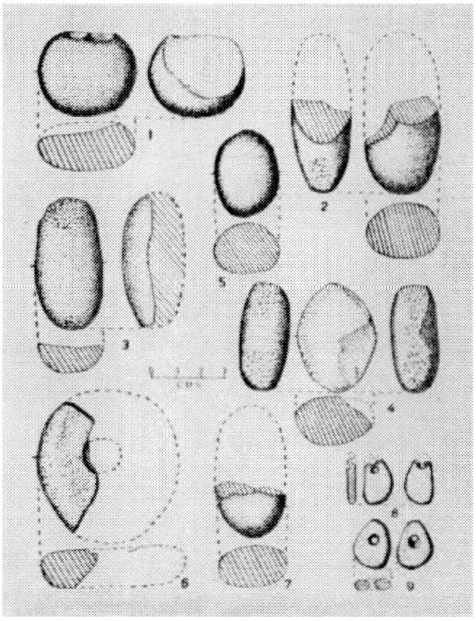

Fig. 5.10: Surface Mesolithic grinding stones, hammerstones and beads

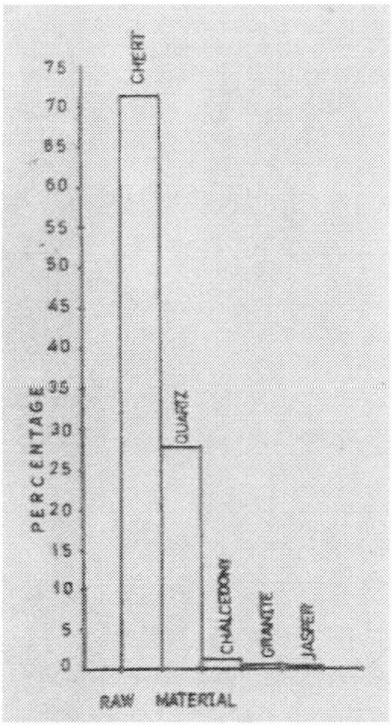

Fig. 5.11: Frequency of raw materials used in microlithic industry (surface)

lateritic soil. The green chert implements are without slightest patination. The shaped artifacts are mainly of chert, with an insignificant proportion of quartz and chalcedony.

Quartz dominant sites are near the granitic outcrops or on granitic hillocks. The quartz is found in nodular and chunk form of different size. These are of two types: crystal quartz and silky quartz. The quartz dominant sites have a low proportion of shaped artifacts and a high proportion of chips and nodules. The flakes from these sites are smaller in size. There is no patination on any of these implements. These observations show that Mesolithic man seems to have used it because it was easily available. The artifacts made on granitic, are worked nodules and chips only. None of the shaped artifacts are of granite. The same is in the case of jasper.

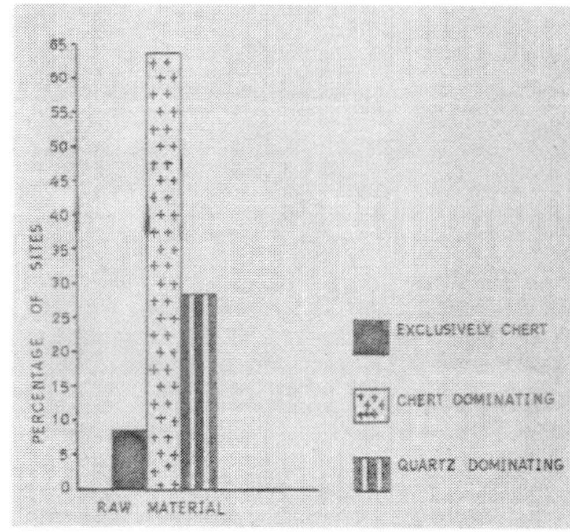

Fig. 5.12: Percentage of sites on the basis of dominance of raw materials

Trial Excavation at the Site of Girla

The presence of large number of microliths on the surface in an area of 42 sq m at Girla A encouraged the present investigator to carry out a small excavation at this site (Plate 5.3 and 5.4). The main aim was to determine the stratigraphic position and to define the nature of the industry. A trench of 2 × 2 m divided into 4 squares of 1 m each was dug to a depth of 75 cm. The entire contents of each square from each dig of 5 cm were sieved and the sorted archaeological materials were recorded on the spot.

Plate 5.3: The site of Girla

Plate 5.4: Excavation at the site of Girla

The method used for the classification of Girla lithic material is primarily analytical basing on morphology, technology and the functional aspect of each piece. The maximum thickness of the cultural deposit is the 0.5 m, but the concentration of the cultural material is more in the top 35 cm. On the basis of hardness and the colour variation of the soils, the deposit can be divided into three layers:

Layer I: It is 5 cm thick and is slightly loose in composition, (Fig. 5.13) yellowish to reddish in colour. The soil colour slowly darkness towards the base.

Layer II: It is 30 cm thick and reddish, slightly darker in color than layer I. This is the main cultural zone and the cultural material does not differ from that of layer I.

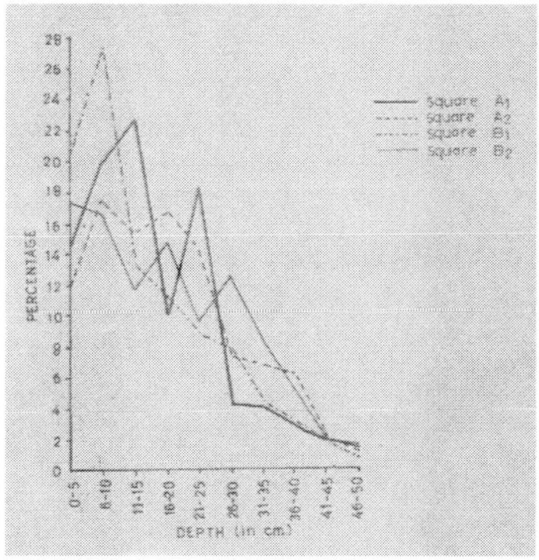

Fig. 5.13: Depth and square wise distribution of Mesolithic artifacts from Girla excavation

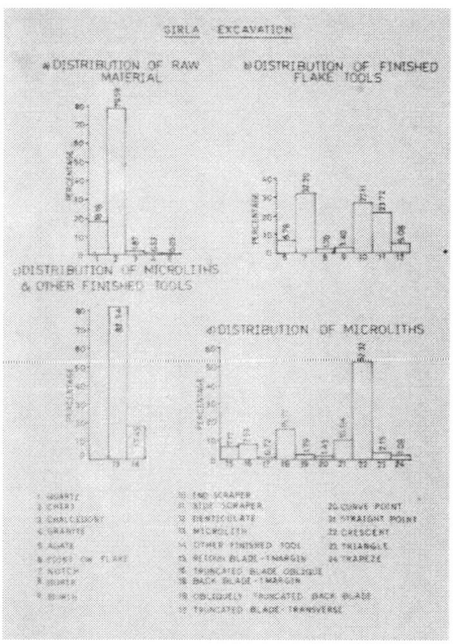

Fig. 5.14: Distribution of artifacts from Girla exacavtion

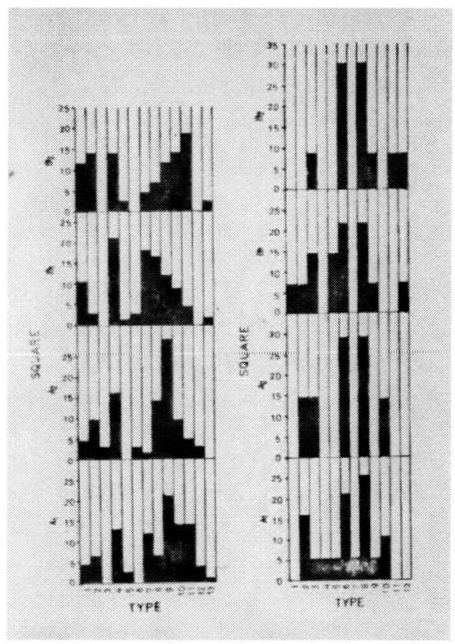

Fig. 5.15: Row diagram of microliths and flake tools from Girla excavation

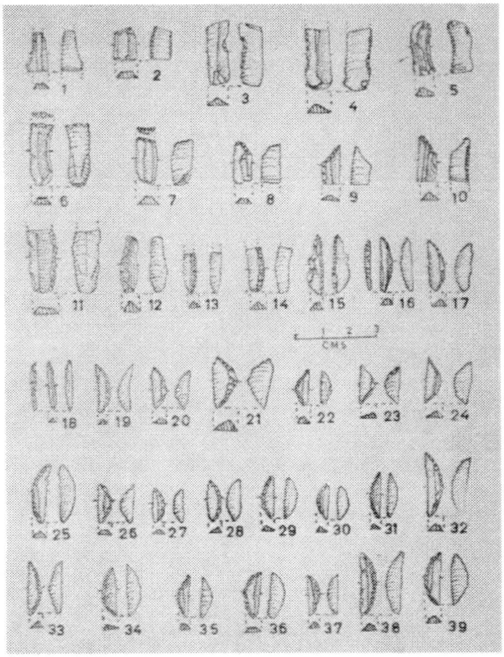

Fig. 5.16: Microliths from Girla excavation

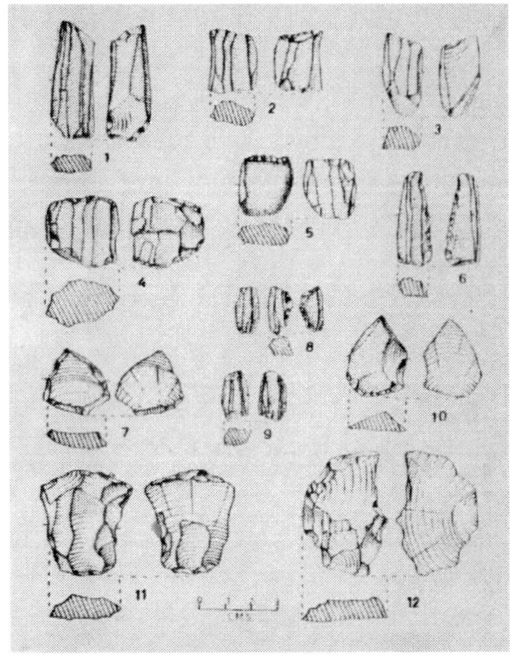

Fig. 5.17: Core and flakes from Girla excavation

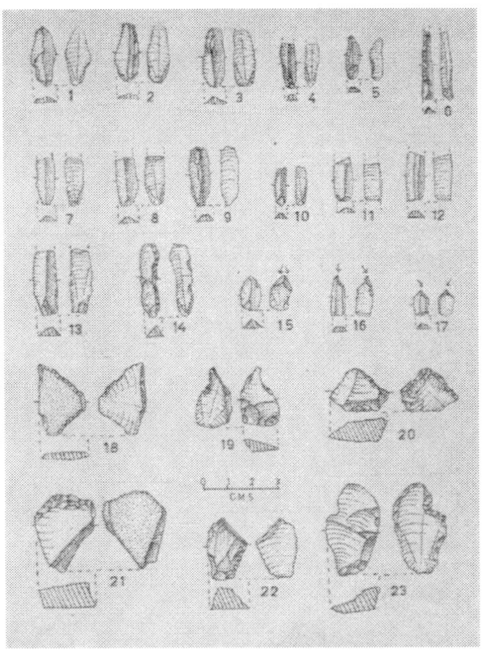

Fig. 5.18: Mesolithic artifacts from Girla excavation

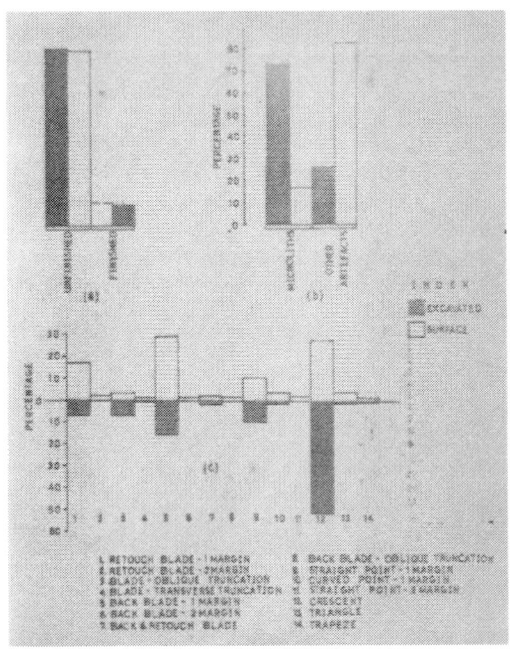

Fig. 5.19: Comparative distribution of Mesolithic artifacts from surface and Girla excavation

Table 5.19: Trench and square depth wise distribution of microliths (simple artifacts) from Girla excavation

Trench/ Square	Depth(in cm.)	M. Bl.C	M. Bl.B	Bl.C	Bl.B	M. Bl.Ut.	Bl.Ut	Fl.Ut.	End. Fl.	Side. Fl.	End. Fl.	Chip	CRF. St.	CRF. Obl	CRF. Top	CRF. Base	M. Bl.1. Core	M.Bl. 2.core	Fl. Core	W.N.	M. Burin	Total
	0-5	2	47			4		2				52	1				10		5		1	124
	06-10	4	51	1	1							122		1			6			1		187
	11-15	5	118			2			3	1	1	82					2			4		218
	16-20	2	39			4						52		1			2					100
	21-25	4	67			2						98					1					172
A1	26-30		16								1	22					2					41
	31-35	2	18									22										42
	36-40	1	9						1			17									1	29
	41-45		5						1			12										18
	46-50		4									9										13
		20	**374**	**1**	**1**	**12**		2	5	1	**2**	**488**	**1**	**2**			23		**5**	**5**	**2**	**944**
	0-5	10	81		1	3		1	1	2	2	52		2	1	1	9			7	1	174
	06-10	5	63		2	1						158					6			2		237
	11-15	11	33			3			5	1		56	1				1					111
	16-20	6	24		4	1		1				50	2						1	4	2	95
	21-25	3	26			1			1			39		1			3					74
B1	26-30	2	17									46					1				2	63
	31-35	2	9					1				20	1				2		1			36
	36-40		5									22										27
	41-45		3			1	1		1			9										15
	46-50		2									6										8
		39	**263**		7	10	1	**3**	**8**	**3**	**2**	**458**	**4**	**3**	**1**	**1**	**22**		**2**	**13**	**5**	**845**
	0-5	4	27			3		1	2	2		32	1				3			4	1	80
	06-10	4	54						3	4	2	49	1			1	1			4	2	125
	11-15	7	42					1	1	2	4	47					4	1		2	3	114

Trench/ Square	Depth(in cm.)	M. Bl.C	M. Bl.B	Bl.C	Bl.B	M. Bl.Ut.	Bl.Ut	Fl.Ut.	End. Fl.	Side. Fl.	End. Fl.	Chip	CRF. St.	CRF. Obl	CRF. Top	CRF. Base	M. Bl.1. Core	M.Bl. 2.core	Fl. Core	W.N.	M. Burin	Total
	16-20	5	47			1			4	1	1	53					4			3	4	123
	21-25	3	28			1		3	4	1		59	2				1	2	1		1	106
A2	26-30		24			1						23			1		4					53
	31-35	4	27									16										47
	36-40	1	20						1			20					1				2	45
	41-45		6						1			9										16
	46-50		1						3			4					1					9
		28	**276**			6		**5**	**19**	**10**	7	**312**	**4**		1	1	19	3	**1**	**13**	**13**	**718**
	0-5	3	24		1			2	4		2	39					6			5		86
	06-10	1	35			3		2	3			34					2			2	1	83
	1115	5	20					2		2		26					2			2	1	60
	16-20	3	24		1	3		3				32	1	1			5			3		76
B2	21-25	2	18						3	1		21					1			1	2	49
	26-30		23						1			29	1			1	2				6	63
	31-35	2	16			1			1			22									3	45
	36-40	1	11						2			10				1	1					26
	41-45		3									5								1		9
	46-50		3			1						4										8
		17	**177**		**2**	**8**		**9**	**14**	**3**	**2**	**222**	**2**	**1**		**2**	**19**			**14**	**13**	**505**

Table 5.20: Depth and type wise distribution of simple (unfinished artifacts) from Girla excavation

	Trench/ Square Depth (in cm.)	M. Bl. C	M. Bl. br	Bl. C	Bl. br	M. Bl. Ut.	Bl. Ut	Fl. Ut.	Ind. Fl.	Side. Fl.	Ind. Fl.	Chip	CRF St.	CRF Obl	CRF Top	CRF Base	M. Bl. Core-1	M.Bl. core-2	M.Bl. core-3	Fl. Core	W. N.	M. Burin	Total
	0-5	19	179			10		6	7	4	4	175	2	2	1	1	28			5	16	3	464
	6-10	14	203	1	2	4		2	6	4	2	365	1	1		1	15				9	3	632
	10-15	28	213		3	5		3	9	6	5	211	1				9	1			8	4	503
	16-20	16	134			9		4	4	1	1	187	3	2			11			1	10	6	394
	21-25	12	139		5	4		3	8	2		217	2	1			6	2		1	1	3	401
	26-30	2	80			1			1		1	120	1		1	1	9					8	225
	31-35	10	70			1		1	1			80	1				2			1		3	170
	36-40	3	45						4			69				1	2					3	127
	41-45		17			1	1		3			35									1		58
	46-50		10			1			3			23					1						38
		104	1090	1	10	36	1	19	46	17	13	1480	11	6	2	4	83	3		8	45	33	3012
	A1	20	374	1	1	12		2	5	1	2	488	1	2			23			5	5	2	944
	A2	28	276			6		5	19	10	7	312	4		1	1	19	3		1	13	13	718
Trench/ Square	B1	39	263		7	10	1	3	8	3	2	458	4	3	1	1	22			2	13	5	845
	B2	17	177		2	8		9	14	3	2	222	2	1		2	19				14	13	505
		104	1090	1	10	36	1	19	46	17	13	1480	11	6	2	4	83	3		8	45	33	3012

Table 5.21: Square wise and type wise distribution of simple (unfinished artifacts) from Girla excavation

	Trench/ Square Depth (in cm.)	*M. Bl. C*	*M. Bl. br*	*Bl. C*	*Bl. br*	*M. Bl. Ut.*	*Bl. Ut*	*Fl. Ut.*	*Ind. Fl.*	*Side. Fl.*	*Ind. Fl.*	*Chip*	*CRF. St.*	*CRF. Obl*	*CRF. Top*	*CRF. Base*	*M. Bl. Core-1*	*M.Bl. core-2*	*M.Bl. core-3*	*Fl. Core*	*W. N.*	*M. Burin*	*Total*
	A1	20	374	1	1	12		2	5	1	2	488	1	2			23			5	5	2	944
	A2	28	276			6		5	19	10	7	312	4		1	1	19	3		1	13	13	718
Trench/ Square	B1	39	263		7	10	1	3	8	3	2	458	4	3	1	1	22			2	13	5	845
	B2	17	177		2	8		9	14	3	2	222	2	1		2	19				14	13	505
		104	1090	1	10	36	1	19	46	17	13	1480	11	6	2	4	83	3		8	45	33	3012

Table 5.22: Trench, square and depth wise distribution of Mesoithic artifacts (shaped) from Girla excavation

P.B.-St.	Long-Sy.Cres.	Long.Asy.Cres.	Short Sy.Cres.	Short Asy.Cres.	Triangle	Trapeze	S.S. 1 Conc.	S.S.1 St.	S.S.1 Conv.	S.S.2	Denticulate	E.S.	T.N.S.	Notch-Fl,	Notch-Bl	Point-Fl.	Borer	Burin	Total
3		8		4		1		2			1	3		2	1	1			33
5		6			3			1		1			1			1			26
1	4	4	2	7										2					25
		3		3					1										8
2	2		11		1							1		1					22
	1		1																4
1				1															2
																			1
1		2																	3
			1																2
13	**7**	**23**	**15**	**15**	**4**	**1**		3	1	1	1	4	1	5	1	2			**126**
1		2	4					1				1		1					14
		8							1							1			15
	2	3			1				1			1				1			9
	4		2									1		1					11
	2													1					7
		1		2								1		1					6
	1	3																	6
		1			1														5
				1															2
								1											1
1	**9**	**18**	**6**	**3**	**2**			2	2			4		4		2			76
2		1	4						1		1			3	1			1	17
2	7					1		1				1							16
1		4		1							1								13
2			1									2							10
1	4		1						1										8
2		1																	5
1				1			1												6
1				1															4

P.B.-St.	Long-Sy.Cres.	Long.Asy.Cres.	Short Sy.Cres.	Short Asy.Cres.	Triangle	Trapeze	S.S. 1 Conc.	S.S.1 St.	S.S.1 Conv.	S.S.2	Denticulate	E.S.	T.N.S.	Notch-Fl,	Notch-Bl	Point-Fl.	Borer	Burin	Total
		2																	2
12	11	8	6	3		1	1	1	2		2	3		3	1			1	81
			3			1								1	1				11
1		2							1			2		1					10
	1			2								1							6
	1		2														1	1	7
				3								1							5
	1	1		2										1					8
		2																	2
				1										1					3
			1																2
1																			1
2	**3**	**5**	**6**	**8**		1			1			4		4	1		1	1	55

Table 5.23: Depth and type wise distribution of shaped (finished) artifacts from Girla excavation

	Trench/ Square Depth (in cm.)	R.B.- 1 m	T.B. obl.	T.B. trans.	B.B.- 1 m	B.B. obl.	B.B. cres.	P.B. St.	Long Sy. Cres.	Long Asy. Cres.	Short Sy. Cres.	Short Asy. Cres.	Tria- ngle	Trap- zee	Total	SS-1 Cnc.	SS-1 St.	SS-1 Conv.	SS-2	Denti- culate	B.S.	T. N. S.	Notch- fl.	Notch- bl.	Point- fl.	Borer	Burin	Total	G. Total
	0-5	5	3		10	1		6		11	11	4		2	53		3	1		2	4		7	3	1		1	22	75
	06-10	4	6		8	1	1	8	7	16			3	1	55		2	2	1		3	1	1		2			12	67
	11-15	4	1		5	2	1	2	7	11	2	10	1		46			1		1	2		2		1			7	53
	16-20	1	3		5		2	2	5	3	5	3			29			1			3		1			1	1	7	36
	21-25	2	3	2	2	1		3	8		12	3	1		37			1			2		2					5	42
	26-30	2	3		3			2	2	3	1	4			20						1		2					3	23
	31-35	1	1		3			2	1	5		2			15	1												1	16
	36-40	1	1		5			1		1		2	1		12								1					1	13
	41-45				2			1		4	1	1			9														9
	46-50				1			1			1				3		1											1	4
		20	21	2	44	5	4	28	30	54	33	29	6	3	279	1	6	6	1	3	15	1	16	3	4	1	2	59	338
	A1	5	7		14	3		13	7	23	15	15	4	1	107		3	1	1	1	4	1	5	1	2			19	126
	A2	3	6	2	10		2	1	9	18	6	3	2		62		2	2			4		4		2			14	76
Trench/ Square	B1	7	2		14	1	2	12	11	8	6	3		1	67	1	1	2		2	3		3	1			1	14	81
	B2	5	6		6	1		2	3	5	6	8		1	43			1			4		4	1		1	1	12	55
		20	21	2	44	5	4	28	30	54	33	29	6	3	279	1	6	6	1	3	15	1	16	3	4	1	2	59	338

Table 5.24: Square wise and type wise distribution of shaped (finished) artifacts from Girla excavation

	Trench/ Square Depth (in cm.)	*R.B.- 1 m*	*T.B. obl.*	*T.B. trans.*	*B.B.- 1 m*	*B.B. obl.*	*B.B. cres.*	*P.B. St.*	*Long Sy. Cres.*	*Long Asy. Cres.*	*Short Sy. Cres.*	*Short Asy. Cres.*	*Tria- ngle*	*Trap- zee*	*Total*	*SS-1 Cnc.*	*SS-1 St.*	*SS-1 Conv.*	*SS-2*	*Denti- culate*	*B. S.*	*T. N. S.*	*Notch- fl.*	*Notch- bl.*	*Point- fl.*	*Borer*	*Burin*	*Total*	*G. Total*
	A1	5	7		14	3		13	7	23	15	15	4	1	107		3	1	1	1	4	1	5	1	2			19	126
	A2	3	6	2	10		2	1	9	18	6	3	2		62		2	2			4		4		2			14	76
Trench/ Square	B1	7	2		14	1	2	12	11	8	6	3		1	67	1	1	2		2	3		3	1			1	14	81
	B2	5	6		6	1		2	3	5	6	8		1	43			1			4		4	1		1	1	12	55
		20	21	2	44	5	4	28	30	54	33	29	6	3	279	1	6	6	1	3	15	1	16	3	4	1	2	59	338

Layer III: It is 40 cm thick, dark red in colour, harder than previous layers, sticky with moisture and with a few angular debris. The upper 15 cm of the layer has cultural materials and the remaining part is sterile.

The detailed typological analysis of the industry is presented in tables and the industry is summarised below.

a) The industry is characterised by micro-blades and tools made on micro-blades. The squares A_1 A_2 B_1 and B_2 have yielded 1070, 794, 926 and 560 artifacts respectively (Fig. 5.13). A total collection 3350 artifacts was made of which 338 (10.1%) are shaped artifacts and 3012 (89.9%) simple artifacts. The ratio of shaped artifacts to simple artifacts is 1:9.

b) The excavation has yielded three pieces of hammerstones, one fragment of ring stone, two pieces of rubber stone and twenty two pieces of rubbed iron oxide.

c) In the shaped forms 279 (82.54%) are microliths and 59 (17.45%) flake tools (Fig. 5.14A). The proportion of microliths (Table 5.19 to Table 5.24) of flake tools is about 5:1. It shows clearly that the Girla Mesolithic culture is of micro-blade tool tradition.

d) The microlith comprise one margin retouched micro-blades 20 (7.17%, Group I), oblique truncated micro-blades 21 (7.53%) and transverse truncated micro-blades 2 (0.72%, Group II), backed micro-blades – one margin 44 (15.77%, Group III) backed micro-blades with oblique truncation 5 (1.79%, Group IV), points 32 (11.47%, Group V), crescents 146 (52.32%, Group VI), triangles 6 (2.15%, Group VII) and trapezes 3 (1.08%, Group VIII) (Fig. 5.14A) and (Fig. 5.16). The row diagram of microliths (Fig. 5.15) displays the squarewise distribution of microliths. The industry is dominated by crescent variant.

e) The components of flake tools (Fig. 5.14 and Fig. 5.18: 18-23) is as follows:

(i) notches 19 (32.20%),
(ii) end scrappers 16 (27.11%),
(iii) side scrappers 14 (23.72%),
(iv) points on flakes 4 (6.78%),
(v) denticulates 3 (5.08%),
(vi) burins 2 (3.39%) and
(vii) borers 1 (1.69%).

And the row diagram of flake tools (Fig. 5.15B) shows the distribution of flake tools in different squares. The types 6 and 8 are the most dominant tool types among the flake tools in all 4 squares. And the distributions of tool types are not uniform in all squares.

f) The components of simple artifacts (Fig. 5.17 and Fig. 5.18: 1-17) is as follows:

(i) micro-blade cores 86 (2.86%),
(ii) flake cores 8 (0.275),
(iii) worked nodules 45 (1.49%),
(iv) micro-blades (Fig. 5.14 to Fig. 5.19) 1194 (39.64%),
(v) blades 11 (0.36%),
(vi) utilised micro-blades 36 (1.20%),

Table 2.25: Trench and depth wise distribution of raw materials

	A1						A2						B1						B2					
Depth/ Trench	*Q*	*Ch*	*Chl*	*Gr*	*Ag*	*Total*	*Q*	*Ch*	*Chl*	*Gr*	*Ag*	*Total*	*Q*	*Ch*	*Chl*	*Gr*	*Ag*	*Total*	*Q*	*Ch*	*Chl*	*Gr*	*Ag*	*Total*
0 to 5	35	118	4			157	14	80				94	48	142	1			191	17	70	7	3		97
6 to 10	48	165				213	23	110	6	1		140	51	197	5			253	15	76	2			93
11 to 15	49	192	2			243	24	97	1	1		123	27	96	1			124	9	57				66
16 to 20	10	98				108	33	95	5	1		134	17	87	1			105	14	64	2	2	1	83
21 to 25	35	158	1			194	14	91	3	5		113	15	67				82	6	45	3			54
26 to 30	13	32				45	7	47	5			59	18	55				73	22	49				71
31 to 35	6	38				44	6	43	4			53	7	35				42	6	41				47
36 to 40	1	29				30	4	41	1	4		50	2	29				31	1	26	2			29
41 to 45	3	18				21	1	17				18	1	16				17	1	10				11
46 to 50	2	13				15	1	8		1		10	1	7				8	2	7				9
	202	861	7			1070	127	629	25	13		794	187	731	8			826	93	445	16	5	1	560

(vii) utilised blade 1 (0.03%), (viii) flakes 99 (3.29%),

(ix) chips 1480 (49.14%) and (x) micro-burins 33 (1.10%).

g) The proportion of micro-blades to micro-blade cores is roughly 13.1.

h) The raw materials (Fig. 5.14A, Table 5.25) used for the manufacture of the tools are yellowish, reddish and greenish chert (79.58%), quartz (18.18%), chalcedony (1.675), granite (0.53%) and agate (0.03%).

To summarise, the Girla Mesolithic industry is characterised by high proportion of microliths made on micro-blades, low percentage of flake tools, complete absence of core tools and well developed blunted back technique. The retouched tools are a few in numbers. Crescent is the predominant type among microliths. Triangle and trapezes occur in a considerable proportion. The use of micro-burin technique is very clear. Notch and end scrappers are two predominant types among the flake tools. Girla Mesolithic culture is a geometric form of microlithic industry fabricated on micro-blades with skilful workmanship.

Comparative Study of Excavated and Surface Collection of Indravati Basin

From above analysis of surface and excavated collections the following inference can be drawn. The typological comparison of the two collections is presented in detail in histograms (Fig. 5.19).

a) There is no significant difference in the proportion of tool and the use of varieties of raw materials in the two collections.

b) The proportion of shaped artifacts (finished artifacts) and simple artifacts (unfinished artifacts) from both the collection are very much similar (Fig. 5.19A).

c) The proportion of flake tools is higher in the surface collection; whereas very low in the excavated collection (Fig. 5.19B).

d) The occurrence of microlithis in the excavated collection is much higher than in the surface collection (Fig. 5.19B).

e) The collection from the excavation is characterised by a lower percentage of flake cores and micro-blades cores while the surface collection consists of a high percentage of flake cores and blade cores.

f) Microburins are more common in the excavated collection than in the surface collection.

g) Among the flake tools, side scrapper variant in the dominant type in the surface collection, while end scrapper is the dominant type in excavated collection.

h) Knife is absent in the excavated collection but it occurs in a significant proportion in the surface collection (Fig. 5.19).

i) Triangle and trapeze are more significant in excavated material than in the surface material.

j) Crescents dominate the microliths in the excavated collection, while the backed blade is the dominant type in the surface collection.

k) There is not such difference on the basis of technology but typological and morphological variations are very much distinct in the two collections.

Comparative study of Indravati Mesolithic Industry with a few Important Surface and Excavated Sites

From the previous discussions on the Mesolithic cultures in India, it is clear that the culture has been reported from varying ecosystem from a large number of sites. A few selected sites (excavated and surface) from different parts of the country have been discussed in the succeeding pages and compared with the Indravati industry to draw some relative affinity of Indravati Mesolithic phase.

EASTERN INDIA

Geographically it is a heterogeneous region. The main units are Chotanagpur plateau, coastal plain of Odisha, parts of Eastern Ghats, Benngal delta and alluvial plain of the Ganga in Bihar. Broadly it includes states of Odisha, West Bengal, Bihar and Assam. The evidence for Mesolithic culture in Eastern India in general and Bihar and Assam in particular is very scanty.

Singhbhum

D. Sen and V. Chaturvedy (1957: 294) had reported microliths from Sanjai valley near Chakradharpur, in Singhbhum. Two sites have yielded 173 microliths. Both are unstratified open air surface sites. The material used is chert, flint or trap rock. The industry mainly consists of flake-blades and corresponding cores. The main tool types are blades 29 (blades with little secondary work, blades with signs of use, backed blades and pen-knife blades), arrowheads 3, points 7 (without retouching and with retouching), lunates 2, semi lunates 2, trapeze 1, scrapers on blade 2, scrapers on cores 4, pseudo-awl 1, utilised flakes 3, unutilised flakes 79 and cores 40. The industry can be briefly described as a non-geometric Microlithic blade tool industry with crude workmanship.

A.K. Ghosh (1959-60) discovered a number of Mesolithic sites in five areas:

(a) near Chandil in northern Singhbhum,

(b) near Sini in northern Singhbhum,

(c) near Ghatsila in eastern Singhbhum,

(d) near Chaibasa in central Singhbhum, and

(e) near Jumda in Southern Singhbhum.

In all 210 specimens were collected from these areas. Agate, jasper and other fine silicious rocks are most commonly used for the manufacture of tools. The industry comprises of choppers 25 (11.91%), scrappers 112 (53.32%), points 25 (11.9%), blades 19 (9.05%), borers 3 (1.43%), knives 4 (1.91%), burins 2 (0.95%) and cores 20 (9.52%). Blades include retouched and unretouched blades and backed blades and cores include flake and blade cores. The industry is dominated by scraper variant. Chopper is also striking character of the industry.

Indravati Mesolithic industry differs from this on the basis of absence of choppers and presence of backed tools, and high proportion of micro-blades and micro-blade cores.

West Bengal

The most important, stratified and well documented Mesolithic sites from Eastern India, is Birbhanpur located on the bank of Damodar river in Burdwan District of West Bengal (Lal 1958: 4). The site is situated on the middle terrace of Damodar River. The artifacts bearing layer lies over a deposit of silty sand, which had been produced by the in situ weathering of the basal sandstone.

Quartz is the primary raw material of the industry, 67.3% small proportions of artifacts are made of chert and chalcedony. In the excavated as well as surface collection the percentage of simple artifacts varies from 93 to 96. The important tool types are blades (flakes with parallel sides, flakes of oval shape, retouched and unretouched), points (pointed stones with or without retouched), lunates, trapezes, borers, scrapers and burins. Blades occur in high frequency both in surface and excavated collection. Point is predominant tool type followed by scrappers. Scrappers include side scrappers (straight and concave), transverse scrappers, discoidal scrappers and end scrappers. The percentages of scrappers among the shaped tools are 11.9% and 25.5% from excavated and surface sites respectively. It suggests that the frequency of scrappers is more in surface collection than in the excavated collection. The crescents are mostly made flakes. It includes symmetric and asymmetric forms of short and long types.

The Birbhanpur industry differs from Indravati industry on the basis of raw material and technology. The microliths are made on micro-blades in Indravati collection and for that micro-burin technique is well developed which is not the case in Birbhanpur. The triangles and trapezes are absent in Birbhanpur collections. These are significantly represented in Indravati collection. One common observation for both industries is the frequency of scrappers is more in surface collection than in excavated collection and typologically both the industries have a lot of common characters.

Odisha

From the earlier review of Mesolithic culture in the beginning of this chapter, it is clear that stray microliths have been found in several districts of Odisha. But no systematic work has been done in any of these areas, except along the river Tel and its tributary (Tripathy 1972), in Kalahandi, Sambalpur and Bolangir districts.

K.C. Tripathy (1972) has discovered 27 open air Mesolithic surface sites located on the river banks. The artifacts were found on the recent alluvium. The total collection consisted of 1781 artifacts. Chert is the most common raw material (53.23%) and cherty quartzite (13.95%), chalcedony (3.82%), jasper 14.095) and oval (12.07%) constitute other raw materials. Of the total collection 63.11% are simple artifacts and 36.88% shaped tools. The microliths are 11.5% of the shaped form. The Table 5.26 gives a comparative analysis of the tool types from Indravati and Tel complex.

Table 5.26: Mesolithic artifacts from Indravati and Tel complex

S. No.	*Tool Type*	*Tel complex*		*Indravati complex*	
		No	*%*	*No*	*%*
1	Worked noudles	–	–	761	9.67
2	Flake cores	–	–	217	2.75
3	Blade cores	–	–	4	0.05
4	Fluted cores	206	18.35	1102	14.02
5	Simple flakes	267	23.75	1043	13.26
6	Blades	–	–	245	3.12
7	Microblades	434	38.70	1036	13.17
8	Utilized flakes	78	6.94	324	4012
9	Utilized blades	139	12.37	–	–
10	Utilized microblades	–	–	57	0.72
11	Chips	–	–	3067	38.99
12	Microburins	–	–	9	0.114
	Total	1124	99.99	7865	99.99
13	Retouched microblades	–	–	45	20.45
14	Truncated microblades	16	21.05	9	4.09
15	Backed microblades	41	53.95	69	31.36
16	Backed and Oblique microblades	–	–	2	0.91
17	Point on microblades	–	–	29	13.18
18	Crescents	19	25.00	59	26.81
19	Triangles	–	–	6	2.73
20	Trapezes	–	–	1	0.45
	Total	76	100.00	220	99.98

21	Hollow scrapers	41	7.05	–	–
22	Side scrapers	105	18.07	336	53.84
23	Dejetes	–	–	3	0.48
24	Denticulates	–	–	29	4.64
25	End scrapers	131	22.55	118	18.91
26	End and side scrapers	–	–	10	1.60
27	Notches	–	–	66	10.57
28	Points on flake	153	26.33	38	6.08
29	Tang points	34	5.85	–	–
30	Borers	36	6.19	13	2.08
31	Burins	20	3.44	2	0.32
32	Knife	–	–	9	1.44
33	Thumb scraper	61	10.50	–	–
	Total	581	99.98	624	99.96

The common characters between these two industries are:

(a) Chert is the most popular raw material.

(b) Blades occur in high proportion.

(c) Fluted core is the dominant type among the core variants.

(d) Backed blade is the predominant tool type among the microliths.

(e) Scrappers occur in high proportion.

The Indravati Mesolithic industry differs from Tel industry on the basis of its occurrence of varying type of microliths as: retouch micro-blades, points on micro-blades, backed micro-blades with oblique truncation triangles trapezes (absent in Tel industry). And among the flake and core tools, dejete scrappers, denticulates, notches and knives are well represented in Indravati collection. While these are absent in Tel collection. Tel industry is dominated by points on flake and end scrappers with a fairly good representation of burins. It suggests that Tel microlith industry has close affinity towards the Upper Palaeolithic culture. But in general the Indravati Mesolithic culture is more advanced than the Tel industry.

SOUTH INDIA

It is roughly a triangular zone, bordered by narrow coastal plain on either side, with a continuous strip of Western Ghat on the west, parallel to the coast and discontinuous hill ranges along the eastern coast. It enjoys tropical climate without much variation. Geographically it includes Andhra Pradesh, Karnataka, Kerala, Tamil Nadu and part of Maharashtra.

Andhra Pradesh

Vedullacheruvu

Microlithic industry occurs widely in this region. One of the important sites is the Vedullacheruvu, on the right bank of the river Rallakalava, 3.8 km north-east of Renigunta (Murty 1970: 115-125). The material employed for making tools is exclusively milky quartz. Therefore it is easy to differentiate this industry from the earlier Upper Palaeolithic of fine grained groomish quartzite of this area.

The industry comprises 1834 artifacts, out of which 11.20% are shaped tools and 88.80% are simple artifacts. The industry includes scrappers (25: 1.36%), awls (24: 1.30%), burins (16: 0.87%), tanged points (7: 0.385), points on cores (10: 0.54%), backed pieces (121: 6.60%), cores (104: 5.67%), flake (331: 18.04%), blades (232: 12.65%) and chips (964: 52.56%). The backed pieces comprise points, lunates, triangles and backed blades. The scrapper is the predominant type among the flake and core tools of this industry and also in Indravati collection. The lunates, triangles, trapezes are quite significant among the microliths in Indravati collection, while these are a few in Rallakalava. Owls and burins occur fairy in a good proportion in Rallakalava collection whereas these are significant in Indravati collection.

Madyakadam

A stratified Mesolithic site had been discovered by Reddy and Prakash (1978) from Madyakadam in Vishkhapatnam. In the river section, 0.47 cm of sterile red soil followed by 33 cm thick deposit of Mesolithic culture in red soil separated from Upper Palaeolithic culture by a sterile dull red soil of 30 cm thick. The Mesolithic artifacts are mostly made on quartz with occasional use of cherty quartzite of blackish brown color. The industry comprises backed knives (21: 0.32%), lunates (93: 1.42%), triangles (18: 0.275), trapezes (3:0.04%), points on blades (18: 0.27%), points on flakes (61: 0.93%), borers (12: 0.18%), microburin (2: 0.03%), scrappers (99: 1.52%), blades (59: 0.90%), flakes (257: 3.94%), cores (223: 3.41%) and chips (2800: 43.36%). The scrappers and lunates are the dominant tool types in this industry whereas backed blades and scrappers are the dominant types in Indravati collection. Retouched blade and truncated blades are absent in Madyakadam but these two types occur fairly with a good proportion in Indravati collection (retouched blades 20.05% and truncated blades 4.09%).

Tirupati

Recently nine Mesolithic sites have been discovered by Jacob (1983) from Tirupati valley in Andhra Pradesh. The sites (Fig. 5.20) are noticed in the hill slopes, on streamside of lakeside, on gorge and plain land. The artifacts are predominantly made on both crystal and milky quartz (1815: 17.02%), with lydianite (95: 4.14%) and fine-grained quartzite (387:16.84%). The total collection comprises 2297 specimens, out of which 14.02% are shaped artifacts and 85.95% simple artifacts. The comparative typological analysis of Indravati and Tirupati collection shows that, side scrapper is the most dominant tool type among the flake and core tools in both the collection. Among the microliths backed blades, crescents and retouched blades occur in descending order in both the industries. Triangle and trapezes are absent in Tirupati collection. The simple artifacts represented with chips, micro-blades and micro-blade cores in descending order in both the industries. The above analysis suggests that typological both the industries have lot of similarity.

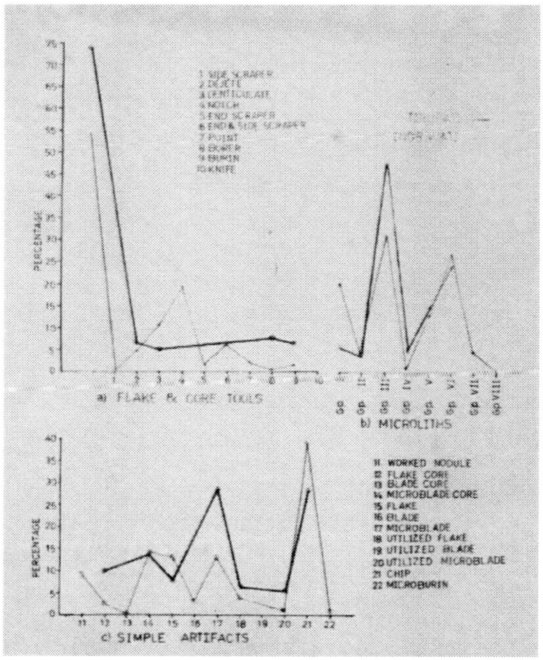

Fig. 5.20: Comparative distribution of Mesolithic artifacts from Tirupati and Indravati

Tamil Nadu

Teri is one of the important Mesolithic sites in Tamil Nadu. Zeunar and Allchin (1956: 4-20) studied on Teri collection. The sites of Teri situated in Tiruchendur taluk in Tinnevelly district and have considerable interest because of their typological, stratigraphical context and typology. Teri consists of 11 sites, located to the south and north of Tambraparni river. These sites are known as Teri sites, on account of their close association with large teris or sand dunes of the region. The use of quartz is common to Teri Mesolithic industry. The implements are heavily stained with red hydrated ferric oxide, which implies that they come from weathered sand of the original soil societies. The industries comprises backed blades, obliquely blunted blades, scrappers (hollow, convex, side, end and thumb-nail), asymmetric points, unifacial points, bifacial points, lunates, transverse arrowheads, triangles, simple points, chopping tools, blade flake, blades and cores.

Teri industry is characterised by poor quality of blades and elaborated preparation of cores, while the blade technique is highly developed in Indravati industry. The typological differences between Teri and Indravati collection are: the absence of transverse arrowheads, bifacial points, chopping tools and thumb-nail scrappers in Indravati collection and the absence of trapezes, dejete scrappers, denticulates, borers and burins in Teri collection. On the basis of raw material also Indravati industry (chert dominated) differs from Teri industry (quartz dominated).

Karnataka

Karnataka is fairly rich in Mesolithic settlements. The sites are generally located on granitic rock, on the river banks and on lateritic formation (Todd 1948: 28-30). A few important sites are reported from Shorapur doab and Shangankallu.

Shorapur doab

Paddayya (1968: 51-117) has reported 33 Mesolithic sites from Shorapur doab in Gulbarga district. The sites are situated in the valleys of the river Bhima and Krishna, on barren patches of land, along the fest of granite hills and on low granite hillocks. Chert is the principal raw material used for the manufacture of the tools, and other materials are chalcedony, jasper, agate and quartz. The industry comprises 9590 specimens, of which 1111 (11.57%) are shaped artifacts and 8979 (88.43%) simple artifacts. Of the total shaped artifacts 763 (68.685) are on blades and 348 (31.32%) on flakes and cores. Among the shaped forms, retouched blades are the dominant type (36.09%), which is not a significant tool type in the Indravati collection (5.335). Typo-technologically there is not much difference between these two industries. And these two industries have some similarity on nature of occurrence of artifacts and the raw material.

Sangankallu

Sangankallu in Bellary district has yielded microlithic industry in a stratigraphical context (Subbarao 1948, Sankalia 1969). The excavated site is locally known as Bangallota, situated on the left side of Bellary-Maka road, about 200 m to the northwest of village school. The upper 23 cm sticky red brown soil has yielded large number of quartz microliths and a few of chert, comprising of 163 specimens. The industry consists of cores (35: 21.47%), core trimmings (31:19.0%), parallel sided flakes (38:23.0%), irregular flakes (19:11.65%), pseudo lunates (5:3.07%), points (3:1.84%), scrapers (3:1.84%) and lunates (29:17.79%).

The industry is completely devoid of micro blades (except a few parallel sided flakes). But micro blade is one of the dominant tool types in Indravati collection. A few types like triangles, trapezes, backed blades, retuched blades and truncated blades of Indravati are absent in Sangankallu collection. In both the collection lunate is one of the dominant tool types.

Kerala

Nine Mesolithic sites were reported by Rajendran (1977), from different parts of Pulghat and Malappuram district of Kerala. These are open air surface sites occurring on the alluvial and lateritic plains. The microliths are exclusively made on quartz. The industry consists of scrapers (50.83%), borers (11.60%), points (10.30%), burins (8.13%), knives (1.00%), choppers (6.65%), discoids (2.66%), lunates (2.33%) and blades (6.31%). Of the total collection of 892 pieces 33.74% are shaped artifacts and 66.25% are simple artifacts. Most of the shaped tools are made on flakes and chips. The industry is of non-geometric type. Blade technique is not well developed. Chopper is absent in Indravati collection. It is well represented in Kerala collection. Typo-technologically there is a considerable difference between Indravati and Kerala collection.

WESTERN INDIA

Maharashtra

Fairly good numbers of Mesolithic sites are known from the coastal zone and the plateau of Maharashtra. The noteworthy sites are Patne and Inamgaon.

Patne

The site of Patne has revealed a cultural sequence from Middle Palaeolithic to Mesolithic period (Sali 1980: 137-160). The Mesolithic culture has been divided into three phases as IIIa, IIIb and IIIc, on the basis of statigraphy and tool composition. Typo-technologically, the Indravati Mesolithic industry is comparable with that Patne IIIa and IIIb. The maximum numbers of Microlithic artifacts have come from phase IIIa (295 specimens); while the phase IIIb and IIIc have yielded 39 specimens each. As the samples from phase IIIb and IIIc are very poor in number compared to Indravati collection, the Indravati collection (from Girla excavation) has been compared with phase A of Patne only. The tool types are simple blades (45.76%), blades with crested ridge (3.39%), flakes (3.36%), fluted cores (2.71%) worked nodules (2.03%) retouched flakes (6.10%), backed blades (8.48%), penknife blades (2.71%), curved backed blades (1.36%), notch on blade (1.70%), lunates (2.03%), triangles (3.05%), trapezes (2.37%), borers (0.34%), tang curved points (0.34%), tanged penknife blades (0.34%), scrapers (4.14%), point on blades (1.02%) and burins (5.72%).

The proportion of shaped artifacts to simple artifacts is about 40:60 in Patne collection, while in Girla collection the proportion is 10:90. It suggests that Patne may be a habitational site and Girla may be factory cum camp site. Among the flake and core tools, burin occurs with highest proportion, 5.72% in Patne collection against 0.05% of Girla. In Microlithic group both the collections exhibit some tool types with a little difference, i.e. the absent of tanged curved points, tang penknife blade and penknife blades in Girla collection.

Inamgaon

The site has been reported by Rajaguru *et al.* (1980: 150-159), at Inamgaon, situated on the right bank of the river Ghod. The trial trench (5 × 2 × 2 m) revealed 25 cm (85-110 cm) thick deposits of microliths along with large number of shells from cross bedded pebble, sandy gravel and brownish fissured clay. The industry comprises 228 artifacts only. The lithic tool complex consists of scrappers (15), points (6), burins (3), lunats (8) triangles (7), blades (86), flakes (48), chips (31), cores (11) and worked nodules (15).

The industry as a whole is a blade based industry, same as Indravati industry. The finished artifacts are fairly large in number (about 54%) in compared to Girla excavated material (10.1%). The scrapper is the most dominant tool type in Inamgaon collection whereas backed blade variant is the dominant tool type in Girla collection. Trapezes are absent in Inamgaon.

Gujarat

Gujarat is rich in Mesolithic settlements. A large number of sites were discovered by Subbarao (1952) and Sankalia (1965). Majority of the sites are located on sand dunes.

Langhnaj

One of the most interesting sites of the Langhnaj, situated north of Ahmedabad; was extensively explored and excavated by Sankalia and others for several seasons in between 1941 and 1963. During 1963, eight trenches were excavated. The main habitational deposit is about 1.5 m but the microliths are found down up to 2.4 m with a lesser concentration. The excavation has yielded 1300 artifacts, out of which 1.92% are shaped tools. The tools are made on chart, chalcedony and quartz. The industry includes amorphous cores (3.61%), core trimming (1.53%), fluted cores (1.70%); crude flakes (85.90%), parallel sided flakes (4.67%), straight blunted back blades (0.38%), lunates (1.00%), triangles (0.0023%), trapezes (0.00107%), scrappers (0.00115%), points (0.00107%) and plenging flakes (0.69%). Apart from this, the site has yielded other objects as ring stones, miniature ground axes, potteries, beads, metal objects and small rubbed stones of hematite with facetted sides. The proportion of shaped tools is insignificant in Langhnaj collection, while it is fairly large in Girla collection. The Langhnaj industry belongs to the late Mesolithic phase in comparison to the Girla Mesolithic phase of Indravati valley.

Rajasthan

A fairly large number of Mesolithic sites have been discovered from east and west Aravali hills in Rajasthan. But the main concentration of sites lies in the Berach basin in Udaypur and Chitorgarh district. Sixteen sites have been reported by V.N. Misra in the year 1961 from the districts of Udaypur, Chitorgarh, Bhilwana and of eastern and western parts of Rajaputana. All sites are surface sites without stratigraphical evidence. These are absolutely non-geometric and non-ceramic assemblages. The common tool types are of various types of scrappers, backed and obliquely blunted blades, points, borers, utilised flakes, blades, blade cores, flake cores, flakes and chips. A significant part of the collection is constituted by the fluted cores as in case of surface collection of Indravati valley. Scrapper is the dominant tool type in both the collection. Later on two more new sites namely Bagor and Tilwara were discovered during 1967.

Bagor

The site Bagor is situated on a sand dune, locally known as Mahasati, on the Kothari river a tributary of the Banas and 25 km west of the town Bhilwara. The habitational deposit is about 1.5 m which is divided into three phases on the basis of cultural material.

Phase I 5000-2800 BC (50-80 cm): The main characters are microliths and animal bones most profuse in this level, the evidence of stone-paved floors and wattle huts or wine breaks and the burials in extended position of east west orientation.

Phase II 2800-600 BC (30-50 cm): The phase is defined by decline of microliths and animal bones, occurrence of metal objects (copper) and handmade pottery with incised decoration burials in east-west direction with food offerings ornaments.

Phase III 600 BC-200 AD (35-75 cm): The phase is characterised by decline of microlithic industry, highly fragmentary animal bones, appearance of iron tools, wheel-made pottery, glass beads, use of bricks, tiles, burial in extended position in north-south orientation.

Quartz is the main raw material followed by chert. Quartz predominance in this simple artifacts and majority of shaped tools are of chert. The industry is based on mass production of micro-blades. Microliths are made out of micro-blades and the bigger tools as scrapers, burins etc. are made on cores and flakes; same as Indravati collection.

The industry comprises 5067 specimens out of which 4.23% are shaped artifacts and 95.77% simple artifacts. The ratio between microliths, flake and core tools is 5:1 at Bagor and 83:17 at Girla excavated collection of Indravati basin. The main tool types in Bagor collection are retouched blades, backed blades, obliquely blunted blades, triangles, trapezes, crescents, points, side scrapers, end scrapers, round scrapers, notched flakes, burins and borers. Blunted back blade is the most dominant tool type among the finished form, whereas crescent is the dominant tool type in Girla collection. And among the flake and core tools, end scrapers occur in highest frequency but in Girla collection notch is the pre-dominant tool type followed by end scrapers. Typo-technologically, Girla microlithic industry of Indravati basin compares well with Bagor phase I microlithic industry.

Tilwara

Tilwara Mesolithic habitational site is located on low sand dune in the old flood plain and Luni river in Barmer district of Rajasthan. The excavation has revealed archeological antiquities from the top 50 cm. The archeological material includes microlithic industry, pottery, stone fragment, baked clay, one small iron piece and animal bones and teeth. Of the total collections 779 specimens, 1.41% are shaped artifacts and 98.58% simple artifacts. Blade constitutes 12.06% of the total collection. The tools are fashioned of quartz and chert. Tilwara and Girla Mesolithic cultures are based on blade tool tradition and microliths are made on thin blades. Both the industries include geometric and non-geometric types.

CENTRAL INDIA

Madhya Pradesh

A large number of sites have been discovered since Hunter's (1935) work at Panchmari in Mahadeo Hills. And a few of them have been excavated.

Adamgarh

Adamgarh is an excavated (Joshi 1978) rock shelter site, located on an isolated quartzite hill, about 2 km south of Hoshangabad. In addition to the Palaeolithic artifacts the site has yielded large amount of Mesolithic artifacts from upper 150 cm of black soil. The dig yielded 5842 artifacts with large number of simple artifacts. The microliths are fashioned on chalcedony and

Table 5.27: Mesolithic shaped artifacts from Adamgarh and Girla

Sl. No.	*Types*	*Adamgarh*		*Girla (Indravati basin)*	
		No	*%*	*No*	*%*
1	Points	1938	77.75	36	10.65
2	Borers & Awls	23	0.92	1	0.29
3	Triangles	186	7.46	6	1.77
4	Trapezes	12	0.48	3	0.89
5	Tranchets	19	0.76	–	–
6	Scrapers	306	12.28	30	0.59
7	Burins	9	0.36	2	0.59
8	Crescents	–	–	146	43.19
9	Notch	–	–	19	5.62
10	Backed blades	–	–	49	14.50
11	Retouched blades	–	–	20	5.92
12	Dentioulates	3	–	3	0.89
13	Truncated blades	–	–	23	6.80
	Total	2493	99.99	338	99.98

chert and a few are on quartz. The industry includes points, borers, awls, triangles, trapezes, trachets, scrapers, burins, blades and cores. Point on blade is the most dominating tool type. The detailed typological account of finished artifacts of Adamgarh and Girla excavation collections are given in Table 5.27.

Typo-technologically, microlithic industry of Girla has a close affinity with that of Adamgarh. The striking difference between these two collections are the, dominant backed blades variant and crescent of Girla collection is absent in Adamgarh collection. The triangle and trapezes are well represented in Adamgarh industry, where as there occurs with a very low proportion in Girla collection. The well developed geometric form, in association with pottery suggest that the Adamgarh Mesolithic industry is more evolved than that of Girla Mesolithic culture of Indravati basin.

Bhimbetka

Bhimbetka is located in the Raisen district of Madhya Pradesh, on the northern margin of the Vindhyan hills. Bhimbetka is a complex of caves and rock shelters. It is one of the most promising prehistoric sites in India. Bhimbetka has revealed a continuous Stone Age culture in undisturbed context. Since 1972, about a dozen of caves have been excavated by V.S. Wakankar (1973) and V.N. Misra (1977, 1978b, 1981). The shelter III F-23 is one of the largest shelters with greatest thickness of habitational deposit of 3.9 m. In all eight layers were recognised in this deposit. The first two layers of 0.6 m thickness have retained microlithic artifacts. Chalcedony is the main raw material associated with a small quantity of chert and quartz. In a total collection of 46948 artifacts, 42407 (90.33%) are simple artifacts and 4541 (9.67%) are shaped tools. Microliths accounts for 95.24% of the shaped artifacts. The main tool types are retouched blades, truncated blades, backed blade, backed with oblique truncated blades, crescents, triangles, trapezes, points, side scrapers, end scrapers, borers, points on flake, burins, and drill. Among the microliths back-blades is the pre-dominant tool type.

Typo-technologically Girla excavated material (of Indravati basin) display a great similarity with that of Bhimbetka III F- 23 collection.

Chitrakot

Recently 49 open air Mesolithic sites have been reported by Cooper (1983), from the surrounding area of Chitrakot waterfall of Indravati river in Bastar district of Madhya Pradesh. CRT 19, the largest site, spread over 18660 sq m and is located on the northern side of the waterfall. The surface collection from this site consists of 28594 pieces, out of which 99.76% are simple artifacts. Milky and crystal quartz forms 82.30% of the raw material and chert is 15.03%. Quartzite, shell, chalcedony and opaline silica occur in negligible quantities.

Among the retouched blades, half of the pieces are crescents and rest half includes points (15.0%), triangles (13.34%), blades blunted on one straight edge (10.0%), penknife blades (8.34%), oblique truncated blades (1.66%) and blades with flat retouched (1.66%).

A comparison of Indravati collection with that of CRT 19 collection indicates that both the industries have similarities with micro variation such as variation in raw material, dominance of backed blades in Indravati collection, absent of penknife blades in Indravati collection, occurance of 9.69% shaped artifacts in Indravati collection against 0.23% of shaped artifact in CRT 19 collection.

Mahanadi Valley

The work on upper Mahanadi valley by Pandey (1982), brought to light 35 Mesolithic sites, mostly concentrated along the Mahanadi proper and a few are on its tributaries. All are open air sites, generally located nearly permanent water bodies and a few sites are on the slop and the bare of hills. The total collection is of 4338 artifacts out of which 735 (17.14%) specimens are shaped artifacts and 3639 (82.86%) are simple artifacts. The number and frequency of shaped artifacts from Indravati and upper Mahanadi valley are given in Table 5.28.

The raw material used for the manufacture artifacts are chert (55.51%), quartz (25.5%), chalcedony (14.68%). Triangles, trapezes, danticulated dejete are all together absent in Mahanadi collection. The frequency of side scraper is 18.62% against 37.09% of Indravati collection and end scraper is 3.85% in Mahanadi collection against 13.02% in Indravati collection. In both the collection backed micro-blades is the dominant microlith, by crescents. Chopper is absent in Indravati collection is fairly similar with those of Mahanadi, in the nature of site, the use of raw material and occurrence of tool types.

Uttar Pradesh

A number of Mesolithic sites had been discovered at late 50s of 20th century. Later several sites have been discovered, and a few cave sites and open air sites have been excavated. The one of the important sites is Sarai-Nahar-Rai.

Sarai-Nahar-Rai

The site of Sarai-Nahar-Rai is located at a distance of 50 m from Pratapgarh in south-westerly direction on the bank of Horseshoe Lake. The site was excavated by G.R. Sharma (1973) in the year 1972. The site has yielded large number of microliths. The other evidences are eleven graves and eight hearths. On typo-technological consideration the evidence can be equated with that of phase II of Lekhahia. Among the geometric form it has yielded triangles only. The tools are generally small in size, firmly retouched. The type consists of symmetrical points, lunates, blunted backed blades, scrapers, triangles. Fine-grained stone, such as chalcedony, agate, jasper, carnelian etc. were used as raw material.

Chopani-Mando

The site of Chopani-Mando is situated on Terrace T_2 of the old channel of the river Belan at a distance of 77 km from Allahabad in east and south-easterly direction in Meja sub-division of

Table 5.28: Mesolithic shaped artifacts from Upper Mahanadi and Indravati basin

Sl. No.	*Tool Types*	*Upper Mahanadi*		*Indravati basin*	
		No	*%*	*No*	*%*
1	Side scrapers-1 margin	129	17.13	336	37.09
2	Side scrapers-2 margin	12	1.59	–	–
3	End scrapers	29	3.85	118	13.02
4	Thumb nail scraper	8	1.06	–	–
5	Combined scraper	9	1.9	–	–
6	Core scraper	56	7.54	–	–
7	Denticulate	–	–	29	3.20
8	Dejete	–	–	3	0.33
9	End and side scrapers	–	–	10	1.10
10	Notch	16	2.12	66	7.28
11	Borer	11	1.46	13	1.43
12	Burin	20	2.65	2	0.23
13	Point on flakes	85	11.29	38	4.50
14	Knife	12	1.59	9	0.99
15	Chopper	17	2.26	–	–
16	Point on microblade	–	–	29	3.20
17	Retouched blade	14	1.86	–	–
18	Retouched microblade	81	10.75	45	4.97
19	Truncated blade	20	2.65	9	0.99
20	Back blade	110	14.61	69	7.61
21	Back & retouched blade	5	0.66	–	–
22	Triangle	12	1.59	6	0.66
23	Crescent	98	13.01	59	6.52
24	Trapeze	–	–	1	0.11
25	Back with oblique truncation	19	1.19	2	0.22
	Total	753	99.98	844	99.97

Allahabad district. It is located within the flood plain of the Belan. The excavation has revealed a total habitational deposit of 1.55 m in thickness comprising 10 layers divisible into three cultural phases as: (i) epi-palaeolithic (ii) early Mesolithic (ii) advance Mesolithic or proto Neolithic.

Epi-palaeolithic: The 20 cm of layer has yielded lithic artifacts of Upper Palaeolithic and Mesolithic culture fashioned on chert (91.83%).

Early Mesolithic: The layers 9 and 8 have yielded non geometric microliths, unassociated with pottery. The artifacts are made on chert (94.82%). Most of the tools (74.4%) are made on blades or blade flakes and the remaining 25.6% have been flakes, cores and nodules. The industry comprises of 88% and 12% finished artifacts.

Early Mesolithic: The layers 7-4 have yielded geometric microliths, unassociated with pottery. The tools are fashioned mainly on chert (91.83%). Of the total collection 85.4% artifacts are made on blades and 4.6% are on cores and flakes. About 90% of the collections are the simple artifacts and 10% are shaped artifacts. The main tool types are parallel sided blades, backed blades, triangles, trapezes, notches, penknife, serrated blades, burins, borers, point and scrappers.

Advanced Mesolithic or proto-Neolithic: Layers 3-1 have yielded geometric microliths made on chert (80%) and chalcedony (20%) and handmade pottery, with the evidence of post holes.

The Indravati collection can be comparable with that early Mesolithic collection of Chopani-Mando. On the basis of raw material and tool types, both the industries are of contemporary period.

Chapter 6

Ethnographic Context of the Study Area

This chapter deals with the economy and socio-cultural life of the tribes of Koraput with special consideration of their dependence on the ecosystem and their subsistence and exploitation pattern. By drawing parallels from the ethnographic present, it is attempted here to postulate on the life ways of the Stone Age hunter-gatherers in the Indravati valley.

According to 1961 census, of the tribal population of 1,75,48,846 in Odisha, 42,23,757 (24.0%) belong to the category of scheduled tribes (ST). There are 62 scheduled tribes. They are concentrated mainly in the undivided districts of Koraput (1.15 million), Baudh Phulbani (0.26 million), parts of Ganjam (0.25 million) and Kalahandi (0.34 million) while the latter consists of the districts of Mayurbhanj (0.84 million), Keonjhar (0.45 million), Sundargarh (0.55 million) and part of Sambalpur (0.52 million).

Koraput has the lowest population. The total population of undivided Koraput district is 15,61,051 of which 9,54,338 are (60.89%) scheduled tribes. Of these 92% live rural area and remaining 8% in the urban area. There are 51 scheduled tribes in Koraput. The list of tribes and the total number of population, which are more than five hundred, are given in the Table 6.1.

Table 6.1: Scheduled Tribes of undivided Koraput District (1961)

Sl. No.	*Name of Tribe*	*Total*	*Male*	*Female*
1	Bagata	1,369	687	682
2	Bhottada	1,56,251	78,687	77,564
3	Bhumia	49,584	24,477	25,107
4	Bhonda Paraja	4,677	2,435	2,242
5	Dharua	4,685	2,393	2,472
6	Didayi	1,976	962	1,016
7	Gadaba	42,035	21,191	20,844
8	Gond	54,760	27,512	27,248

9	Holva	3,955	1,898	2,056
10	Jotapu	10,583	5,263	5,320
11	Khond or Kandha	2,69,901	1,34,812	1,35,089
12	Kolha	743	405	340
13	Kondadora	15,301	7,627	7,674
14	Kotia	3,447	1,790	1,657
15	Koya	53,583	26,421	27,162
16	Mahali	947	464	485
17	Matya	1,119	567	552
18	Mirdhas	732	343	389
19	Munda	5,887	2,961	2,926
20	Omanstya	14,096	6,946	7,150
21	Parenga	6,702	3,262	3,440
22	Paraja	1,37,740	68,698	69,051
23	Pentia	4,112	2,067	2,045
24	Sajntal	990	431	559
25	Saora	36,161	18,085	18,076
26	Shabar	16,628	8,362	8,266

The centrality index (the extent of maximum concentration in a tribal community in any areal unit is its centrality index) of the domicile of the total communities of Koraput district are Bhottada (99), Bonda (100), Didayi (100), Holva (89), Omanstya (98), Parenga (99), Paraja (83), Dharua (68), Gadaba (84), Bhumia (62), Pentia (43), Gandia (66) and Khond (32).

The majority of the tribal's of the district depend on agricultural labour. They engage in part-time hunting, fishing and gathering to support their economy. In the following pages, while a few selected tribes like Paraja, Didayi, Saora, Omanastya, Bonda are discussed in brief, a detailed description of Gadba is given for the reason that they are still primitive and the Stone Age sites are located close to their habitat.

PARAJA

Paraja or Parjas are hill cultivators. According to the1961 census, of the 1,59,866 Paraja in the states 1,41,694 (88.63%) are inhabitants of Koraput district. The name Paraja appears to be derived from the Sanskrit term Praja, a subject. And the term Paraja is not a tribal denomination but a class denomination. The Parajas are not a compact group but rather a conglomerate, and up of several endogamous sections and speaking a language, which varies according to locality.

They are divided into different sections as:

(a) Barang Jhodia (who eat beef and speak Oriya),

(b) Ponga Paraja (eat buffalo and their language is close to Khonda),

(c) Kondi Paraja (section of Kandha, eat beef and buffalo, speak Konda or Kodu),

(d) Parenji Paraja (section of Gadaba, two sub-groups, one eats buffalo and the other does not, speak a Gadaba dialect),

(e) Kanga Paraja (section of Gadaba, call themselves Bonda),

(f) Tagona Paraja (section of Koya, speak Koya dialect) and

(g) Dur Paraja (known as Didayi Paraja, who speak Oriya) (Thurston 1909: VI).

The Parajas have a number of totemistic steps as tiger, tortoise, goat, dog, dove and big lizard. Marriage is strictly prohibited between the members of the same clan. Five main types of marriages found in the Paraja community are *Haribel* baha (by arrangement), *Udlia baha* (love marriage), *Jhina-Utra baha* (marriage of widows and the divorces) and *Gharjwain* (marriage, where the male is adopted as a son by the wife's father). The principle of free love is recognised among them. The bachelors and unmarried girls sleep together in separate quarters called Thenga Ghar in the village.

The main occupation of the community is plain land agriculture and shifting cultivation and many of them are agricultural labourers. Forest products are collected and fishing is resorted to at times. Paddy is sufficient for a part of the year. They manage with edible roots, tubers, fruits, flowers and nuts of the forest. Liquor of various types like ricebeer, salope, and pahua are their favorite drinks. They are very fond of dance and music. The girls dance to the sound of musical instruments played by the boys.

DIDAYI

Didayi inhabits the Koraput district of Odisha at 1,213 m plateau of the Eastern Ghat. According to Thurston (1909: 11, 171), Didayi are a subdivision of Paraja. The primary distribution of the tribe is the hilly and forested zones of Malkangiri police station area of Koraput district. The total population is 1,978 persons. The Didayi speaks a dialect closely akin to the language spoken by the Gadaba and Bonda, who belong to the Mundari group.

They are grouped into classes on the basis of their settlement in relation to the geographical setting, 'Hill people' and 'Plain people'. The houses of hill top villages are not arranged in any order whereas plain land village houses are arranged in arrows with a narrow path in between. They live in low-roofed rectangular houses of two rooms. The walls are made of spilt bamboos plastered with mud and the roof is thatched with *sabai* grass or with straw.

The Didayi kinship system is based on two distinct exogamous clans known as Ghia and Rata. The groups of each class are exogamous and can have marriage relations only with any of the groups of the next clan. And the marriage can be *bihay* (by negotiation), *dube* (by capture), and also there are instance in which the girl forcibly gets into the groom's house and enters into sexual relation.

The economy is based on settled agriculture (plain people), shifting cultivation (both plain and hill Didayi) and agricultural labour. The Didayis are addicted to *saolap* wine and also wine prepared out of Ragi and Mahul. They supplement their cereal diet with edible roots, fruits, flowers, leaves and tubers. Digging stick and the collecting bamboo basket are the main articles used by the Didayis in gathering wild natural products collected by them during February to May. This is used for food, curry, edible oil, oil for lamp and for liquor. The important forest products are *amba, kendu, tala, dimiri, baunssaja, bars-kanda, dor-kanda, toraj-kanda, neta-kanda, sargi kanda, nota kanda, tarls roots, kondals roots, sarails* roots and *kiral* roots. Didayi eat a kind of red ants called *tapenga*. Males, females and children go for food collecting.

In hunting, only adult males participate. Didayi are remarkably skillful in locating, chasing and killing game. Before going for hunting they pray to forest deity for the success of their expedition. Generally they go for hunting during the months of April-June. The main preys of Didayi are sambar, deer, wild cat, jungle fowl, peacock, squirrel, hare, pigeon and birds of different types.

In summer, when the water is less in the ponds they go for fishing. They do not use large nets. They use fish traps of varying types and hand nets. Fishing is also done by poisoning the pond water by dropping the powder of fruits, locally known as *ponoralaslo*.

Rice is their principal diet; it is cooked with a kind of leaf locally known as *samiliyabad*. During the time of hunting expedition the hunted meat is roasted in the jungle over an open fire while in village it is boiled and eaten.

SAORA

The Saora are one of the hill tribes of Odisha. The main concentration of this tribe is in three districts of Ganjam (96,128), Sambalpur (82,575), and Koraput (36,329). Saora are divided into two broad groups, on the basis of geographical division such as Hill Saora and Plain Saora. They practice terrace and shifting cultivation.

The Saora family is patriarchal and patrilineal. The clan organisation, which is common to tribal society is totally absent among the Saoras. The most common form of marriage is of the arranged type. They have also marriage by capture and service. Polygamy is widly prevalent among the Saoras. The main source of livelihood for Saora is shifting cultivation. But the essential economy, in the broadest sense may be termed as collecting, hunting, fishing and cultivation. They collect different type of edible roots, tubers, nuts, fruits, leaves, flowers, shoots, mushrooms and shells. Honey is occasionally collected from the forest. Hunting as a means of subsistence has lost its importance. It has become a very irregular feature in their economy because of scarcity of game in the adjoining area. Generally hunting start after harvesting and ends before ploughing. Only men take part in hunting. In individual hunting only small game like hare and sometimes wild fowls, birds etc. are procured. But group hunting is very interesting. The group takes the helps of dogs during hunting to chase the game. The main hunting appliances are bow, arrow and traps. In group hunting the participants are entitled to take equal share of the animal hunted. Saoran are fond of fish also.

They do not know any other type of cooking except boiling the things together with salt and chilies. They do not know the use of oil or fat in preparing food. For them the autumn is the worst period when there is acute food shortage. At that time they mainly depend on a powder prepared from the trunk of the sago-palm tree and Mahul flowers stored earlier and on forest product.

OMANSTYA

The main concentration of the tribes is in Koraput district. The total population of Omanstya is 14,365 in the state, and out of it 14,145 are found within the Koraput district. They are thickly settled at Nowrangpur (3,022), Kotpad (2,519) Tentulikhunti (2,135) and Bhairava Sirghpur (1,896) area. This tribe forms roughly ten percent of the total population at those stations. They live in villages of multi-ethnic composition. In a few villages, there are separate hamlets with exclusive concentration of Omanstya. They are not deemed as untouchables by the neighbouring caste Hindus.

The tribe is divided into two sections, called *bada* and *sana*. They have a number of exogamous clans called Bagh (tiger), Dhuda (milk), Nag (cobra) etc. Nuclear families are the chief social units, but there are extending and joint families. Marriage of Bada with the Sana is prohibited. Child marriage and widow marriage are permitted in the society. The marriage by consent is more frequent than by negotiation. There are rare instances of marriage by service and elopement. Cross-cousin marriage is the general rule. Polygamy is allowed.

Omanstya is the most developed tribe among the tribes of Koraput district. They are basically agriculturists. Landless people usually get employed as agricultural labourers. Fishing is usually carried out and fishing implements are different sizes of nets, traps of single valve and multi-valves made on split bamboo. Hunting is practiced at leisure.

BONDA

Bonda live on the high hills to the north-west of river Machkund in Khair block of Jeypore Tahsil of Koraput district. The Bonda call themselves 'Romo' (men) and speak an Austro-Asiatic language belonging to Mundari group. The total population of the tribe is 4,677.

Bonda houses are individual huts with some enclosure around it. The walls are of mud and the roof is of bamboo or wooden frame, thatched with grass. The house is of two rooms only. The entrance room is for cooking and living and next room is for storage. The house-hold articles are very limited, a few bows and arrows, axes, a few agricultural implements, fishing traps, leaf and bamboo baskets of different sizes, 3 to 4 earthen pots for cooking and storing water.

The dress and ornaments of Bonda women are distinctive. They wear the scantiest cloths which they weave themselves, out of *Kerans* fiber, collected from the forest. The size of the cloth is eight to ten inches in width and two to three feet long. They shave their heads and wear two three fillets of Palmyra palm. They cover their upper parts of the body with large number of bead necklaces of different sizes, which hang up to the navel. The male members move with scanty cloth only.

Bonda (Plate 6.1) economic life depends on shifting and terrace cultivation and on food gathering, hunting and fishing. The Bondas sell some of the forest products in weekly market to buy the iron arrow heads, axes and beads.

Plate 6.1: Bonda girl extracting fibres from a palm trunk

Every Bonda village has two dormitories; one is for girls and one for boys. The real aim of dormitory is to give opportunity to the boys and girls to select their life partner. Once selection is made the consent of the parents is subsequently obtained and the marriage rite is performed. The regular marriage called *sehung* is very expensive; it is practiced by a few rich people. But majority of the Bonda marriages are performed through capture, known as *gubai godo-rungone*. Widow marriage is permitted. Usually the Bondas cremate their dead, excepting exceptional cases of death caused by smallpox or cholera or during pregnancy.

GADABA

Gadaba, a hill tribe, live in inaccessible mountainous areas of Koraput district of Odisha and the folk adjoining mountainous tracts of Andhra Pradesh and Madhya Pradesh also. Their total population in Odisha is 4,393 of which 4,256 (96.86%) live in Koraput district. The main concentration of this tribe is in Lamptaput, Jeypore, Nandapur, Semiliguda, Sunabeda and Pottangi mixed with other tribes and castes.

Their language belongs to Austro-Asiatic linguistic family. The Gadaba tribe (Plate 6.2) is broadly divided into three groups such as Bada Gadaba, Sana Gadaba and Ollar Gadaba. The

Sana Gadaba includes the Parenga Gadaba. In another way they are grouped into a number of divisions like Bada, Sanda, Ollar, Kalavi, Kanu, Kateni, Juruma and Parenga.

Social Organisation

Plate 6.2: A Gadaba woman

The family is the smallest unit. After the marriage of a son, he gets separated from parents. The family is patrilineal, patrilocal and patripotestal. There are a few clans in Gadaba community. The clans are named as *kora* (sun), *nag* (cobra), *bagh* (tiger), *collari* (monkey) etc. Every village has a secular head known as *naock*, an attendant to *naock* known as *challan* and a bearer called *barik*. The village has a *desari*, who officiates as the priest for all worships in the village. He is consulted in illness and calamities of the village.

Gadabas worship a goddess whom they call *thakurani* or *gramadevati*. The Goddess is respresented by slabs of stones and worshipped by *desari*. The place is known as hundi. They observe a few festivals like *chaita parba, nuakhia* (observe eating of new rice), *nusambakhia* (observe eating of new mango), *dasahara* etc. *Chaita parba* is the most important festival among them. This is a community festivals associated with hunting. This festival lasts for eleven days. The male members of the village go for hunting on the second day of festival. The festival date is fixed by the *desari*. This is observed in the month of March-April. After hunting the male folk come back to the village with the animal and they are received by the women. Then the meat is distributed by *desari*. Then they enjoy the day by dancing after taking a lot of wine. The boys and girls dance in circles. On *Dasahara*, they make offerings to the arrows and bows and sacrifice a type of fish called *magara*. The Gadabas are very fond of music and dance. The main themes of the songs are of love and natural beauties.

Settlement

Gadaba villages are generally located on flat topped small hills, or hill slopes, on the bank of rivers, by the side of hill springs or on the elevated river terraces. They build houses in two rows facing each other with a broad street left between them. Generally the house has two rooms, one rectangular in plan and behind it a circlar one with conical roof and with verandah in front. The building materials for house construction are obtained from the jungle. The foundation day is fixed by the *desari* and on that day *hundi* (village deity) is worshiped by *desari* by offering eggs and hen.

The walls are made of bamboo and wood, plastered with mud. Sometime the walls are made of mud only. Final plastering is done by the women with cowdung and coloured clay. The houses are thatched with wild grass or leaves.

The head man's house is centrally located. At one end of the village near the river is the burial ground and at the other end of the village is *hundi*. Sometime *hundi* is centrally located in the villages. Every village possesses dormitory for boys and girls, separately but closely located.

Household Articles

Earthen pots are used for cooking and storage of water. These are small to medium in size. For boiling water, bigger pots are used. For storage, leaf backets (Fig. 6.1) and bamboo baskets are used. Different shapes and sizes of gourds are used for carrying liquid things. For carrying oil they use bamboo containers known as *nala*. The wooden articles of Gadaba generally consist of the mortar; pestle; agricultural implements like yoke, plough, digging stick; hunting implements; musical instruments and weaving implements. Gadaba eat on leaf plates (Fig. 6.2) locally known as *khali* and *dana* respectively. They make raincoats of leaves, known as *talara* (Fig. 6.1).

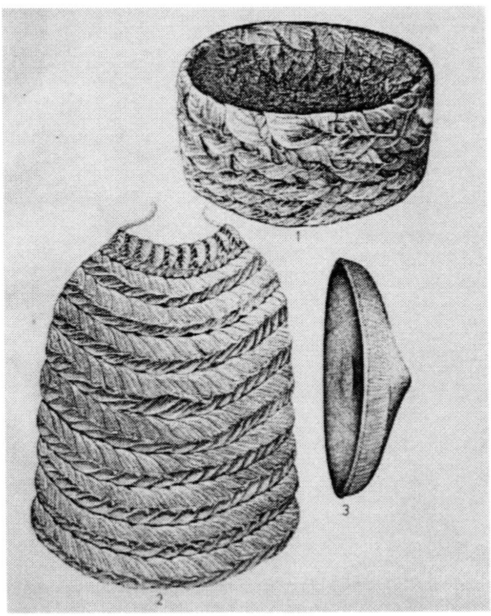

Fig. 6.1: 1. Leaf basket, 2. raincoat and 3. cap used by the local tribes

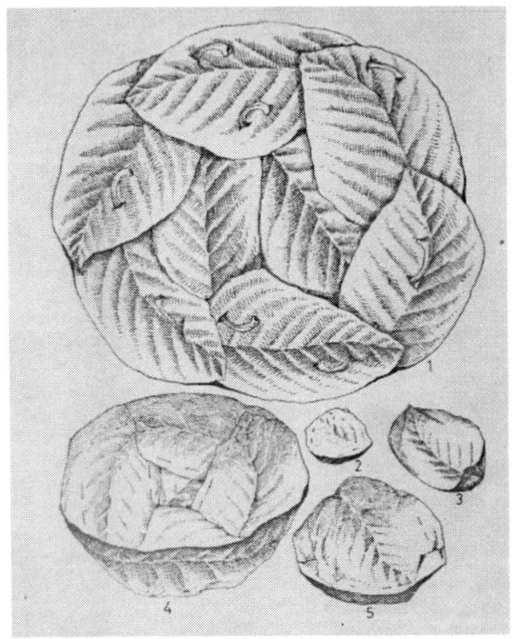

Fig. 6.2: Leaf plates and cups used by the local tribes

Dress

The cloths which the Gadaba females require are manufactured by themselves from cotton thread and the fiber of *silloluvada* and *sakude chettu* (*Cholarrhana antidysenterica*) and *bedaluvada* or *bad chettu* (*Ficus glomarata*). Every Gadaba women must know how to weave her cloth before she is eligible for marriage.

A bundle of twigs is brought, and the leaves are removed, then the stems are twisted to loosen the bark and then left for two to three days for drying. The bark is removed and beaten with a heavy stick to get smooth fibres. Again the fibre is carefully dried after dying it in blue or reddish brown colour. Then the Gadaba woman weaves her cloth on her miniature loom. The edges of the cloth are white; a blue stripe comes next, while the middle portion is reddish brown with narrow stripes of white on blue.

Why Gadaba women use fibre cloth? There is a legend behind it. When 'Sita' was moving with 'Ram' in the 'Danda-Karnya' forest, she was wearing small piece of cloth made of fibre only, which was laughed at by Gadaba women. 'Sita' cursed them and from that day Gadaba women are dressed up in fibre cloth. At present, due to the influence of modern culture they are using sari, but they have to weave the fibre cloth at the time of marriage and on special occasions. The Gadaba women do not like elaborate ornaments like the Bondas. They wear ear-rings made of brass which reach to the shoulders (earlier the ear-rings wear of wood). The head dress consists of shell and beads of various sizes and colours with a pendant at the centre. They use bead necklaces, sometimes of coins. Tattooing is common in case of women. Generally women tattoo on their head, chin, forehead and fingers. The women are great admirer of flowers.

The dress of males is very simple. They wear small cloth of one meter length and 0.5 m width to cover the lower part of the body. They use ear-rings of brass of small size.

Subsistence pattern

The Gadaba depends on five fold subsistence pattern as: (a) gathering, (b) fishing, (c) fowling, (d) hunting, (e) agriculture, plain land, shifting and terrace cultivation (as these are recent adaptation, these sections are not discussed here).

Gathering

Gadabas collect different types of edible roots, tubers, nuts, fruits, flowers, leaves, shoots, barks, mushrooms, honey, crabs and other minor forest products for their food, clothing and shelter as well as curing of diseases. The major part of the collection is consumed and a small part of it is sold or bartered for food grains, cloth, salt another commodities.

The natural products from the neighbouring forest areas (Plate 6.3) exploited by Gadabas for their need are discussed in details below under three headings, as (a) for food, (b) for

Plate 6.3: A view of rocky Indravati river bed with the background of evergreen forest near Tentulikhunti

Plate 6.4: Distribution of tamarind shares among the Gadaba man and woman

medicinal use and (c) for miscellaneous use. And a list of tubers, roots, flowers, fruits, berries, leaves, mushrooms, medicinal plants and miscellaneous articles is given in Table 6.4, with local and botanical names (whatever possible), the habitat and habit and season of availability (Plate 6.4 to 6.15).

a) For food

This category includes, (i) tubers and roots, (ii) flowers, fruits and berries, (iii) leaves, (iv) mushrooms and (v) seeds and grains.

Tubers and roots

1. *Kesari Kanda:* It grows near ponds and swampy areas. The tuber is darkish brown or black in colour with plenty of thin roots over the thick cover. The tuber is boiled, peeled and then consumed. It is sold in weekly markets.
2. *Pita Kanda:* It is plentiful in the forested valley and plain land also. The size of the tuber is that of a tomato, it is more or less round in shape and has a thick dark cover. Tuber is eaten, boiled or roasted.
3. *Katha Kanda:* It is a long naroow tuber, growing in forested valley. The tuber is brownish in colour. Thin slices are cut and boiled and after removing the skin the slices are eaten with salt. The tubers are also roasted and eaten.
4. *Kau Kanda:* It is a long tuber of irregular forms and grown in forested valley. After removing the skin of the tuber, slices are cooked as a vegetable with salt, turmeric powder and chillies. Sometimes it is roasted, powdered and cooked with water and eaten as a full diet.

5. *Simili Kanda:* Commonly found near the bank of ponds, water ditches or streams. It appears like a ginger but is hard to bite. The tuber is boiled or roasted, peeled and eaten. Rarely it is cooked as a curry.
6. *Kultudamudi Kanda:* It grows along the banks of ponds or water ditches. The tubers are small, rounded in shape. It comes in large numbers at the roots and is yellowish brown in colour. The Kanda is boiled, peeled and then eaten.
7. *Pita Boranda Kanda:* It grows near water, and is irregular in shape and a dark brown in colour. Thin slices are cut and boiled with ash, then the skin is peeled off and washed in clean water and again boiled, then slices are eaten with salt and chilly.
8. *Puruni Kanda:* It grows in ponds. It is the stem of lily. It is sold in plenty in valley markets. The Kanda is cut into pieces and cooked as a vegetable.
9. *Garsi Kanda:* It grows along the banks of ponds. The size of the tuber is rounded to irregular, it is dark brown to light brown in colour. The tubers are washed, boiled, peeled and then vegetable is prepared with salt, chilly, turmeric powder and tamarind.
10. *Dora Kanda:* The plant grows along the banks of ponds or near water ditches. It is tubular in shape. The Kanda is boiled, peeled and eaten.
11. *Das Kanda:* It grows near the banks of ponds, streams or water ditches. These are irregular in shape with rough surface. It also has medicinal values and is eaten for regular motion.
12. *Mati Kanda:* It is plentiful in the forested valley. The tuber is yellowish brown in colour, long tubular in shape with a thin cover. The tuber is sliced into small pieces and cooked as a vegetable.
13. *Bara kanda:* The tuber is found widely in forested hilly area. It is boiled or roasted and then eaten. The tuber is also sold in the weekly market.

Plate 6.5: Tubers and roots used by the locals

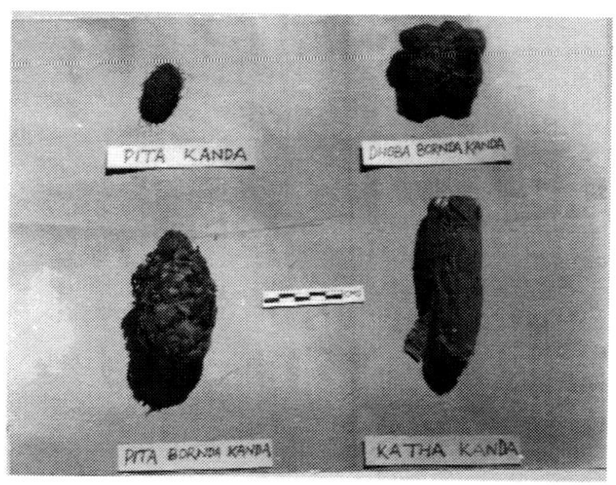

Plate 6.6: Tubers and roots used by the locals

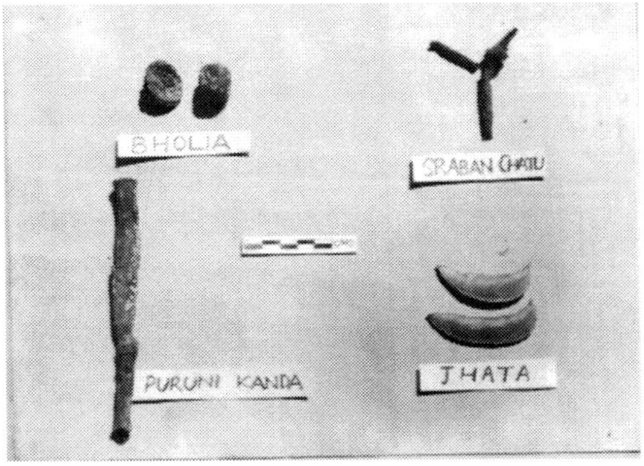

Plate 6.7: Plant resources used by the locals

Plate 6.8: Kanteikoli, a kind of berry

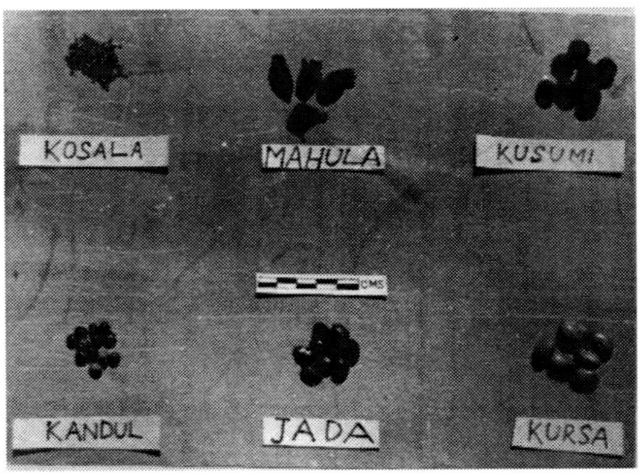

Plate 6.9: Varieties of oil seeds

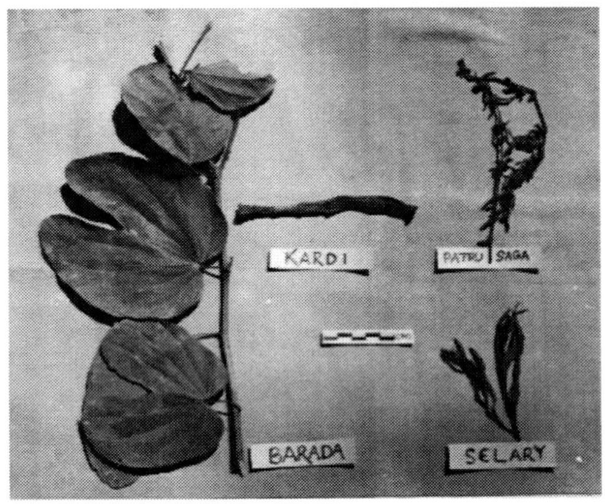

Plate 6.10: Different parts of edible plants

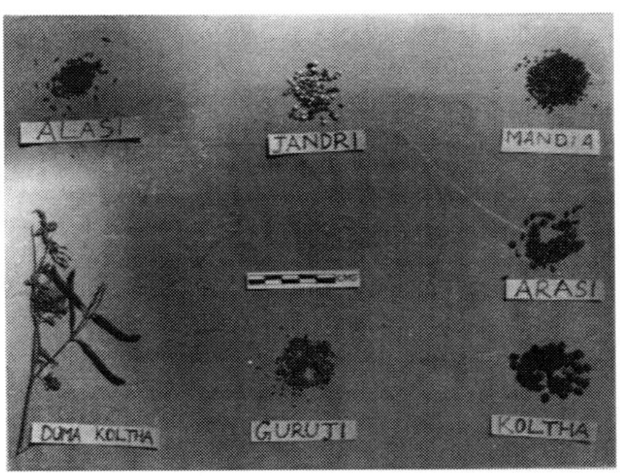

Plate 6.11: Plant resources used by the locals

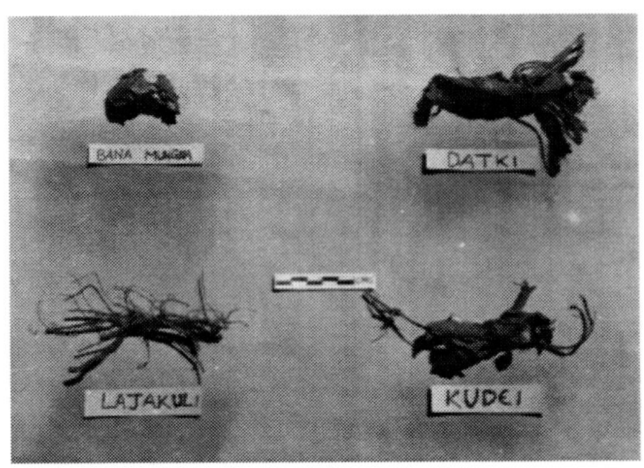

Plate 6.12: Plant resources for medicinal use by the locals

Flowers, fruits and berries

1. *Barada:* The flowers and seeds are cooked as vegetable. Sometimes the tender leaves are also used for vegetable.
2. *Bholia:* The ripe fruit is eaten. Occasionally the fruit is roasted and eaten. The nut is roasted and the hard cover is removed and eaten.
3. *Ambada:* Both unripe and ripe fruit is eaten. The unripe one is used for making chutney and pickle. The unripe fruit is cut into small pieces and dried and stored for consumption during the off season. The ripe fruit is eaten raw, but in rare cases after roasting. It is sour in taste.
4. *Kendu:* It is found very widely and has great value during scarcity of food. The tribal depend for days together on this fruit. It is a yellowish, sweet fruit, eaten when ripe. The leaves are sold in the market, for making bidis.
5. *Tala:* The tender fruit is eaten after removing the brownish skin. And the pulp of the fruit is eaten after roasting the ripe fruit. The juice is used as an intoxicating drink, collected from the tree trunk.
6. *Bela:* Ripe fruit is eaten directly, but tender one is eaten after roasting or boiling.
7. *Amba:* Both unripe and ripe fruit is eaten raw. The unripe one is used for making chutney and pickle. The unripe fruit is out into pieces and stored after sun drying. The ripe fruit juice is dried and made into small thin cake and kept for consumption during off season. The kernel is dried and powdered and used as flour to make roti.
8. *Amla:* The fruit is eaten raw and rarely after roasting. Chutney and pickles are made out of the fruit.
9. *Tentuli:* Both ripe and unripe fruit is eaten. The ripe fruit is dried and stored. The fruit is sour in taste. Tribal's use it as vegetable. Chutney is made out of unripe fruit. The seed are fried and powdered and used as flour.
10. *Waou:* The raw fruit is cooked with turmeric powder, chilli and salt. The slices fruit are dried and stored. It is sourish in taste. Pickles are made out of this.
11. *Panasa:* The unripe and ripe fruit is eaten. The unripe one is cooked as vegetable. The seeds are also cooked as curry or are roasted and eaten. Therefore the dry seed are stored for future use.
12. *Karamanga:* It is sour in taste in ripe stage. When it is ripe it is slightly sweet in taste. The ripe one is eaten raw and the unripe fruit is made into chutney and pickle. The dried fruit is store for future use.
13. *Lewa:* The ripe fruit is eaten. It is sweet in taste.

14. *Jamokoli:* Only the ripe fruit is eaten. The tender leaves and fruits are used as medicine to stop loose motions.
15. *Kanteikoli:* Ripe fruit is eaten.
16. *Barakoli:* The fruit is eaten both ripe and unripe. Ripe fruit is stored after sun drying for future consumption.
17. *Khajurikoli and Bhuin Khajourikoli:* Ripe fruit is eaten raw but the unripe fruit is boiled and eaten. The leaves are used for mat making and used as straw for roof thatching. The khajourikoli differ from Bhuin khajurikoli in size only. The earlier is bigger than the latter.
18. *Kujiborandakoli:* Ripe fruit is eaten as it is.
19. *Kantakoli:* Ripe fruit is eaten. It is sour in taste.
20. *Charkoli:* The ripe fruit is eaten as it is.
21. *Dimbiri:* Ripe fruit is eaten. It is sweet in taste.
22. *Singhada:* The inner white soft part of the fruit is eaten after peeling the thick dark green skin or the fruits are boiled and peeled, then eaten. After boiling it is easy to peel the skin. After peeling the raw fruit get dried and powdered and made into cake.
23. *Baunsagaja:* Baunsagaja (karadi) is a bamboo shoot. It is sliced into thin pieces and cooked with salt, turmeric powder and tamarind and eaten as curry.
24. *Mahula:* The flower of Mahula tree is one of the most important edible forest products. Cake are prepared out of this flower and at times cooked as curry. Liquor is also distilled from the flowers. The flowers are collected drying. The oil extracted from the seed is used in lamp.
25. *Salapa:* A strong intoxicating drink is extracted from this tree. The new stem carrying the flowers is cut, leaving one foot from the main trunk and an earthen pot is fixed ner the cut end, as a result the juice is collcted in the pot. It takes 4 to 6 hours to get 1.5 liters to 2.0 liters of juice in the beginning but slowly the amount of juice decreases. The same cutting gives juice for 20 to 30 days.

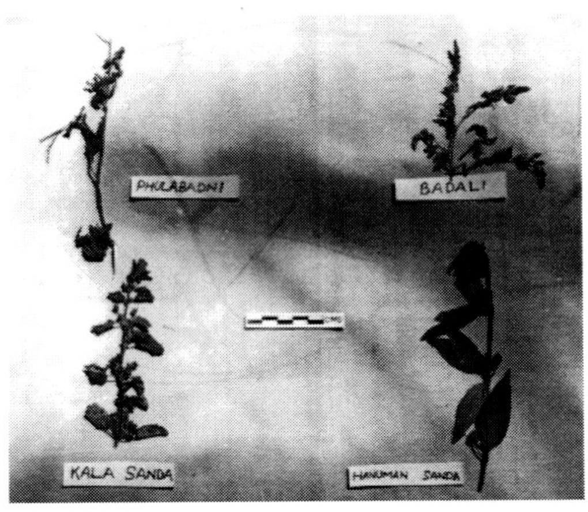

Plate 6.13: Leaves for medicinal use

Leaves

Leaves are eaten as vegetable, prepared separately or mixed with other vegetables. But occasionally the leaves are cooked with rice. When the rice is

Plate 6.14: Leaves for medicinal use

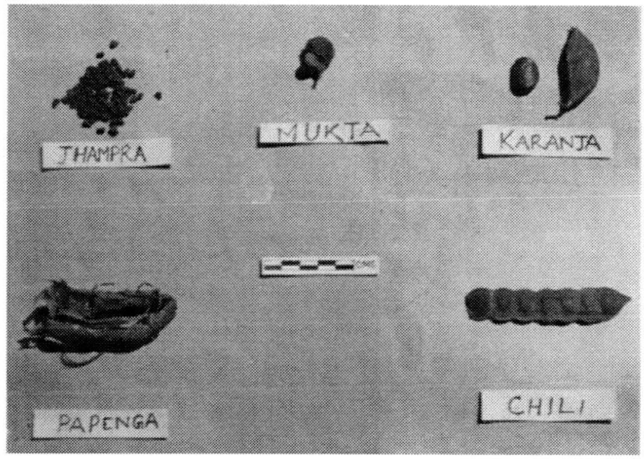

Plate 6.15: Plants resources used for varius purposes like colouring, cleaning hair, extraction of oil

cooked the salt is added and eaten. It is known as *peja*. Sometime tamarind and chilly powder are added for better taste.

Mushrooms

Mushrooms are abundant in the rainy season. They grow after a shower of rain. These are roasted with salt and turmeric powder and eaten. Rarely, these are cooked with other vegetables.

Seeds and Grains

The seeds are grouped into three categories as oil seeds for cooking, oil seeds for lamp and seeds cooked as main food or diet. The seeds of *karanja, mahula, kusumi, hursa* and *jada* are slightly roasted and ground then squeezed by a locally made fibre sac to extract oil. The sac is known as *kola* (Plate 6.16). This oil is used in lamps. The oil extracted from *alsai* and *jada* is used for cooking. The seeds of *arasi, jandri, guruji, mandia, kolath* and *kandula* are cooked like rice with a lot of water. This is the main food of the Gadaba as well as most of the local tribes. This food is known as *peja*. The seeds of *jhata* and *kandula* are cooked as curry. Except *jhata* all other seeds are cultivated on the hill slopes or on top of hills (occasionally) by shifting cultivation or terrace cultivation. A variety of containers are made of natural products such as leaves etc. (Plate 6.17 and 6.18)

Plate 6.16: Kola, a sac used for oil extraction

Plate 6.17: Leaf basket

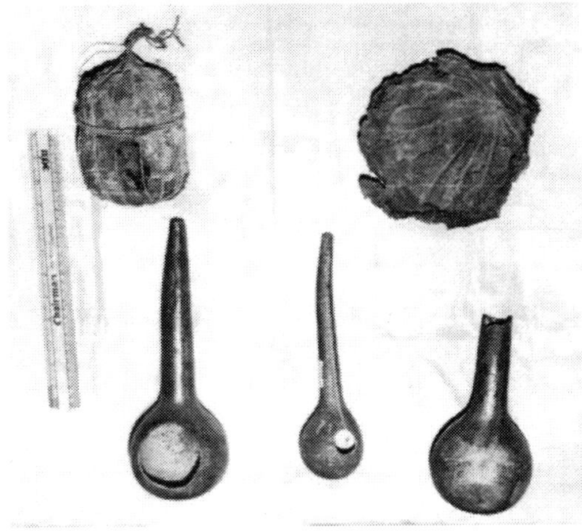

Plate 6.18: Leaf container for tobacco, leaf plate, gourd spoon and container

b) For Medicinal Use

Medicinal plants and herbs, collected, are of high importance in the day-to-day life of tribals. A few important medicinal plants are described in detail below.

1. *Banamuninsa:* The juice of the bark is put in the nose of the patient to get relief from headache.
2. *Bajarmali:* To get relief from eye pain, the juice of the leaves is applied to the outer part of the eye.
3. *Hanumansanda, Kamunisanda, and Kalasanda:* The leaves of these shrubs are ground and then mixed with water, and applied on the body of the patient to get relief from fever.
4. *Phulabadini and Sabitrisanda:* The flowers of phulabadini and the leaves of sabitrisand with turmeric powder are made into a paste with little water, then it is given to pregnant women for easy delivery.
5. *Dhatki:* The flowers are boiled in water, after it is cooled, the water is given to cure fever.
6. *Kantamalali:* The tender leaves are boiled with water. After cooling, the water is mixed with honey and given to cure fever.
7. *Sargi:* The seeds are boiled in water and the water is given to cure dysentery. Pitabada ripe fruits are given to cure dysentery.
8. *Neema and Haladi:* The paste of Neema leaves is mixed with turmeric powder and applied over the body of a small pox patient to avoid itching feeling and to cause the sores to dry easily. The same paste is also eaten and externally used to cure certain skin diseases, like scabies etc.

9. *Kumi:* The juice of the bark is given to cure blood dysentery.
10. *Badali:* A few drops of the juice of tender leaves are put into the eye to get relief from eye pain.
11. *Matikanda:* To stop bleeding from nose, a few drops of juice of the leaves are put into the nose.
12. *Papenga:* The paste of the bark is externally applied on boils for healing.
13. *Kudai:* The juice of the bark is applied on tooth for relief in toothache.
14. *Lajakuli:* The paste of the leaves is eaten to cure fever.
15. *Bahada:* The fruit is boiled in water, the extracted juice (water) is used to obtain cure in dysentery.
16. *Arakha:* A few drops of Arakha juice is mixed with 25 gm. Of Guda (Jaggery) and 5 gm. of Hengu and Til given to pregnant women of up to 5 months for easy abortion.
17. *Balakuinri:* To get sufficient milk for child, mother takes a paste made out of these leaves and a kind of fish, locally known as pita machha, roasted in fire.
18. *Dumakolath:* The paste of the root is mixed with castor oil then given to get cure from dysentery.
19. *Malckanda:* The paste of the leaves is eaten to get relief from chest pain.
20. *Chili:* The paste of the leaves is mixed with raw milk and sugar and then taken to get relief from headache.
21. *Tulasi and Duba:* The leaves are ground together with water, then the paste is given to cure fever.
22. *Chilagaruda:* The leaves of chilagaruda with ginger are ground with water, then the paste is take to get relief from cough.
23. *Karanja:* The extracted oil from seeds is used to get cure from skin diseases.

Miscellaneous

House Construction

Forets supply enough timber and thatching grass for house construction. *Baunsa, sala, kurua, badhan, kani* are the trees which supply timber, used for frame of the house and the grasses like *benaghasa, sabaighana* and the *khajuri* leaves are used for roofing. The bank of *siali* creeper is used as rope in house construction. Frequently they sell these wood as firewood to get an income.

Other Purposes

The wood from *mahula, kurchi, kelikadamba* is used for making combs. The fibre of *nidli* is used to decorate combs. Chilli seeds are used for washing. The Jhampra seeds are used for colouring. The seeds give red colour like vermilion. At present the tribals collect the *jhampra* seed from the forest and sell it in market.

Fishing

Fishing is an important activity for Gadabas as they live near hill streams, ponds, and rivers (Plate 6.19 amd 6.20). Fish plays an important role on all occasions of their life. After the disposal of the dead, Gadabas go to the stream, take a bath, catch fish, cook it and leave the cooked fish near to place of cremation, to satisfy the soul. In the marriage and birth ceremony there has to be a fish dish. Dry fish is used as barter for commodities. The Gadaba have intimate knowledge of habits and varieties of fish available in nearby area. The locally available fishes are given in Table 6.2.

Fishing is mainly a male activity. But there is no restriction on females joining the males in fishing. Though it is also done in group, individual fishing is very common. Group fishing is done by small nets, hooks and traps. The main season for fishing is the summer, when the water is less in ponds or pools. Secondly, the Gadabas do not have such work during this period. Scarcity of food-grains also indirectly forces them to go for fishing.

Fishing implements

The important fishing implements are (a) angling rod, (b) traps (without valve, with valve, with net), (c) nets, (d) bow and arrow, (e) poison and (f) container for collecting fishes.

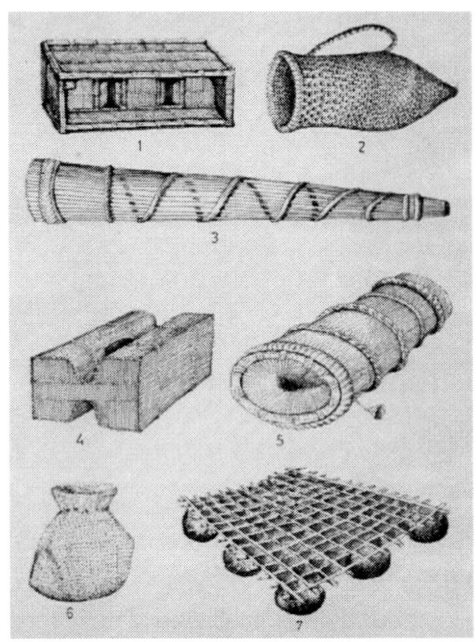

Fig. 6.3: Fish traps

a) Fishing by angling rod

This is the most commonly practiced with easy technique. The angling rod constitutes a long bamboo of 1 to 1.5 m, with a string of two to three meter, tied to one end of the rod. To the other end of the string is tied an iron hook and at some point on the string is tied a float. For catching fish, a piece of earthworm is fixed to the hook and the string is thrown into the water. When the fish attracted by the earthworm gets caught on the hook, the float starts sinking; line the angler then retrieves the fish.

Table 6.2: Various types of fishes

Sl. No.	*Local Name*	*Scientific Name*
1	Dandakiri	*Esomus danricus*
2	Sarana	*Puntius sarana*
3	Jeela	*Rasbora daniconius*
4	Rang Chandi	*Ambassis ranga*
5	Jalla	*Oxygaster bacaila*
6	Gundi	*Ambassis nama*
7	Kujee kerandi	*Puntius chola*
8	Pita kerandi	*Puntusophara*
9	Balia	*Wallago attu*
10	Magur	*Clarias batrachus*
11	Seula	*Ophicephalus striatus*
12	Singli	*Heteropneustes fossilis*
13	Phali	*Notopterus notopterus*
14	Rohi	*Labeo rohita*
15	Bhakur	*Caltor buchanani*
16	Chilala	*Notopterus chitala*
17	Adi	*Mystus seenghala*
18	Kamtia	*Mystus cavasius*
19	Mahurali	*Amblygaster sirm*
20	Chenga	*Ophicephalus gachua*
21	Kevandi	*Puntius chola*
22	Sala	*Ophicephalus marulius*
23	Bodari	*Nandus nandus*
24	Kocliea	*Amphipnous cuchia*
25	Adisa	*Ophiocephalus lata*
26	Kau	*Anabas testudineus*
27	Jaila	*Pangasius pangasius*
28	Chingudi	*Penaeus indicus*
29	Pobata	*Ompok bimaculatus*

b) Fishing with trap (Fig. 6.3)

Trap without valve

1. *Tati:* This is made out of bamboo strips and fibre of *sargi* creeper and looks like a mat. The approximate length is about 2 m and breadth is 1 to 1.5 m. Two people are required for fishing with a Tati. Fishing with this trap is possible in the hill streams only. The Tati is kept in flowing water on two boulders on either side in such a way that it forms an angle of less than 30° with the surface of the stream. Two persons hold the two higher ends of the Tati, the flowing water gets filtered through it and the fish gets trapped on the Tati. These are collected and carried away in a bamboo container called Tati. Medium to small sized fishes fall a prey in this method.
2. *Pohals:* This is a conical shaped bottomless trap, and of thin bamboo strips. It is used for fishing in shallow still water. The fisherman stands in water holding the trap and whenever a fish is sighted he puts the trap on the fish and collects it with his hand through the opening at the top.
3. *Khaichi:* It is an elongated funnel-shaped trap, made of bamboo staves with one end closed. This is kept in a longitudinal position in running water against the current. The fish which enter the trap along the stream of water get caught at the closed end and the water drains out.

Trap with valve

1. *Dandar:* This is a tubular trap, made of bamboo staves, with a valve in the centre through which fish can enter but cannot come out. The length of the trap varies from 12 cm to 20 cm. This trap is used for catching small fish in the narrow hill streams, when the water current is very slow. Generally it is used by grown up children.
2. *Tandra:* It is rectangular in shape and is made of split bamboo. These are of varying sizes. The number of valves varies from one to four (depending upon the size of the trap). The trap is kept, with the open end of its valve against the current of the water. Therefore the fish that move along the water current into the trap through the valves get caught in the trap. With a time interval of an hour or two, the fisherman removes the trap and collects the fish and then fixes the trap again. This trap is helpful in catching small fishes.

Trap with net

1. *Chaukhada:* It is a semicircular bamboo frame of two spilt bamboo with a net tied to the four free ends of split bamboo. This is usually used in shallow slow running water like that of a nallah or canal and is also sometimes used in tanks and ponds for catching fish. The fisherman fixes the trap in the water and after an interval of half-an-hour to one hour he removes the trap and collects the catch of fish from the trap, and refixes the trap in the water. It this trap small to medium sized fishes are caught.

Plate 6.19: A Gadaba man catching fish with fish trap and net

Plate 6.20: A Gadaba man catching fish with net

2. *Phelans:* It has a triangular bamboo frame with a sack-like net, it is used in shallow still water. Once the fish is sighted, this is put in the water and lifted out in such a way that the fish get caught in the sack-like net. This needs such skill of manipulation.

c) *Fishing with Net*

1. *Phinga Jala:* It is a circular net with iron sinkers at the edge. It is thrown by a single man in ponds or pools on canal in such a way that before it sinks in the water, the net opens completely and the free end of the rope remains in the fisherman's hand. Then slowly the net is gathered in and the fishes caught in the net are collected.
2. *Teka Jala:* It is used in group fishing. The net is of about three to four metres in length and one and a half metres to two metres in breadth. Four persons are involved in catching fish with this net. This net is used in shallow still water. The fisherman hold the four corners of the net and get into the water, then drag the net slowly from one end of the pond or the pool to the other end. Then they collect the fish from the net.

d) *Fishing with bow and arrow*

Bow and arrow (Plate 6.21) is used for catching medium to big sized fish in shallow, still and clear water. The bow is known as *bangso* (in Gadaba language). It is made of bambo shaft of about one meter length and the string is of strong thread or fibre. The arrow is made of cane or bamboo, and is of 50 cm length. To this a small iron arrowhead is fixed. The fisher man shoots at the fish after locating it under water.

e) Fishing by using poison

In summer when the water in ponds or pools is less, the Gadabas poison the water by putting the powder of seeds of *Ponoralasla* plant. This method is very common in Didayi community also. At hour or so after putting the poison in the water the dead fish start floating on the surface of water. The fish is removed from the water.

f) Fishing by hand

This is a very simple method, practiced by villagers for fishing. They drain out the water from small ponds or water ditches and catch the fish from the muddy clay with their hands. Usually the Gadaba eat fish after cooking or roasting. The method of cooking is very simple. They boil the fish with turmeric powder, salt and chilli and eat it. They cook a part of the catch for food required immediately and preserve the rest for the future after drying them. The preservation and storage of fish are done with great care. The fish is kept in the sun or; then it is kept in baskets of leaves or bamboo, without salt or sometimes with it. Subsequently, occasional sunning is required to keep them free from worms. This dry fish is used as a medium of barter for other commodities.

Fowling

The Gadabas go to hunt birds when they have some leisure to do so. They have good knowledge about the habitat of local birds. Generally they hunt birds for their own consumption; rarely do they sell the birds. They roast the bird and eat it with chilli and salt, but sometime they prepare a curry. The birds most frequently hunted by the Gadabas are given in Table 6.3.

Table 6.3: Birds hunted by Gadabas

Sl. No.	*Local Name*	*Scientific Name*
1	Badudi	*Pteropus medius*
2	Para	*Columba intermedia*
3	Bana Kukuda	*Gallus ferruginous*
4	Harada Chadhei	*Crocopus phoenicopterus*
5	Baga	*Bubulcus coromandus*
6	Dahuk	*Amaurornis phoenicurus*
7	Bani	*Acridotheres tristis*
8	Haladi basanta	*Gymnopus asiatica*
9	Hansa	–
10	Kapata	–
11	Gunduri	–

The important methods of bird catching are: (a) by applying a sticky juice to bamboo strips, (b) with bow and arrow, (c) with a net, and (d) by laying snares.

By using sticky sticks

Split bamboo strips, 30 to 40 cm long, are coated with natural gum (Ficus juice) up to ¾ of the stick. About 15 to 20 of these sticks are kept separately in a vertical position, keeping the sticky part up, near the bank of a pond, water ditch or swampy area. When the bird sits on a stick, its feathers get struck and it cannot fly. The Gadaba in wait catches the bird. Gadabas carry these gummy sticks in a bamboo container known as '*Chapanala*'.

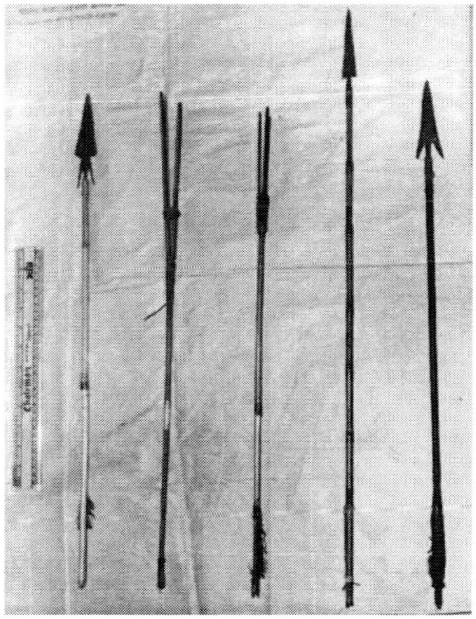

Plate 6.21: Arrows with iron tip and splitted bamboo

With bow and arrow

The bow is made of spilt bamboo about one metre long and tied with a bow string at both ends. The arrow (Plate 6.21) are of two types: (i) arrow shaft with a wooden or bamboo bolt at the hitting end and (ii) arrow with two or three pointed bamboo strips tied at the hitting end. Gadaba usually shoot *Columba intermedia, Crocopus phoenicopterus, Bubulcus coromandus, Bubulcus coromandus* birds with their arrows, with bow and clay beads or small stone pebbles. The size of bow is the same as that described in the preceding para but the strings are of two pieces, centrally woven forming a net of 3 cm × 1 cm. Clay beads or small rounded pebbles are used in hitting the birds.

3) With a net

The net is locally known as *gunduri net.* This particular type of net is meant for catching 'Gunduri' bird only. The net is square in form; framed with bamboo at edges and also crosswise. There is an opening of 0.5 m diameter at the centre of the net. A man carries the net on his shoulder to the place where the birds (Gunduri) are generally available in large numbers, then slowly the person moves near them and puts the net over them. As the birds (Gunduri) move in large numbers it is easy to get a few by this process.

4) By laying snares

a) *Upadi:* The snare (Plate 6.22) is a funnel-shaped trap made of bamboo staves with two rows of rectangular openings guarded with a noose made of the buffalo or cattle tail. This is the most common type of snare used by the Gadabas. The bird catcher fixes the snare near swampy area and keeps a small insect (grasshopper) tied at the centre of the trap. Long-necked birds like the crane try to get the insect through the nooses and get trapped in the noose.

b) *Chadheiphasa:* This kind of snare (Plate 6.23) consists of several rectangular frames, made of bamboo staves with 4 to 5 nooses tied at the gaping openings of each rectangular frame. These nooses are made out of the hair of buffalo or cattle-tail. This snare is arranged near bushes with some food grain around. As the birds move about in search of the grain, they get caught in these nooses.

Hunting

Hunting has become a very irregular feature in Gadaba economy because of the scarcity of game in the adjoining area. The main cause of this is deforestation, by shifting cultivation and fire-wood collection. So hunting is becoming a cultural activity rather than an economic activity of the Gadabas. On some particular day (*chaitaparba*) all the male members of the village go for hunting in a group and the women go for collecting money from non-Gadaba villages. After the male members return from the hunting expedition all the villages join together and enjoy the day.

But still, whenever the Gadaba get time, particularly in summer they go for hunting to supplement a part of their economy. Only men take part in hunting. There are two types of hunting prevalent among Gadabas, i.e. individual hunting and group hunting. In individual hunting small game is generally procured. Sometimes more men than one go for small-game hunting also. The small game is easily and very frequently available in the nearby scrub jungle. Therefore small game hunting is more frequent than big game hunting.

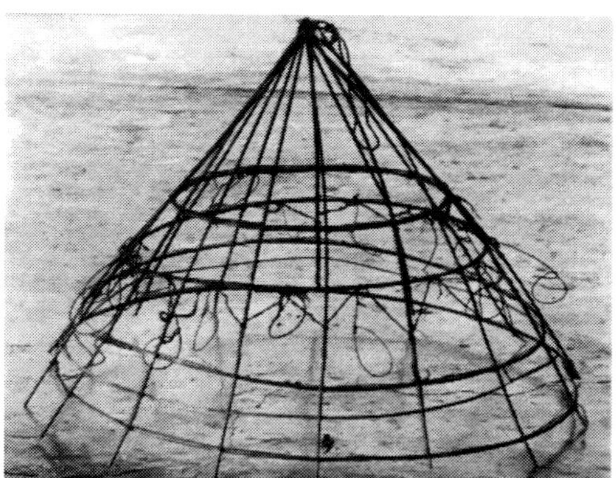

Plate 6.22: Upadi, a bird trap

Plate 6.23: Chadheiphasa, a bird trap

The small games hunted by Gadabas are Indian squirrel, Indian hare, Indian porcupine and grey mongoose. Among the big game spotted deer, samber, mouse deer, black bear, Indian fox and wild bear are hunted by Gadabas at time.

Hunting implements

The major hunting implements are knife, bow and arrow, rope, bamboo stick and traps.

Small game hunting

Small game hunting is usually done by single or two male. Children generally try to hunt rats (Plate 6.24 and Plate 6.25) and squirrel by throwing stones but very rarely get success. Rat catching is very common phenomenon in Gadaba community. If the Gadabas see the rat holes they postpone their work; and get engaged in digging those holes, till they get the rats. Sometimes they catch 7 to 8 rats and at the least 2 to 3 rats. Not only Gadabas but also other tribes, as Paraja, Gonda and Saora are fond of rat meat. Sometime they catch small rats and keep them in earthen pots by feeding grains and whenever they feel to have rat meat, they kill them. On special occasions rat meat is fried. Rats are eaten after roasting or by making curry.

Hare is commonly hunted by using nets, locally the net is known as '*Khada jala*'. Two to three people try to locate the area of hunting, than they fix the net in a predetermined spot. After driving the animal out of the surrounding scrub jungle they chase it towards the net in a semicircular form and finally hare is caught in the net.

Big game hunting

In recent years big hunting has become very rare. This is because it is difficult to get any big animals in the nearby forest. Secondly there is official ban on killing of several animals. Among the big game the more common animals are spotted deer, mouse deer, samber and wild bear.

Plate 6.24: Two Gadaba men catching rats

Plate 6.25: A Gadaba boy with three rats

Before going for hunting Gadabas pray to forest deity for the success of their expedition. Generally 20 to 30 persons participate in a single hunting expedition. Again they form sub groups of 8 to 10 persons. In most of the hunting expedition they take two hunting dogs, bow and arrow, and bamboo sticks with them. Only adults join in this type of expedition. They have very good idea about animals' habitat of the adjoining area. They can predict the particular animal movement in a particular area by examining the foot prints and dung of animal. Then by the help of dogs, bow and arrow and fire they kill the animal. They cut the animal by knives and part of it is roasted in the fire and eaten in the forest. Then the meat is shared among the participants in equal amount.

Table 6.4: List of Tubers, Roots, Flowers, Fruits, Berries, Leaves, and Mushrooms

Sl. No.	*Local Name*	*Botanical Name*	*Habitat*	*Habit*	*Season of availability*
			Tubers and Roots		
1	Kesari Kanda	–	Near water resources	Shrub	December to March
2	Pita Kanda	*Dioscorea species*	Foot of the hills	Creeper	October to December
3	Katha Kanda	*Manihot usitatissimum*	Foot of the hills	Shrub	October to December
4	Keu Kanda	–	,,	Shrub	September to November
5	Simili Kanda	–	,,	Shrub	January to March
6	Kukudamundi Kanda	–	Aquatic	Aquatic Plant	November to March
7	Pita Boranda Kanda	–	Near water resources	Aquatic Plant	August to June
8	Puruni Kanda	–	Aquatic	Aquatic Plant	October to January
9	Sargi Kanda	–	Near water resources	Creeper	August to September
10	Bora Kanda	–	,,	Creeper	February to March
11	Dasa-Karanda	–	,,	Shrub	October to December
12	Mati Kanda	–		Creeper	November to January
13	Bera	–		Creeper	August to October
			Flowers, Fruits and Berries		
14	Barada	*Bauhinia purpurea*	Foot hills/ Plain area	Tree	March to May
15	Bholia	*Anacardium occidentale Linn.*	,,	Tree	March to May

16	Ambada	*Spondias species*	,,	Tree	July to September
17	Tandu	*Diospyros melanoxylon*	,,	Tree	May to April
18	Tala	*Borassus flabelliformis*	Plain area	Tree	April to June
19	Bela	*Aegle marmelos*	,,	Tree	April to June
20	Amba	*Mangifera indica*	Hills & Plains	Tree	March to July
21	Amla	*Phyllanthus emblica*	,,	Tree	January to March
22	Tentuli	*Tamarindus indica*	,,	Tree	October to April
23	Maou	*Dillonais indica Linn.*	Plains	Tree	—
24	Panasa	*Artocarpus integrifolia*	Foot hills & plains	Tree	March to June
25	Karamanga	*Averrhoa carambola*	Plain land	Tree	April to June
26	Jamakoli	*Eugenia jambolana*	Foot hills & plains	Tree	June To July
27	Sal	*Shorea robusta*	Hills & plains	Tree	March to April
28	Kantsikoli	*Caesalpinia sepiaria*	Foot hills	Shrub	November to January
29	Barakoli	*Ziziphus jujuba*	Foot hills	Tree	December to March
30	Khajurikoli	*Phoenix sylvestris*	Plain area	Tree	June to July
31	Bhuin Khajuri	*Phoenix acaulis*	Foot hills	Shrub	May to June
32	Gujibaranda koli	—	Hill slopes	Shrub	May to June
33	Leva	*Annona squamosa*	Plain land	Tree	November to December
34	Kanta koli	*Ziziphus rugosa.*	Foot hills	Shrub	April to June
35	Dimbiri	*Ficus glomerata*	Plain land	Tree	January to June
36	Singhada	*Trapa bispinosa*	Aquatic	Aquatic plant	March to June
37	Charkoli	—	Foot hills	Tree	March to May
38	Kahula	*Bassia latifolia*	Plain land/Foot hills	Tree	March to April
39	Baunsagaja	*Bambusa arundinacea*	,,	Tree	August to September
40	Salpa	*Caryota urens*	,,	Tree	Throughout the year

41	Barada	*Bauhinia purpurea*	Plain area	Tree	Throughout the year
42	Sunusunis	*Marsilea quadrifolia*	Aquatic	Aquatic plant	Throughout the year
43	Chakunda	*Cassia tora*	Plain area	Shrub	Throughout the year
44	Muringa	*Moringa oleifera*	Plain area	Tree	Throughout the year
45	Khadasnga	*Amaranthus gangeticus*	Plain area	Shrub	Throughout the year
46	Sirili	—	Plain area	Shrub	Throughout the year
47	Salary	—	Plain area	Shrub	Throughout the year
48	Patru	*Alternanthera sessilis*	Near water resources	Creeper	Throughout the year
49	Kantalcutia	*Amaranthus spinosus*	Plain area	Shrub	Throughout the year
50	Leutia	*Amaranthus tenuifolius*	Plain area	Shrub	Throughout the year
51	Kalamsag	*Ipomoea aquatica*	Aquatic	Aquatic plant	Throughout the year
52	Neem	*Azadirachta indica*	Hills/plains	Tree	March to April
53	Kukta	*Sapindus trifoliatus*	Foot hills	Creeper	—
54	Karanj	*Pongamia glabra*	Foot hills plain land	Tree	March to June
55	Jhata	*Dolichos lablab*	Plain area	Creeper	January to February
56	Kandula	—	Foot hills	Shrub	—
57	Jandri	*Sorghum bicolor*	,,	Shrub	December to January
58	Jada	*Ricinus communis*	Foot hills/Plain area	Shrub	—
59	Kolath	*Dolichos biflorus*	,,	Shrub	—
60	Arsi	*Linum usitatissimum*	Foot hills	Shrub	April to May
61	Alasi	*Guizotia abyssinica*	,,	Shrub	December to January
62	Mansia	*Eleusine coracana*	,,	Shrub	—
63	Guruji	*Setaria species*	,,	Shrub	November to December
64	Kuasumi	—	,,	Shrub	—
65	Kosala	—	,,	Shrub	—
Mushrooms					
66	Palachhatu	—	On straw	Mushroom	July to September

67	Balichhatu	—	Sandy land	,,	,,
68	Sargichhatu	—	On the trunk or root of Sargi tree	,,	,,
69	Badachhatu	—	Plain land	,,	,,
70	Sravanachhatu	—	Plain land	,,	,,
71	Baunsachhatu	—	On bamboo	,,	,,
			Medicinal plants		
72	Banamuninga	*Moringa species*	Hilly forested area	Tree	Throughout the year
73	Sajeramali	*Sida rhombifolia*	,,	Tree	Throughout the year
74	Ranusansanda	*Lantana indica*	,,	Shrub	Throughout the year
75	Keusanda	*Hyptis suaveolens*	,,	Shrub	Throughout the year
76	Phulabadini	*Sida acuta*	,,	Shrub	Throughout the year
77	Kamusisanda	*Chenopodium album*	,,	Shrub	Throughout the year
78	Dhatki	*Woodfordia fruticosa*	,,	Shrub	December to January
79	Kantamalati	*Barleria prionitis*	,,	Shrub	Throughout the year
80	Sargi	—	,,	—	Throughout the year
81	Neema	—	,,	—	Throughout the year
82	Patagiril	—	,,	Tree	July to March
83	Kumi	—	,,	Tree	July to March
84	Badali	—	,,	Creeper	July to March
85	Matikanda	—	,,	Creeper	July to March
86	Papenga	—	,,	Tree	July to March
87	Kudei	—	,,	Tree	July to March
88	Lajakuli	*Mimosa pudica*	Hilly/plain area	Creeper	July to March
89	Bahada	*Terminalia Bellerica*	,,	Tree	November to February
90	Arakha	—	,,	Shrub	Throughout the year
91	Balakuainri	—	Hilly forested area	Creeper	Throughout the year
92	Dumakolath	—	Hilly slopes	Shrub	March to April
93	Malakanda	—	Hilly forested area	Creeper	July to December

94	Chili	—	Plains/Hills	Creeper	November to December
95	Tulasi	—	Plain	Shrub	Throughout the year
96	Chilagaruda	—	Aquatic	Aquatic	September to February
97	Haladi	—	Hilly slopes/plain	Shrub	—
98	Sabitrisanta	—	Hilly forested area	Creeper	July to March
99	Duba	—	Plains/Hills	Grass	July to March
100	Karanja	—	Hilly forested area	Tree	Throughout the year
101	Baunsa		Hilly slopes/Hills	Tree	Throughout the year
102	Sala	*Shorea robusta*	,,	Tree	Throughout the year
103	Kurua	—	,,	Tree	Throughout the year
104	Bandhan	*Ougeinia oojeinensis*	,,	Tree	Throughout the year
105	Kasi	*Bridelia retusa*	,,	Tree	Throughout the year
106	Benaghass	—	Forested area and Near water resources	Grass	November to March
107	Sabaighass				
108	Siali	*Bauhinia vahlii*	Hilly forested area	Creeper	Throughout the year
109	Kurchi	*Holarrhena antidysenterica*	,,	Tree	Throughout the year
110	Kelikadamba	*Adina cordifolia*	,,	Tree	Throughout the year
111	Jhampra	—	,,	Tree	November to December

Chapter 7

Summary and Conclusion

In the preceding pages the detail analysis of present environment of the study area, the material culture of the two stages of lithic industries and the ethnography of the local tribes in general and Gadaba in particular has been presented to establish: (a) the evidence of human habitation from the pre-historic times in Indravati basin, (b) the typo-technological evaluation of the lithic industries of the area and (c) the visualisation of the probable way of life of prehistoric man by drawing ethnographic analogies. In the following pages an attempt has been made to summaries these analyses to bring out the culture and chronology of the people in sharp focus.

The Indravati basin of undivided Koraput district lies between 19°00' and 19°40' N latitude and 82°1' and 83°16' E latitude and covers an area of about 2,400 sq km. The river Indravati is the second largest river of Koraput district. It originates near the village Madriguda in Kalahandi district. It flows through Kashipur, Nawrangpur and Kotpad tahsils of Koraput district and then enters in Baster district to join the Godaveri. The main tributaries of the river are Fodaguda nullah, Muran nullah, Teligiri nullah and Bhaskel.

The average annual rainfall of the district is 1,522 mm and the main annual temperature is 17.8° C. The vegetation of the district is of northern tropical moist deciduous and northern dry deciduous type the present day flora and fauna of the district suggested the favourable environment for the human settlements in the past as it is in the present.

Till 1975, the Indravati basin was not explored systematically by prehistorian. The archaeological findings made till then belong to the historical period except a solitary Neolithic celt and a few Mesolithic artifacts from Jeypore tahsil of the district. The intensive explorations carried out by the present author in a small geographical area (2,400 sq km) have brought to light 17 Upper Palaeolithic and 85 Mesolithic sites. The evidence of the Upper Palaeolithic culture has come to light for the first time from the study area and also from the Odisha as a whole.

The Upper Palaeolithic sites are located in varied geographical settings. These are found near the river banks, on the plain land and the elevated rocky waste land. However, the main concentration of the sites is along the river Indravati and its main tributary Bhaskel. These are all open air sites. The sites are located within 1 to 7 km distance from the main river course. The artifacts are largely made on the yellowish chert which is available right on the site or within a distance of 1 to 2 km.

There is no marked difference among the artifacts from 17 Upper Palaeolithic sites, even though they are located in different geographical settings. They represent a single homogenous industry. The total number of artifacts is 1,282 of which 129 (10.06%) are shaped artifacts and 1,153 (89.94%) simple artifacts, the ratio being 1:9. The industry is based on blade technology. The shaped artifacts comprise side scrapers (21.70%), notches (14.28%), burins (4.65%), borers (2.33%), denticulates (2.33%), knives (1.55%), backed micro-blades (0.77%) and micro-blade crescents (3.10%). The simple artifact group is represented by cores (11.88%), flakes (20.55%) chips (42.58%) and blades (14.57%).

The blades are generally irregular or parallel. Some of them have retained the damage mark on the edge. The blades with plain platform (44.07%) and tiny prominent bulb suggest the application of indirect percussion or punch technique. Nearly 60% of the blades fall within the length range of 41 to 60 mm and 43% fall within the breadth range of 12 to 17 mm and 50% fall within the thickness range of 4 to 9 mm. Majority of the blades are triangular in cross-section. Four blades retain complete cortex on the dorsal surface with a single ridge. It shows that the natural ridge has been exploited for the removal of blades. Twenty blades possess single blade scar with cortex, having a single ridge suggesting a second round of blades removal. Further, 88 blades have two blade scars with a single mid-ridge suggestive of third round of the removal of blade. Thirty nine blades with 3 scars having trapezoidal cross-section suggest the fourth round of the removal of blades. The small percentage of blade cores (1.17%) can be explained by the further use of blade core for the removal of micro-blades. The micro-blade cores account for 4.33%. The Upper Palaeolithic industry is dominated by scraping artifacts among the shaped tool. The scraping tools (scraper and notches) account for 62.01% of the total collection. Of this 50% are concave and notched scraper.

Study of the functional aspects of the stone artifacts (Gould *et al.* 1979) indicates that the Upper Palaeolithic industries of the Indravati basin represent the combined activity of hunting-gathering camp and tool preparation. The absence of any datable material from the open air surface sites leaves no alternative, but to draw parallels from the other dated Upper Palaeolithic sites of India. The C-14 dates available for the different Upper Palaeolithic sites are given in Table 7.1.

The above C-14 dates suggest a date bracket of 20,000-10,000 BP for all the sites of India. Thus, the Upper Palaeolithic culture of the Indravati basin can be put somewhere in this date bracket.

Table 7.1: C-14 dates from Upper Palaeolithic sites in India

Sl. No.	*Site*	*C14 dates*	*Half life 5730 ± 40 years*
1	Patne	CRN 7200	25000 ± 200 BP
2	Inamgaon	TF 1003	21725 + 630 –585 BP
3	Inamgaon	TF 1117	19290 ± 360 BP
4	Belan Valley	TF 1245	19160 ± 330 BP
5	Asla	TF 1178	10036 ± 125 BP

The evidence for Mesolithic culture comes from 85 sites in the study area. These are located on hill top, hill slope, foot hills, elevated rocky land and plain land. Some of the sites are disturbed due to cultivation. Majority of the sites occur within 1 to 7 km distance from the rivers. Average distance between the two sites is 2.5 km and the area of the sites varies from 8 sq m to 1,250 sq m. The sites are generally located near the present day tribal settlements.

The artifactual material from 85 sites displays a general homogeneity and has been treated as a single cultural entity. Of the total sites 54 (63.52%) have yielded less than 99 artifacts, 21 (24.79%) between 100 and 199 artifacts, 7 (8.23%) between 200 and 299 artifacts and 3 sites have yielded more than 300 artifacts.

The raw material is dominated by yellowish red chert of poor quality, available in vein form at the site or within 1 to 2 km distance. The use of chalcedony, quartzite, jasper and quartz are only occasional.

The industry comprises of 8,709 artifacts of which 884 (9.69%) are shaped artifacts and 7,865 (90.31%) are simple artifacts. The shaped artifacts include 220 (26.07) microliths and 624 (73.93%) flake artifacts. On the basis of retouch on microliths, they have been classified into eight broad groups retouched blades (31.36%), truncated blades (0.91%), points (31.36%), blunted backed and truncated blades (0.91%), points (13.18%), crescents (26.81%), triangles (2.73%) and trapezes (0.45). Blunted backed blade is the dominant tool type followed by crescents. Probably these were used as composite tools, which have been depicted in microlithic rock paintings in the caves of central India.

The flake tools include side scrapers (53.84%), dejete scrapers (0.48%), notches (10.57%), end scrapers (10.19%), points (6.08%), borers (2.98%), burins (0.32%) and knives (1.44%). These occur in 4:1 ratio with micro-blade tools (microliths). Among the scraper variants side scrapers (18.10%) with convex working edge are the most common type followed by the straight (14.0%) and concave (11.0%) working edges. The functional analysis shows that for butchering, straight and convex edges are prepared while the concave edge is the result of wood working (Tainer 1979: 465). The presence of larger number of convex and straight scrapers and smaller number of concave scrapers, retouched edge artifacts and the larger number of unutilised debitage suggest that the lithic scatter might have been the site of combined activities of the tool preparation and hunting camp.

The simple artifacts and shaped artifacts ratio is 9:1. The simple artifacts comprise nine main groups such as flake cores (2.76%), blade cores (0.05%), microblade cores (14.01%), flakes (17.38%), blades (31.11%) microblades (13.17%), chips (38.99%), worked nodules (9.67%) and microburins (0.11%). The ratio between the blade core and microblade core is 1:275 and the ratio between the micro blades and microblade core is 1:1.

The blades of Mesolithic culture show some differences from that of the Upper Palaeolithic blades. The metrical values of the blades from the Mesolithic and Upper Palaeolithic cultures show that the majority of the blades from Mesolithic collection are shorter and narrower than the Upper Palaeolithic blades. However, the thickness range of the blades is nearly the same in both the industries. This shows that there has been a gradual reduction in the length and the breadth of the blades from Upper Palaeolithic to Mesolithic culture.

The trial excavation (2 × 2 m) at Girla has yieled 3,350 artifacts. In the excavation, upper 0.35 cm thick layer is the main cultural horizon. After this depth the concentration of artifacts starts decreasing and below 0.75 cm from the surface no artifacts were found. Of the total collection 10.1% are the shaped artifacts and 89.9% simple artifacts the ratio being 1:9. Among the shaped artifacts 82.54% are microliths and 17.45% flake tools. Microliths includes retouched blades, truncated blades, blunted backed blades, blunted backed and oblique retouched blades, points, crescents, triangles and trapezes. Among these, backed blades are the most dominant types.

The flake tools comprise of side scrapers, dejete scrapers, denticulates, notches, end scrapers, points, borers, burins and knives. These occur in 1:5 ratios with microblade tools (microliths). The simple artifact group represents the ratio of 9:1 with shaped tools. The simple artifacts include cores, flakes, blades, microblades, chips, worked nodules and microburins.

Of the total excavated material microblades (including simple microblades, microliths and utilised microblades) account for 1,509 (45.04%) pieces. Of these only 18.49% were used for the manufacturing of microliths and 2.38% retained the use mark. The proportion of microblades to microblade cores is 7:1. The occurrence of micro-burin shows that its preparation technique was well known to the Mesolithic people of Girla.

The limited excavation yielded 3 pieces of hammer stones, a fragment of ring stone, 2 pieces of rubber stones and 22 pieces of rubbed iron oxide. The presence of above cultural material suggests that Girla Mesolithic site was occupation site.

There is no significant difference between the excavated and surface collections in the proportions of tools, use of the type of raw material and the proportion of shaped and simple artifacts. The difference is indeed very minor. The proportion of flake artifacts is higher in surface collection where as the proportion of microliths is higher in the excavated collection.

In the excavated collection the percentage of flake cores and microblade core is low while it is higher in surface collection. Among the flake tools side scraper is the dominant type in the surface collection while the end scraper is the dominant type in the excavated collection. Knife is absent but triangles, crescents, microburins and trapezes are more in excavated material. The backed blade is the dominant type in the surface collection.

There is no significant difference in technology, typology and morphology of the artifacts in the two collections. The Mesolithic culture of the Indravati basin is a geometric form of microlithic industry. It is closer to the microlithic industry of Bhimbetka of Madhya Pradesh and the microlithic industry of Tirupati valley of Andhra Pradesh.

For dating this industry no direct evidence is available from the study area. The C-14 dates for the Mesolithic cultures from other parts of India are given in Table 7.2.

Table 7.2: C-14 dates from Mesolithic sites in India

Sl. No.	*Sites*	*C-14 dates*	*Half life 5730±40 years*
1	Bagor	TF 786	6245 ± 200 (6430 ± 200) BP
2	Bagor	TF 1007	5620 ± 125 (5783 ± 130) BP
3	Langhnaj	TF 744	3875 ± 105 (3990 ± 110) BP
4	Lekhahia	TF 419	4240 ± 110 (4367 ± 113) BP
5	Sarai-Nahar-Rai	TF 1104	10050 ± 110 (10345 ± 110) BP
6	Adamgarh	TF 120	7240 ± 125 (7450 ± 130) BP

These dates suggested that the Mesolithic culture of India can be dated between 8500 BP to 2500 BP. The absence of pottery and the crested guided ridge technique suggest that the Indravati Mesolithic culture belongs to pre-Chalcolithic geometric form of microlithic industry.

Ethnographic analyses are one of the best parameters for interpreting the archaeological evidence. The present work is confined with the evidence of the stone artifacts from the prehistoric settlements. The hunter-fisher-gatherer of prehistoric time must have depended on environmental and other natural resources for their survival. The subsistence activities must have been confined to food collection, hunting and gathering for which different types of stone artifacts might have been used. To understand the subsistence strategies of those people, a few local tribes, especially Gadabas have been studied.

The tribes inhabiting the Indravati basin are Paraja, Gadaba, Bonda, Bhatra etc. who are still practicing some sort of primitive way of life and economy. The subsistence pattern is based on shifting cultivation, hunting, fishing and gathering. These tribes represent the pockets of population who have not been affected much by the advanced group of people. For this reason the tradition in these societies continues even today.

The Gadabas, the hill tribe, live in hamlets of 20 to 30 houses generally located on the flat topped small hills, or hill slopes, on the bank of rivers and by the side of hill springs. The material possession is mainly confined to earthen pots for cooking, leaves and bamboo baskets for storing, gourd for carrying water and liquid, and leaf plates and cups for daily use. They make rain coats and caps from leaves. The cloths which Gadaba women require are made by themselves from the cotton threads and the fibres of *ankude chettu* (*Holarrhena antidysenterion*) and *badda chettu* (*Ficus glomerata*). Gadabas have good knowledge of local flora and fauna. They collect different types of roots, tubers, nuts, fruits, flowers, leaves, barks, honey and other forest products for their food, clothing and shelter as well as for medicines.

Fishing is an important activity for Gadabas as they live near ponds and rivers. They have intimate knowledge of a variety of fishes available in the pond and rivers. They have also acquired good knowledge of the habitat of the local birds and they catch then either with the help of nets or various types of traps.

At the time of scarcity of other food resources like plant foods, the food is supplemented by meat of wild animals. The small games hunted by Gadabas are Indian squirrel, Indian hare, Indian porcupine and grey mongoose. Among the big game, spotted dear, samber, black bear, fox and wild boar are hunted. Rat catching is very common among the Gadabas. Often they catch small rats and keep them in earthen pots by feeding grains and eat them (whenever they need) by roasting or making curry.

The intimate and wide knowledge of the environment and the resources around them for the survival shows that this knowledge has been passed from generation to generation in the tribal communities. These tribes represent a continuity of a long tradition and thus a good analogy for understanding the way of life of Stone Age people.

Bibliography

Acharya, P. 1969. *Studies in Orissan History, Archaeology and Archives*. Cuttack: Cuttack Student's Store

Agrawal, D.P. 1982. *The Archaeology of India*. Scandinavian Institute of Asian studies Monograph series No. 46. London: Curzon Press Ltd.

Agrawal, D.P. and S. Kusumgar. 1974. *Prehistoric Chronology and Radiocarbon dating in India*. New Delhi: Munshiram Manoharlal Publishers.

Agrawal, D.P., R.P. Dhir, R.V. Krishnamurty, V.N. Misra, S.C. Nanda, S.N. Rajaguru, G. Singh and S. Sinha. 1978. Multiples Evidence for climatic change in Rajasthan. Paper presented at the International Symposium on Arid Zone Research and Development, held at Jodhpur, Rajasthan, India, during 14–18 February 1978.

Allchin, B. 1958. Morhana Pahar: a rediscovery. *Man* 58:153-55.

Alichin, B. 1960. Central Indian Prehistory - The Carlyle collection. *Man* LX: 153-156.

Alichin, B and S. Satyanarayan. 1959. A Late Stone Age site near Kordapur Museum, A.P. *Man* LIX: 197-198.

Alichin, B., A. Goudie and Karunakara Hegde. 1978. *The Prehistory and Palaeography of the Great Indian Desert*. London: Academic Press.

Ball, V. 1876. On Stone Implements found in the tributary states of Orissa. *Proceeding of the Asiatic Soceity of Bengal* 12: 122-23.

Banerji, R.D. 1930. *History of Orissa from the earliest times to the British period*: Vol. I. Calcutta: R. Chatterjee.

Bordes, F. 1961. *Typologie du Paléolithique ancien et moyen*. Bordeaux: Impr. Delmas.

Bordes, F. 1968. *Paleolithique dans le monde (The Old Stone Age)*. Translated from the French by J.B. Andersan. London: Weidenfeld & Nicolson and New York: McGraw Hill Book Company.

Bordes, F. and D.B Crabtree. 1969. The Corbieve blade technique and other experiments. *Tobiwa* 12(2): 1-21.

Bordes, F. and Denise de Sonneville-Bordes. 1970. The Significance of Variability in Palaeolithic assemblages. *World Archaeology* 2(1): 61-73.

Bose, N.K. and D. Sen. 1948. *Excavation in Mayurbhanj*. Calcutta: Calcutta University Press.

Bose, N.K., D. Sen and G.S. Ray. 1958. Geology and Cultural Evidences of the Stone Age in Mayurbhanj. *Man in India* 38(1): 49-55.

Brown, J.A 1889. On some small highly specialized forms of stone implements, found in Asia, North Africa and Europe. *Journal of the Royal Anthropological Institute of Great Britain and Ireland* XVIII: 134-139.

Brown, J.A. 1893. On the continuity of the Palaeolithic and Neolithic Period. *Journal of the Royal Anthropological Institute of Great Britain and Ireland* XXXI: 66-98.

Burkitt, M.C. 1929. *Our Early Ancestors: An Introductory Study of Mesolithic, Neolithic and Copper Age Cultures in Europe and Adjacent Regions*. Cambridge: Cambridge University Press.

Census of India, 1961. Vol. XII, Part IXB. Orissa: Orissa Administrative Atlas.

Clark, G. 1967. *The Stone Age Hunters*. London: Thames and Hudson.

Clark, J.D. 1954. *The Prehistory of Africa*. New York: Praeger.

Clark, J.D. 1959. *Prehistory of Southern Africa*. Harmondsworth: Penguin Books.

Clark, J.G.D. 1932. *Mesolithic Age in Britain*. Cambridge: Cambridge University Press.

Clark, J.G.D. 1936. *The Mesolithic Settlement of Northern Europe*. Cambridge: Cambridge University Press.

Clark, J.G.D. 1954. *Excavations at Starr Carr: Early Mesolithic site at Seamer near Scar Borough, Yorkshire*. Cambridge: Cambridge University Press.

Clark, J.G.D. 1958. Blade and Trapezes Industry of European Stone Age. *Proceedings of the Prehistoric Society* XXIV: 24-42.

Clark, J.G.D. 1963. *World Prehistory: An Outline*. Cambridge: Cambridge University Press.

Clark, J.G.D. 1965. *Archaeology and Society*. London: Metheun.

Clark, J.G.D. 1967. *Stone Age Hunters*. London: Thames & Hudson.

Clark, J.G.D. 1969. *World Prehistory: New Outline*. Cambridge: Cambridge University Press.

Clark, J.G.D. 1970. *Aspects of Prehistory*. Berkeley: University of California Press.

Collins, D. 1970. Stone artifact, analysis and the recognition of cultural tradition. *World Archaeology* 2(1): 17-27.

Commiad, L.A. 1924. Pygmy implements of the Lower Godavary. *Man in India* IV: 83-105.

Commiad, L.A. and M.C. Burkitt. 1930. Fresh light on the Stone Age of Southeast India. *Antiquity* 4: 327-339.

Cooper, M.Z. 1983. *Prehistoric Habitation patterns around Chitrakot falls, Bastar District, Madhya Pradesh*. Unpublished PhD Dissertation, submitted to Poona University, Poona.

Dani, A.H. 1960. *Prehistory and Protohistory of Eastern India, with a detailed account of the neolithic cultures of South East Asia.* Calcutta: Firma K.L. Mukhopadhyay.

Das, G.N. (ed.) 1964. *Adibasi.* Orissa: Tribal Research Institute.

Daniels, S. 1967. Statistics, typology and Cultural dynamics in the Transvall Middle Stone. *South African Archaeological Bulletin,* XXII: 114.

de Terra, H., and T.T. Paterson 1939. *Studies on the Ice Age in India and Associated Human Cultures.* Washington: Carnegie institution of Washington, Publication No. 499.

District Statistical Hand Book, Koraput 1976-77. Government of Orissa. District Statistical Office, Koraput.

Foote, R.B. 1884. Rough Note on Billa Surgam and other caves in the Kurnool district. *Records of the Geological Survey of India* 27(2): 27-34.

Foote, R.B. 1961. *The Foote Collection of Indian Prehistoric and Protohistoric Antiquities: Notes on their ages and distribution.* Madras: Madras Govt. Press.

Ford, J.A. and Julian H. Steward. 1954. On the Concept of types. *American Anthropologist,* New Series 56(1): 42-57.

Gaussen, H.P.L. *et al.* 1967. *Notes on the sheet Jagannath (International map of vegetation and environment conditions.* (Scale 1/10,00,000). New Delhi: ICAR.

Gazetteer of India, 1966, Orissa district Gazetteers Koraput, Orissa. Cuttack: Orissa Government Press.

Ghosh, A. 1948. Prehistoric Explorations in India. *Indian Historical Quarterly* 24(1): 1-18.

Ghosh, A.K. 1970. The Palaeolithic Cultures of Singhbhum. *Transactions of the American Philosophical Society* 60(1): 1-68.

Ghosh, H.N., A.K. Dasgupta, G.C. Deo and S.C. Nanda. 1977. Early Man in the little Rann of Kutch. *Paper presented at the National Seminar on Quaternary Environments with special Reference to Western India,* organised at the University of Baroda, Baroda.

Gordon, D.H. 1938. The microlithic Industries in India. *Man* XXXVIII: 21-24.

Govinda Rajan, S.V. and H.G. Gopala Rao. 1978. *Studies on Soils of India.* New Delhi: Vikas Publishing House Pvt Ltd.

Hole, F. and R. Heizer. 1977. *Prehistoric Archaeology: A Brief Introduction.* New York: Holt, Rinehart and Winston.

Hunter, G.R. 1935. Interim report on an Excavation in the Mahadeo Hills. *Nagpur University Journal* 1: 28-57.

Hunter, G.R. 1936. Final Report on the Excavation in the Mahadeo Hills. *Nagpur University Journal* 2: 127-144.

IAR 1958-59. *Indian Archaeology - A Review.* Annual Bulletin of the Archaeological Survey of India, New Delhi, 37-38, 73.

IAR 1959-60. *Indian Archaeology - A Review.* Annual Bulletin of the Archaeological Survey of India, New Delhi.

IAR 1960-61. *Indian Archaeology - A Review.* Annual Bulletin of the Archaeological Survey of India, New Delhi, 22-24, 60.

IAR. 1961-62. *Indian Archaeology - A Review.* Annual Bulletin of the Archaeological Survey of India, New Delhi, 36.

IAR 1963-64. *Indian Archaeology - A Review.* Annual Bulletin of the Archaeological Survey of India, New Delhi, 2, 90.

IAR 1965-66. *Indian Archaeology - A Review.* Annual Bulletin of the Archaeological Survey of India, New Delhi, 8.

IAR. 1968-69. *Indian Archaeology - A Review.* Annual Bulletin of the Archaeological Survey of India, New Delhi, 68.

ICAR- National Bureau of Soil Survey and Land Use Planning. 1958. *Final report of the all India Soil Survey Scheme*, pp. 81-85. Nagpur: Indian Council of Agricultural Research (ICAR).

Isac, H. 1960. *The Stone Age Cultures of Kurnool.* Unpublished PhD Dissertation, Poona University, Poona.

Jacob, S. Jaya Raj. 1983. *Early Hunter-Gatherers adaptation in the Tirupati valley, South India.* Unpublished PhD Dissertation, University of Poona, Poona.

Jacobson, J. 1970. *Microlithic contexts in the Vindhyan Hills of Central India.* Unpublished PhD Dissertation, Columbia University, New York.

Joshi, R.V. 1968. Late Mesolithic Culture of Central India. *La Prehistoric: Problems of Tendances* Paris: 245-251.

Joshi, R.V. 1978. *Stone Age Culture of Central India: Report of the Excavation of Rock Shelters at Adamgarh, Madhya Pradesh.* Poona: Deccan College Post-graduate and Research Institute.

Joshi, R.V. and M.D. Khare. 1966. Microlith bearing Deposit of Adamgarh Rock-shelters. In *Studies in Prehistory: Robert Bruce Foote Memorial Volume*, eds. D. Sen and A.K. Ghosh, 90-95. Calcutta: Firma K.L. Mukhopadhyay.

Joshi, R.V. and R.S. Pappu 1979. Bhokar: An Upper Palaeolithic Factory site from Central Godavari Basin, Maharashtra. *Man and Environment* 3: 86-91.

Khatri, A.P. 1958. *Stone Age Culture of Malwa.* Unpublished PhD Dissertation, Poona University, Poona.

Krieger, Atex D. 1944. The typological Concept. *American Antiquity* 9(3): 271-288.

Krishnan, M.S. 1956. *Geology of India and Burma*. Madras: Higgin-Bothams Private Ltd.

Krishanaswami, V.D. 1947. Stone Age in India. *Ancient India* 3: 11-57.

Krishnaswami, V.D. and K.V. Soundara Rajan. 1951. The Lithic tool industries of the Singrauli Basin. District Mirjapur. *Ancient India* 7: 40-65.

Lal, B.B. 1958. Birbhanpur - A Microlithic site in the Damodar Valley, West Bengal. *Ancient India* 14:4-48.

Lal, B.B. and S.B. Lal 1961. The Microlithic site of Birbhanpur: A Geo-chronological Study. *Ancient India* 17: 37-45.

Leakey, M.D. 1971. *Olduvai Gorge, Vol. 3: Excavations in Beds I and II 1960-63*. Cambridge: Cambridge University Press.

Misra, V.N. 1961. *The Stone Age Cultures of Rajputana*. Unpublished PhD Dissertation, University of Poona, Poona.

Misra, V.N. 1965. Mesolithic phase in the Prehistory of India. In *Indian Prehistory: 1964*, eds. Misra V.N. and M.S. Mate, 57-85. Poona: Deccan College.

Misra, V.N. 1971a. Two Late Mesolithic Settlements in Rajasthan- A Brief Review of Investigations. *Journal University of Poona* 35: 59-77.

Misra, V.N. 1971b. Two microlithic sites in Rajasthan - A Preliminary investigation. *The Eastern Anthropologist* XXIV (3): 237-288.

Misra, V.N. 1973. Bagor - A Late Mesolithic Settlement in Northwest India. *World Archaeology* 5 (1): 92-110.

Misra, V.N. 1974. Archaeological and Ethnographic Evidence for the Hafting and use of Microliths and related tools. *Puratattva* 7: 3-12.

Misra, V.N. 1976. The Acheulian industry of Rock Shelter III F-23 at Bhimbetka, Central India: a Preliminary Study. *Puratattva* 8: 13-36.

Misra, V.N. 1978. The Acheulian industry of Rock Shelter III F-23 at Bhimbetka, Central India: a Preliminary Study. *Bulletin of the Indo-Pacific Prehistory Association* 1: 63-106.

Misra, V.N. 1980. *Evolution of the Blade element in the Stone Age Industries of Rock-Shelter III F-23, Bhimbetka*. Paper Presented at XI Annual Congress of the Indian Society for Prehistoric and Quaternary Studies, Bhopal.

Misra, V.N., Y. Mathpal and M. Nagar 1977. *Bhimbetka - Prehistoric man and his art in Central India*. Poona: Bhimbetka. Souvenir Committee.

Misra, V.N. and S.C. Nanda. 1977. *Mesolithic Industry of Rock-Shelter III F-23 at Bhimbetka (Dist. Raisen, Madhya Pradesh)*. Proceedings of III Annual Conference Ethnographic and Folk Culture Society and Indian Association of Physical Anthropologist, held at Lucknow, on January 23-15, 1977.

Misra, V.N., M. Nagar and S.C. Nanda 1978. *Typology of Indian Microlithic Industries*. Proceedings of IV Annual Conference of Ethnographic and Folk Culture Society, held at Ahmedabad, 8-10 January 1978.

Mohapatra, G.C. 1962. *The Stone Age Cultures of Orissa*. Poona: Deccan College.

Movious, H.L. Jr., N.C. David, H.K. Bricker and R.B. Clay. 1968. *The Analysis of Certain Major Classes of Upper Palaeolithic tools*, ed. H. Hencken. Cambridge, Massachusetts: The Peabody Museum.

Murty, M.L.K. 1966. *Stone Age Cultures of Chittoor District, Andhra Pradesh*. Unpublished PhD Dissertation, University of Poona. Poona.

Murty, M.L.K. 1968. Blade and Burin Industries near Renigunta on the Southeast coast of India. *Proceedings of the Prehistoric Society* 35: 85-101.

Murty, M.L.K. 1970. Blade and Burin and Late Stone Age Industries around Renigunta, Chittoor District. *Indian Antiquary* 4 (1-4): 106-128.

Murty, M.L.K. 1974. A Late Pleistocene Cave site in South India. *Proceedings of the American Philosophical Society* 118(2): 196-230.

Murty, M.L.K. and K.T. Reddy 1976. The significance of Lithic finds in the Cave Areas of Kurnool. *Asian Perspectives* 18(2): 214-226.

Murty, M.L.K. 1978. *Use of plant foods by some hunter-gatherer communities on the southeast coast of India: its possible relevance to Prehistory*. Paper Presented at Symposium on Recent Advances in Indo-Pacific Prehistory, held at Pune.

Murty, M.L.K. 1979. Recent Research on the upper palaeolithic phase in India. *Journal of Field Archaeology* 6(3): 301-320.

Murty, M.L.K. 1981. Hunter-gatherer ecosystems and archaeological patterns of subsistence behavior on the southeast coast of India: an ethnographic model. *World Archaeology*, 12: 47-98.

Nagar, M. 1978. *The use of wild plant foods by Tribal communities in Central India with special reference to Bastar and Bhimbetka*. Paper Presented at Indo-Pacific Prehistoric Association Xth ICAES, Post-Plenary Symposium on "Recent Advances in Indo-Pacific Prehistory", held at University of Poona, Poona.

Nagar, M. 1980. *Fishing and fishing gear among the tribal communities of Central India, and their implication for Archaeology*. Paper Presented at Seminar on Indian Prehistory, held at Allahabad.

Nagar, M. 1982. Fishing among the tribal communities of Baster and its implications for Archaeology. *Bulletin Deccan College Research Institute* 41: 116-125.

Nanda, S.C. 1977. *Microlithic Industry of Koraput District, Orissa.* Proceedings of III Annual Conference Ethnographic and Folk Culture Society and Indian Association of Physical Anthropologist, held at Lucknow, on January 23-15, 1977.

Nanda, S.C. 1978a. *Microlithic Industry of Daitary, Keonjhar District of Orissa.* Proceedings of IV Annual Conference of Ethnographic and Folk Culture Society, held at Ahmedabad, 8-10 January 1978.

Nanda, S.C. 1978b. *Mesolithic Culture of Indravati Valley, District Koraput, Orissa.* Paper Presented at Indo-Pacific Prehistoric Association X[th] ICAES, Post-Plenary Symposium on "Recent Advances in Indo-Pacific Prehistory", held at University of Poona, Poona.

Nanda, S.C. 1981. *Upper Palaeolithic Culture of Orissa.* Paper Presented at 7th Indian Society for Prehistoric and Quaternary Studies and XIIIth Indian Archaeological Society.

Nanda, S.C. 1982. *Stone Age Succession of Indravati Valley, Koraput District, Orissa.* Proceedings of First Annual Conference of Orissa Anthropological Society, Bhubaneswar.

Oakley, K.P. 1957. *Man - The Tool Maker.* Chicago: University of Chicago Press.

Paddayya, K. 1968. *Pre and Proto-historic investigations in Shorapur Doab.* Unpublished PhD Dissertation, University of Poona. Poona.

Paddayya, K. 1970. The Blade tool industry of Shorapur Doab. *Indian Antiquary* 4(1-4): 165-190.

Paddayya, K. 1978. *The Acheulian Culture of Hunsgi Valley, South India: Settlement and Subsistence Patterns.* Paper Presented at Indo-Pacific Prehistoric Association X[th] ICAES, Post-Plenary Symposium on "Recent Advances in Indo-Pacific Prehistory", held at University of Poona, Poona.

Pandey, R.P. 1980. Geomorphology and Prehistory of the Upper Mahanadi Valley, Central India. *Bulletin of the Deccan College Research Institute* 39: 135-146.

Pandey, R.P. 1982. *Archaeology of the Upper Mahanadi Valley Madhya Pradesh, (India).* Unpublished PhD Dissertation, University of Poona, Poona.

Pappu, R.S. 1974. *Pleistocene Studies in the Upper Krishna Basin.* Unpublished PhD Dissertation, Poona University, Poona.

Pascoe, E.H. 1973. *A Manual of Geology of India and Burma,* Vol. I. Delhi: Government of India.

Prater, S.H. 1965. *The Book of Indian Animals.* Bombay: Bombay Natural Historical Society and Prince of Wales Museum of Western India.

Rajaguru, S.N. 1970. *Studies in the Late Pleistocene of Mula Mutha Valley.* Unpublished PhD Dissertation, Poona University, Poona.

Rajaguru, S.N., R.S. Pappu, A.R. Marathe and B.C. Deotare. 1980. The terminal Pleistocene Mesolithic Industry of Inamgaon, Maharastra. *Bulletin of the Deccan College PG and Research Institute* 39: 150-159.

Rajendran, P. 1979. *Environment and Stone Age Cultures of North Kerala*. Unpublished PhD Dissertation, Poona University, Poona.

Raju, D.R. 1981. *Early settlement Pattern in Cuddapah District, Andhra Pradesh*. Unpublished PhD Dissertation, Poona University, Poona.

Ray, G.C. 1960. *Prehistory of Orissa*. *Man in India* 10(3).

Reddy, K.T. 1968. *Prehistory of Cuddapah*. Unpublished PhD Dissertation, Saugor University, Saugor.

Reddy, K.T. 1970. Vemula Industry in the Cuddapah Basin. *Indian Antiquary* 4(1-4): 227-234.

Reddy, K.T. 1980. Billasurgam: An Upper Palaeolithic Cave site in South India. *Asian Perspectives* XX(2): 206-22.

Reddy, K.T. and V. Sudarsan. 1978. Prehistoric Investigation in Sagileru Basin. *Man and Environment* 2: 32-40.

Reddy, K.T. and P. Vijaya Prakash. 1978. *Mesolithic Culture: A revolution? Technological Evolution? A case study from Gambhiram River Valley*. Paper Presented at Indo-Pacific Prehistoric Association Xth ICAES, Post-Plenary Symposium on "Recent Advances in Indo-Pacific Prehistory", held at University of Poona, Poona.

Sali, S.A. 1967. Quaternary Stratigraphy in the Kan Basin at Bhadne and Yesar - Results of Preliminary exploration. *Journal of the Asiatic Society of Bombay* 39-40: 157-167.

Sali S.A. 1978. *The Upper Palaeolithic Culture at Patne, District Jalgaon, Maharashtra*. Paper Presented at Indo-Pacific Prehistoric Association Xth ICAES, Post-Plenary Symposium on "Recent Advances in Indo-Pacific Prehistory", held at University of Poona, Poona.

Sali S.A. 1978. The Upper Palaeolithic research since Independence. *Bulletin of the Deccan College PG and Research Institute* 34(1-4): 147-169.

Sali S.A. 1980. *Stone Age Culture Sequence at Patne, District Jalgaon, Maharashtra*. Unpublished PhD Dissertation, University of Poona, Poona.

Sankalia, H.D. 1942. In search of Early Man along the Sabarmati. *Journal of the Gujarat Research Society* 4: 75-80.

Sankalia, H.D. 1946. *Investigations into the Prehistoric Archaeology of Gujarat*. Baroda: Baroda State Press.

Sankalia, H.D. 1944. The Second Gujarat Prehistoric Expedition: A Preliminary account of the search of Microlithic Man in Gujarat. New Indian *Antiquity* 7: 1-5.

Sankalia, H.D. 1956. Animal fossils and Palaeolithic industries from the Pravara basin at Nevasa, District Ahmednagar. *Ancient India* 12: 35-52.

Sankalia, H.D. 1956. The Microlithic Industry of Langhnaj, Gujarat. *Journal of the Gujarat Research Society* 18 (40): 275-284.

Sankalia, H.D. 1960. *From History to Prehistory at Nevasa, 1954-56*. Poona: Deccan College Post-graduate and Research Institute.

Sankalia, H.D. 1965. *Excavation at Langhnaj 1944-63, Part II, Archaeology*. Poona: Deccan College.

Sankalia, H.D. 1969. *Mesolithic and Pre-mesolithic Industries from the Excavation at Sangankallu, Bellary, 1965*. Poona: Deccan College.

Sankalia, H.D. 1974. *The Prehistory and Protohistory of India and Pakistan*. Poona: Deccan College Post-graduate and Research Institute.

Sankalia, H.D. and I. Karve. 1949. Early Primitive Microlithic Culture and People of Gujarat. *American Anthropologist* 51: 28-34.

Semenov, S.A. 1964. *Prehistoric technology: Experimental study of Oldest Tools and artifacts from traces of manufacture and wear*, translated by M. Thompsons. London: Adams and Mackary.

Sen, D. and V. Chaturvedi. 1957. Microlithic industry of Singhbhun. *Man in India* 37(4): 294-304.

Seshadri, M. 1962. Stone Age tools from Salvadgi, Bijapur District, Mysore State. *Journal of the University of Mysore* 25(2): 1-5.

Sharma, G.R. 1965. Mesolithic phase in the Prehistory of India. In *Indian Prehistory*, eds. V.N. Misra and M.S. Mate, 76-79. Poona: Deccan College Post Graduate and Research Institute.

Sharma, G.R. 1973. Stone Age in the Vindhyas and the Ganga Valley. In *Radiocarbon and Indian Archaeology*, eds. D.P. Agrawal and A. Ghosh, 106-110. Bombay: Tata Institute of Fundamental Research.

Sharma, G.R. 1973. Mesolithic Lake cultures in the Ganga Valley, India. *Proceedings of the Prehistoric Society* 39: 129-146.

Sharma, G.R., V.N. Misra, D. Mandal, B.B. Misra and J.N. Pal. 1980. *Beginning of Agriculture (Epi-Palaeolithic to Neolithic: Excavations at Chopni-Mando, Mahadaha and Mahagara)*. Allahabad: Abinash Prakashan.

Sinha, B.N. 1971. *Geography of Orissa*. New Delhi: National Book Trust, India.

Soundara Rajan, K.V. 1952. Stone Age sites near Giddalur District, Kurnool. *Ancient India* VIII: 64-92.

Soundara Rajan, K.V. 1953. Studies in the Stone Age of Nagarjunakonda and its Neighbourhood. *Ancient India* 14: 49-113.

Subbarao, B. 1948. *Stone Age Culture of Bellary being a report of the excavation at Sanganakallu*. Poona: Deccan College.

Subbarao, B. 1952. Archaeological explorations in the Nahi Valley. *Journal of the Maharaja Sivajirao University of Baroda* 1: 33-69.

Subbarao, B. 1958. *Personality of India.* Maharaja Sayajirao University. Archaeology series no. 3. Baroda: Maharaja Sayajirao University.

Tainter, J.A. 1979. The Mountainair lithic scatters: Settlement Patterns and Significance Evaluation of low Density surface sites. *Journal of Field Archaeology* 6: 463-469.

Thurston, Edgar. 1909. *Castes and Tribes of South India,* Vol. II & VI: Madras: Government Press.

Todd, K.R.U. 1932. Prehistoric man round Bombay. *Prehistoric Society of East Anglia* 8(3): 35–42.

Todd, K.R.U. 1948. A microlithic industry of eastern Mysore. *Man* 48: 28–30.

Tripathy, K.C. 1972. *Lithic Industries of South-Western Orissa.* Unpublished PhD Dissertation, Utkal University, Orissa.

Wadia, D.N. 1975. *Geology of India.* New Delhi: Tata McGraw-Hill Publishing Co.

Wakankar, V.S. 1973. Bhimbetka Excavation. *Journal of Indian History* 51(1): 23-32.

Wilkins, J. 1959. The Mesolithic. *Antiquity* XXXIII: 130-131.

Zeuner, F.E. and B. Allchin 1956. Microlithic sites in Tinnevalley district, Madras State. *Ancient India* XII: 4-20.

Index